THE WORKING PARENTS' SURVIVAL GUIDE

Sally Wendkos Olds

Prima Publishing & Communications
P.O. Box 1260WP
Rocklin, CA 95677
(916) 624-5718

Copy Editing by Betty Duncan-Todd
Typography by Miller Freeman Publications
Production by Bookman Productions
Cover design by The Dunlavey Studio

Prima Publishing & Communications
Rocklin, CA

Library of Congress Cataloging-in-Publication Data

Olds, Sally Wendkos.
  The working parents' survival guide / Sally Wendkos Olds;
    p. cm.
  Reprint, with new introd. Originally published: Toronto : New
York : Bantam Books, 1983.
  Bibliography: p.
  Includes index.
  ISBN 0-914629-82-4
  1. Working mothers—United States.   2. Parenting—United
States.   3. Children of working parents—United States.   I. Title.
HQ759.48.045   1989
646.7'8—dc19   88-38558
                                                                   CIP

89 90 91 92 RRD 10 9 8 7 6 5 4 3 2 1

Printed in the United States of America

to David Mark Olds, because . . .

. . . you said at first that you would change only the wet
diapers—and then when the time came, you changed
all kinds;

. . . you sent me a telegram on my first day back at *paying*
work after six years at home with the children, telling
me it was about time;

. . . you believed in my ability to write before I had
thought of it myself;

. . . you told me never to worry about the possibility of my
earning more money than you—and then told it to me
again when it looked as if it might really happen.

. . . you've always come through—as a working parent
and as one working parent's best friend.

ABOUT THE AUTHOR

Sally Wendkos Olds worked in a Cleveland (Ohio) advertising agency until three weeks before the birth of her first child. She then launched her writing career during the six years she was home full-time with her daughters, Nancy, Jennifer, and Dorri. She has worked continuously since then, at a variety of part-time and full-time jobs, mostly with activist or social welfare organizations, before turning to freelance writing as her full-time profession.

An award-winning author or coauthor of eight other books and more than 200 articles that have appeared in major national magazines, Sally Olds is a former president of the American Society of Journalists and Authors. Two of her books, *The Complete Book of Breastfeeding* and *Raising a Hyperactive Child*, have become classics in their fields, and her college textbooks (*Psychology*, *A Child's World*, and *Human Development*) have been read by more than 1 million students. Her most recent book for general readers is *The Eternal Garden: Seasons of Our Sexuality*. She lives on Long Island, New York, with her husband, a professor of communications.

also by Sally Wendkos Olds

The Complete Book of Breastfeeding
   (with Marvin S. Eiger, M.D.)
A Child's World (with Diane E. Papalia, Ph.D.)
The Eternal Garden: Seasons of Our Sexuality
Helping Your Child Learn Right from Wrong
   (with Dr. Sidney B. Simon)
The Mother Who Works Outside the Home
Raising a Hyperactive Child (with Mark A. Stewart, M.D.)
Human Development (with Diane E. Papalia, Ph.D.)
Psychology (with Diane E. Papalia, Ph.D.)

CONTENTS

Preface: Help Is On the Way!

"You have to talk about the guilt," Louise, a city planner and the mother of three teenagers, told me. "I never thought it would be so hard to find somebody I could trust to take care of my son," said Alan, an accountant and father of a preschooler. "Time. There's never enough. The housework piles up, and I don't have time to do what I want, even sleep!" said Monica, a medical secretary and single mother of a toddler. And Gary, a division manager for a Fortune 500 company and the father of four, is stressed from other pressures. "I know I've been passed over for promotion because I care about my family. Some people—unfortunately, some at my own company—assume you aren't committed enough to your professional life if you show more than a passing interest in your children's welfare."

Time—there's never enough. *Guilt*—there's always too much. *Child care*—it's hard to find, hard to evaluate, and hard to pay for. And *stress*—from the combination of these three, along with fatigue, task overload, and career concerns. These seem to be the biggest problems working parents face.

The bad news is that they are not the only ones. Many of the problems of today's working parents stem from the fact that they live in a time of transition. Never before have so many American women worked outside the home. Never before have so many American men been so active in caring for their children. As a result, these hardworking, family-oriented men and women have few models to show them how to handle all the conflicts between family and work. The questions are sometimes soul-searching and global, but the answers are usually rooted in the tiny details of everyday life. How to resolve the practical problems. How to find the best child care. How to see that everyone is fed, clothed, bathed, transported, and having some fun in the process. How to enjoy life at home while advancing on the job. What to do when advancing on the job means being in one place when enjoying life at home would have you at the other end of town. How to juggle roles as parent, worker, spouse, all-around adult.

But the good news is that millions of working parents are dealing with these issues and enriching their lives and the lives of their children in the process. And that's what this book is about—how you can do it, too. This is not a book written in an ivory tower for people who live in the best of all possible worlds, where Mary Poppins flies in to take over a household and where there's always enough money and time to do it all and have it all. This is a book for real people in a real world. When sometimes things go wrong on the job. When sometimes you want to scream at your kids. When sometimes you fight with your spouse—or wish you had one to fight with. When sometimes you wonder why you're trying to do it all.

The miracle is that so many people succeed at combining the two things that Sigmund Freud said were the most important in life: love and work. Either because they have to or because they want to, millions of men and women are filling their lives with the challenges and gratifications of both work and family. How do they do it? What problems do they need the most help with? To get the answers to these two questions, I asked. I asked the experts—the family counselors and the time-management experts, the psychologists and the psychiatrists, and the professionals in the field of child care. Most of all, though, I asked the people who know the most—the working parents themselves.

I have been in close touch with more than 250 working parents. One hundred and fifty busy mothers and fathers took the time to answer the questions I posed in a long questionnaire. The other 100 or so spoke with me directly, usually with regard to one specific aspect of their lives—child care, marriage, money or time management, and the like. I am grateful to all these people because I know how precious their time is and how generous they were in giving it to me. I am especially grateful because they came up with some of the most helpful suggestions in this book.

Few of these parents feel they're doing as well as they could. (Do any of us feel we ever do anything as well as we could?) Most feel they have a lot to learn. Many underestimate how much they can teach others. And yet we can all learn from each other. From the mother who said to me, when I asked her what shortcuts she could pass on to other working parents, "I'm waiting for your book to come out so *I* can find out how everyone else is doing it!" (Still, her personal solutions are in these pages, and they are creative and helpful.) From the father who confessed, "Sometimes I lie awake at night wondering how I can make it come together better." (It seemed to me as if he was making it come together very well—and so *his* ideas are in this book, too.) Despite their doubts, these pioneers are untangling knots every day of their lives. And ending up with smooth results that the rest of us can apply to our lives.

The key to coming up with solutions is in looking at life as one big puzzle—one that *can* be solved—rather than as a stone wall made up of insoluble problems. In looking at each new roadblock as a challenge to get around, not a barrier to keep you back. In facing these challenges flexibly, bending to stay strong rather than snapping under self-imposed demands for rigid, permanent arrangements. Nothing is forever. A solution that works today may not work tomorrow. What works for one child may be disastrous for another in the same family. This is why, throughout this book, you'll see different options, so that you can pick and choose from them to select the solution that fits your family's needs.

My own children are now grown. While I am still a working parent, my parenting these days is on the emotional level rather than the nitty-gritty, day-in-day-out, logistical one. The topic, though, is close to my heart and always will be. For those years when I was changing a diaper with one hand and making notes with the other constituted a richly textured span of my life. During that period, my ideas about work and parenthood and marriage and women's roles changed enormously. So did my work, my parenting, my marriage, and my life as a woman. In some ways then, this book is the culmination of a long gestation during a time of exciting change. My hope is that it will help working parents today as much as my commitment to being a working parent has helped me to lead a richly fulfilling life.

Sally Wendkos Olds
Port Washington, New York

PROLOGUE: THE HISTORY OF THIS BOOK

Back in 1961 the Child Study Association of America, a highly respected educational organization, published a pamphlet titled, "The Mother Who Works Outside the Home." The pamphlet was advanced for its time in the support it gave to working mothers, who were then being roundly criticized from many quarters for neglecting their children.

In 1974 the association asked me to write a completely new version of this pamphlet. Thirteen years after it had originally been published, there had been so many changes in women's lives and in societal attitudes that the original had a quaint, old-fashioned air. As good as it was, it still said things like "a wife with children who wants to work outside her home certainly should have her husband's approval," "you must face the fact that you will still have to do most of the home chores you do now," and "the care of the household is your responsibility, just as the burden of its support is your husband's."

My pamphlet, with the same title, appeared in 1975. Among other changes, I had dropped the notion that women should ask their husbands' permission before going out to get a job, or the advisability of a wife's being everlastingly grateful to the husband who "helps" her with "her" work of caring for children and house, or any implication at all that a wife's job was less important than her husband's. Apparently, the pamphlet addressed the concerns of many working mothers; it was among the most popular publications of Child Study Press. By 1980, however, the Child Study Association had disbanded its publishing operations, and since Bantam Books was interested in publishing a book on this topic, I set out to expand and update the booklet.

A funny thing happened on my way to the typewriter. As I began to write, I realized that something was wrong. As I was writing about the concerns of working mothers and the ways that they could juggle their career and family obligations, I realized that it didn't make sense to address *only* the mother. By doing so I would continue to perpetuate the stereotype that she was the parent who was expected to consider and meet the family's needs, on top of her job obligations. Yes, although most women still were shouldering most child care and housekeeping chores, and although most men still were earning more than their wives, major changes had taken place in family life and it no longer made sense to address only the female working parent. Or to assume that she had a husband at home to provide most of the family's financial support. Accordingly, the first edition of *The Working Parents' Survival Guide*, published in 1983, was the first "how-to" book for working parents of both sexes and the first to put major emphasis on the single working parent—of either sex.

This time, only six years later, when Prima Publishing (a firm founded and operated by working parents), wanted me to revise this book, I thought that I would do just a very minor updating of facts and figures. But once again, societal changes dictated more sweeping editorial changes. Much of the emphasis in the previous edition of this book was on the concerns of women who had been at home with their children for some years and were now going back to work; now those women are a minority as most mothers continue to work after taking only brief leaves (weeks or months) after the birth of each baby. This is only one of a number of changes that have occurred in recent years.

As this edition of the book goes to press, it is my fervent hope that in a few years it, too, will become outdated. If society provides more of the supports that working parents need for themselves and their children, many of the problems that loom large in their lives today will evaporate into nothingness. But to reach that point, we need to continue to work out our own solutions and to continue to press our employers, our governments, and our community agencies to respond in ways that will make life better for working parents and their children.

1

WHO ARE THE WORKING PARENTS?

"Sometimes the balancing gets to me," Joan Alyce Maynard, age thirty, educational director of a New York City daycare center, told me. "Coming home bone-tired from work but knowing you have to struggle through because supper has to be cooked, and Joseph has to be bathed, and the checkbook has to be balanced . . . and on and on. But even though there *are* nights like this, I am happier working than I would be staying home. Both my husband and I have had the opportunity to complete our educations, to pursue our interests, and to share our duties. As a result, we're a close family unit."

Her husband, William, age thirty-one, a nuclear medical cardiology technician, added, "While we thought at first that Joan wouldn't go back to work till Joseph was in nursery school, she went back when he was six months old, and we've both worked steadily ever since. Things have worked out well. The two of us have a sense of independence, and all three of us enjoy the special times we plan on weekends. One of the biggest benefits has been showing our son what two mature people can do when they set their minds to it."

"The most important thing for a working parent is knowing your children are happy and well taken care of," says

1

accounting clerk Ann Marie Leal, divorced mother of three children, ages eleven, nine, and four. "I'm lucky that my four-year-old is in an excellent day-care center that I don't have to pay for, but since I have to commute two hours a day to get him there and back, besides the two hours I spend getting to and from my job, I never have enough time to spend with the children or to finish the household chores. If I were starting all over again, I would have gone to college and had my children later so that I'd be better able to support a family. Still, it's good to know that I can survive as a working single mother."

When either Michael or Karen Weymouth has to stay home from school, they're equally likely to be cared for by their psychoanalyst father, Arthur, or their teacher/law student mother, Doris. "It's not so much a question of whether the mother or the father stays home," says Art, "but of whose schedule allows for it more. I've missed some appointments because of the children's needs, and Doris has missed some classes, but over all, our arrangement of sharing work and parenting has been good. Doris and I have many interests and many sources of self-validation, and our children have developed a view of a world in which activity is more significant than status."

"The biggest problem for us," says Doris, who left her job as a high school teacher to become a full-time law student, "has been getting good child care. But even this has been more of a tedious responsibility rather than a serious problem. All in all, I have the sense of having it all—personal work success, marriage, and parenthood—and I feel our whole family has benefited."

There is, of course, no one kind of working parent. We all have our children for different reasons, look at parenthood from different viewpoints, and show these differences as we bring up our children. We all view our work differently, too. Some people fall into their jobs by accident and then keep them only because they desperately need the pay, whereas others plan their professions carefully and get career rewards that go far beyond the figures on their paychecks.

And yet, no matter how different working parents may seem on the surface, we all have the same basic concerns. "How can I be a good parent?" "How does my job affect my family?" "How can I manage best on both fronts?" "How much do I deserve out of life—and how can I get it?"

Who *is* the working parent? Every parent is. We change diapers; we launder overalls; we tie shoelaces; we cook mashed potatoes and spoon them into little mouths. We wrench ourselves out of a warm bed in the middle of the night to comfort a child scared by a nightmare; we play endless games of Candyland when we want to curl up with a good book. In short, as parents we do all kinds of things that are described better as "work" than as "play."

But besides this family work, most parents take on other work, too. Across the world and throughout history, most parents of both sexes have always worked. They have labored in the fields; they have spun and woven; they have hunted and fished and manufactured articles for use by their own families and for sale to others. Until relatively recent times, much of this work could be done without both parents having to leave their children in the care of others.

With the coming of the Industrial Revolution, however, the kind of work that was needed from women and available to them changed. By and large, to earn money they now had to leave their homes. When faced with the choice between earning a salary and staying close to their children, many who could afford to stay home did so. In families like this, the work was usually divided: the man left the house to do work that yielded dollars, and the woman stayed home to do the unpaid work of child rearing and household management.

THE WORKING PARENT IS HERE TO STAY

Over the past twenty-five or thirty years, this picture has changed again; now the great majority of all American children live either with two working parents or with one single parent who works outside the home. Today only one family in ten is the Dick-and-Jane household of the old schoolbooks—a breadwinning father, a homemaker mother, and two or three children. The typical family is made up of two or more wage earners. Furthermore, the family type that has mushroomed the most in recent years is the one headed by a single woman. As of March 1988, about one in five children were living with a single parent—usually a working mother.

It is, of course, the great increase in the number of working women that has increased the likelihood of a child's being raised by parents who work outside the home as well as in it. This increase, called by economists "the greatest economic revolution of our time," has been occurring ever since the Civil War and has soared since World War Two. One turning point was the year 1969 when more mothers of school-age children (between ages six and seventeen) were holding down jobs than not. A more recent turning point was 1987, the first year when more mothers of babies under one year old were working outside the home instead of in the home.

By March 1988, 64 percent of married mothers whose youngest child was under six years old were out working, compared to fewer than 50 percent ten years earlier. The proportion of single working mothers of children under age six—63.5 percent in 1988—had not changed substantially. Most of the increase in the number of women in the labor force has been among married women with children, that very group who, in the past, were considered the least likely to seek outside employment.

SOCIETY GIVES NOD TO WORKING PARENTS

All over the country, this change is recognized:

- In the 1988 presidential campaign, both the Democratic and Republican platforms came out with strong statements on the need for child care. Even though neither party came through with proposals for enough funding to make their proposals make much of a difference, when politicians pay lip service to these needs, we have proof that there are enough of us to command attention. The Democrats urged family-leave policies "that no longer force employees to choose between their jobs and their children" and major increases in government assistance so that low- and middle-income families could have access to more child care—and be able to afford it.

- The Girl Scouts of America have radically restructured the organization's program. Because so few mothers have time to volunteer these days, scouts meet in different ways and take part in different activities. A major thrust is on serving the needs of children who are alone after school (see the appendix, "Helpful Organizations").
- In 1986 the United States Department of Labor and the Bureau of National Affairs, together with the AFL–CIO and the National Association of Manufacturers, held a landmark symposium called "Work and Family: Seeking a New Balance." Here some 400 union officials, government managers, and corporate executives discussed ways business and labor can and should respond to the needs of the new American family.
- Psychologist Margaret W. Matlin, Ph.D., and her husband, pediatrician Arnold H. Matlin, M.D. (both working parents), asked pediatricians around the country when they would advise new mothers to go back to work. Of the 234 doctors who responded, more than half believed that it was appropriate for a mother to go to work when her baby was three months old, and an additional 35 percent chose ages between four months and one year. Only four pediatricians responded that the mother should not be employed at any time, and neither the doctors' ages nor genders affected their answers.

The only unfortunate part of this change is that now those women who do stay at home with their young children protest that they constantly have to justify their lives. "I'm so tired of hearing that you need to have a career or job to be fulfilled," says Donna Brauner of Sublimity, Oregon. "I have two daughters, ages three years and seven months, and have had the pleasure of being home with them all their lives. Sure it's trying at times, but what job isn't? It's been so rewarding to watch each and every new discovery, development, and phase of their lives."

And Marion Hook of Bethel, Pennsylvania, a former English teacher who left teaching to devote her time to the care of her two small daughters and to a host of other home-related activities, told me, "I'm tired of dealing with the preconceived notions so many people have, that any woman at home has minimal intelligence, can't think for herself, or is just plain lazy."

It's a shame that individual families so often have to defend their personal life-styles to family, friends, and society in general. We need to give people credit for doing what seems best to them. Just as pressure was once put on working mothers to stay home, the reverse is now true. But those women—and men—who can afford to devote themselves full-time to keeping a home and raising children, and who choose this occupation, should be respected for the valuable contribution they can make not only to their own families but also to society in general. The more we recognize the value of child rearing, the better will be the quality of substitute care for those parents who do not take care of their children themselves.

In a society truly committed to the family and the welfare of children, the government would support the needs of working parents, as our government does not do today. And employers would stop insisting on work schedules that don't mesh with family obligations; avoiding reasonable child-care arrangements. "Because of the way we run our world of work, parents either have to be in it all the way or not at all—or suffer second-class citizenship for being part-time workers," says Dr. Urie Bronfenbrenner, professor of human development, family studies, and psychology at Cornell University's College of Human Ecology. Why, then, in the face of such monumental pressures from society, do so many parents take on the obligations of outside work?

WHY PARENTS WORK

"We get to eat regularly."

"I love my job."

"We would both become bored and depressed without outside stimulation—and we need two incomes."

"You don't get promoted in my firm by taking time out to bring up children."

"We have more bills than we have money."

These are just a few answers to the question, Why do you work?—a query usually addressed only to women, in the (usually false) assumption that they're the ones who have a choice. When men answer the same question, however, we find that—as in so many other aspects of life—men and women are more alike than they are different.

One recent study found that although small children in the home often keep a mother out of the labor market, the more older children a woman has, the more likely she is to look for work. Because both parents can usually earn more money on a job than they can save by staying home—even with child-care, commuting, and other job-related expenses—certain traditional household activities have now become expensive hobbies. These include baking bread, sewing clothing, cleaning house, and even growing one's own vegetables. Most parents can earn more money outside the home than they would have to pay for these goods or services.

In the 1970s, as men's earnings declined with the disappearance of many highly paid manufacturing jobs, more women went to work for the first time, switched from part-time to full-time work, or got better jobs. Still, in terms of constant dollars, the income of families with children, headed by an adult under age thirty, fell by about one-fourth between 1973 and 1986 according to a report by the Children's Defense Fund.

Only with a second income are many parents able to offer their children what they consider basics of the good life—a nice home, music lessons, a couple of weeks of summer camp, the chance to go to college. And even *with* two incomes, these amenities are out of the question for many families, in which the second job is the lifesaver that lets them just get by. Then there are single parents who have to do it all themselves.

Many single working parents are the sole support of their families. During the 1970s, the number of single-parent families headed by women rose by 80 percent, while those headed by men rose by more than 70 percent. These more than 7 million single-parent families are dependent for survival on the income of the head of the household. Although almost all these families are headed by women, more and more men have sought custody of their children in cases of divorce and separation, and the single father is becoming a more familiar figure.

Still, neither single nor married parents live by bread alone. While money ranks high—and usually highest—among reasons for working, personal fulfillment follows close behind. In 1980 Catalyst, a national organization originally founded to further women's corporate and professional roles, established the Career and Family Center to explore issues that affect two-career families. In a 1981 survey of employers and working couples, the center asked 815 couples, in which both partners had careers that were very important to them, why they worked. Both men and women put money first but rated "autonomy" and "personal growth" close seconds.

In a similar survey of seventy-five professional employees of General Electric Company, the major motivations for working were personal fulfillment, the ability to use special skills, and money, with no difference between men and women. And in the nationwide study done for the General Mills American Family Report, "Families at Work," almost all workers (90 percent of men and 87 percent of women) name a "personal sense of accomplishment" their most important reason for working, followed by "helping to make ends meet" and "improving the family's standard of living."

When asked what they would do if they had enough money to live comfortably, 58 percent of working women said they would continue to work, although more than twice as many would prefer to work part-time (41 percent) than full-time (17 percent). Surprisingly, the women with the best jobs—executive, managerial, and professional—are even more likely to want part-time over full-time work (51 percent vs 19 percent), probably reflecting the pressures they feel. When working men were offered the same hypothetical option, 78 percent said they would continue to work, with the preference for full-time over part-time work, almost the reverse of the women (50 percent to 28 percent). If the option of working at home and caring for the family were available, 10 percent of the men and 28 percent of the women said they'd like to do that.

WHY WORKERS HAVE CHILDREN

Despite the death knell for the family that doomsayers have been sounding in recent years, this ancient human institution is still alive and well. Marriage is still very much in style—and so is parenthood. Almost all adults marry, and almost all have children. Why? For one reason, because even in today's high-tech world, the family is as much a unit of survival as it was in the days of cave dwellers.

Even today people who live in families live longer and healthier lives than those who live alone. Families also provide emotional sustenance, a sense of security, the knowledge that you are loved and cared for.

As feminist writer Betty Friedan recently wrote, "Family is not just a buzz word for reactionaries; for women, as for men, it is the symbol of that last area where one has any hope of control over one's destiny, of meeting one's most basic human needs, of nourishing that core of personhood threatened now by vast impersonal institutions and uncontrollable corporate and government bureaucracies. Against these menaces, the family may be as crucial for survival as it used to be against the untamed wilderness and the raging elements, and the old, simple kinds of despotism."*

CAN A MAN COMBINE
FAMILY AND CAREER?

The changes in men's lives over the past few years are not nearly as dramatic nor as well documented as those in women's. Yet change has come, often in subtle ways. Television commercials now show fathers diapering and bathing their children; stores sell strollers with long, man-sized handles; and airports are beginning to install diaper-changing tables in men's restrooms. *The New York Times* now features an "About

*Betty Friedan, "Feminism's Next Step." *New York Times,* 5 July 1981, p. 33.

Men" column in its Sunday magazine as a forum for men to write about the emotional issues in their lives, many of which concern their relationships with their children. The "strong, silent" ideal is giving way to the "emotional, sensitive" one as the model of masculinity. Even guilt has turned unisex: this emotion, which used to be the exclusive province of working mothers, is now bedeviling working fathers, too.

Survey after survey of current male attitudes shows that more and more men say they put their families ahead of their careers. Furthermore, many men very literally put their money where their mouths are by spending time with their children, by turning down assignments involving excessive travel and overtime, by giving up their own jobs to relocate for their wives' jobs, by occasionally reversing roles so that they stay home with their children while their wives work full-time, and by carefully examining their own promotion and transfer offers to weigh their effects on their families.

This message is getting across to employers. In response to Catalyst's survey of employers, 83 percent of the representatives of 374 major corporations said they believed that men were increasingly feeling the need to share parenting responsibilities; 67 percent had found it harder to get employees to move to another city.

As men take their fathering seriously, they tend to undergo the same kinds of doubts that trouble women when they think about what having children means to their careers. When the man assumed that his primary role was to support the family financially and the woman's was to stay home and tend the family, his decision about having children was easier. Assuming that his income stretched far enough, his basic life-style changed hardly at all with the advent of one, two, three, or more children. Today, for one thing, his income is less elastic. For another, he is more likely to want to play an active role in his children's lives. And the more active he wants to be as a father, the more carefully he examines their impact on his career.

This pressure is hard, as one lawyer told a *New York Times* reporter: "Society hasn't lowered its level of job performance, but it has raised its expectations of our roles in our children's lives." And as one employment manager of a high-tech company said, "There's an expectation that you will give up your family for your job."

Thirty years ago most men accepted this expectation. Men with children behaved the same on the job as men without them. Women picked up the slack, handling a double load. Even today, when many husbands' attitudes are different from what they had been, wives still bear most of the responsibility for bringing up the children and managing the home. And they do the lioness's share of the work, too. But not as much as they had been doing.

Two recent surveys by advertising agencies found that while men still see taking out the garbage, mowing the lawn, and fixing things around the house as their principal domain, they also do some child care, as well as dishwashing, grocery shopping, cooking, and vacuuming. (In fact, more than one father has told me that he felt his wife didn't do her share of the work—and should take out the garbage more, or cook more, or do more household repairs.)

Husbands of working women feel they should do more around the house than men whose wives are not employed, and they actually *do* do more. More than half of the husbands surveyed feel that if the wife is working, husband and wife should be equally responsible for household chores.

Yet with all this change, many men still have one foot trapped in the bog of tradition. In one survey of 452 husbands—from different geographic locations and at different income levels, 62 percent of the men agreed that "the family is stronger if husband and wife share responsibilities, including providing family income." However, 70 percent also agreed with the exact opposite: "Unless it's an economic necessity, a family is better off if the woman of the house does not work."

This kind of conflict and ambivalence is typical of people in the process of change. Working families are still charting new paths, picking up on-the-job training. Few of today's working parents learned in their own families how to share the work of the family, how to respect each other's career and personal needs, how to live in a totally new context. As executive assistant Jane Brandon Garbo, mother of a five-month-old baby, told me, "This generation of parents are the Columbuses of this new type of parenting. The only difference is that he *wanted* to do it!" Her husband, Mitchell, a social service administrator, is making his own discoveries. He and his contemporaries are learning how to recognize and revel in the advantages of their life-style and how to overcome its difficulties.

PLUSES FOR WORKING PARENTS

Despite all the problems working parents have—and not even the most fulfilled denies that there are problems—the benefits can be great. Says Massachusetts attorney and mother Janet McCabe, "I'm better at both my jobs because I have—and love—the two of them." And lingerie sales manager Linda Wasserman told me, "For me the benefits have been tremendous. I love my work and love my family and feel I have the best of both worlds. I don't know many people as fortunate as I am."

Love and work. Sometimes, of course, the two get in each other's way. Sometimes the time and energy we put into one aspect of our lives seem to crowd out the other. But always the two are there, intertwined, posing challenges and delivering gratifications.

The combination of family and work seems to be the healthiest and most gratifying life-style for many people. Research has shown that both men and women who have more than one role (that is, as parent, paid worker, spouse, volunteer, and so on) are better adjusted and happier than those who concentrate only on family or only on work. In fact, some studies show that the more roles a person handles, the healthier that person is from a psychological viewpoint. This is partly because the different roles give people the chance to express the different parts of their personalities—the assertive and the nurturing, the creative and the expected, the serious and the silly.

When we look specifically at women, it's worth noting that evidence is piling up to show that the most stressful role a woman can have is that of "mother"—no matter what the rest of her life is like. Rosalind C. Barnett and Grace K. Baruch, directors of the Wellesley College Center for Research on Women, have conducted extensive research on women between ages thirty-five and fifty-five. They have found that it's not the number of roles that matter to a woman—it's the quality of those roles that determine how stressed she'll be. As far as working is concerned, working women don't seem especially stressed. Furthermore, the better a woman's job—the more money she makes and the more decision-making power she has—the less stressful her work is. Women who are *not* employed often feel inadequate because they have too much time available. Of course, the women in this group of studies are past the years when their children are making the greatest demands of time and energy, a point we'll be coming back to in Chapter 4, which talks about designing a job that fits in well with raising small children.

When asked what they like about work, most people point first to the money. Enough money is a great stress reducer. But working parents also point to other pluses—to pride in their accomplishments, to a greater understanding within the family, to a sense of sharing family responsibilities, to raising more independent children, to a measure of personal fulfillment.

PROBLEMS OF COMBINING WORK AND PARENTHOOD

Say bankers Barbara and Salvatore Mirrione, "We both work to realize 'the American dream'—house, family, all the rest. However, we are disillusioned because the sacrifice and stress are too much to manage."

Other parents' voices echo some of the pressures:

- "Between work and caring for my son, all my waking hours are devoted to a 'must do' activity. By keeping my job after he was born, I surrendered all my free time."

- "I'm more tired and more stressed than I ever could have imagined. I never have enough sleep or enough time to myself—and sex is a thing of the past."
- "I feel guilty all the time. I always want to be in two places at once."

Although both fathers and mothers acknowledge the problems, in every survey of working couples, women report more of them than men do. Society still expects more of women. Their heritage from the past is a greater responsibility for their families, and their "gift horse" of the present is the privilege of working two full-time jobs—the one they get paid for and the one they do for love. For example, when a child gets sick, who stays home? According to a survey by the University of Michigan's Institute for Social Research, 80 percent of the time the mother does. Everyone expects her to lose the day of work—and yet her attendance record is compared with her male co-worker's—whose wife stays home with *his* sick child.

The married working mother generally handles 70–80 percent of the child-care and household responsibilities, even though she may be working as many hours as her husband. And even when men pitch in, they typically do it with an attitude of "helping" their wives, leaving her with the responsibility of thinking about what has to be done. The single parent (a woman in nine out of ten cases) is even more burdened because she has to handle 100 percent of these duties—as well as the ones traditionally done by men.

But men, too, are sailing through uncharted seas these days. The man who wants to immerse himself in the care of his children and wants to assume his rightful share of household management usually worries—often with reason—that his family involvements may keep him out of the fast lane at work. And what about the man who grew up expecting to have a wife like a flashlight battery (ever ready, ever available) to do errands, cook his favorite meals, and listen to his job worries? He may say all the right words in recognition that he needs and values his wife's income and respects her right to fulfillment through work—yet still feel on some deeper, inexpressible level that she's not giving him the kind of emotional support he deserves.

Both men and women know that the more of themselves they invest in their work, the further they're likely to advance—and the less they'll have available to invest in their children and their personal lives. In fact, some critics have blamed the numbers of women in the workforce for the rising divorce rate over the past several decades. However, the chain of causation seems to be just the reverse. The rising rate of divorce made more women realize that they need to be economically independent. As a result, more women sought jobs. Many other women didn't—until their marriages fell apart and they had to support themselves and their children. The major way in which women's presence in the workforce contributes to divorce is in the knowledge that a woman who can earn her own living doesn't have to remain in a bad marriage.

For both married and single parents, work and love both need time, energy, and commitment. And often—especially when children are young—they need them at the same time. This sounds like an impossible order to fill, but the full lives of so many successful working parents show how possible it can be when the will is there. So let's look first at the biggest concern of working parents—how their work affects their children. Then we'll tackle the nuts and bolts of making that work have a happy effect on your own lives, as well as those of your children.

2

WHAT ABOUT
THE KIDS?

———

On this unremarkable Tuesday afternoon, Tara, eight, had gone to a neighbor's house after school, as she did every week-day. By and large, this arrangement worked out well. She liked to play with Mrs. Lee's children; she stayed there only about three hours until her mother or father came to pick her up, and she spent the evenings with her parents and two older brothers. But today the Lee children were sick in bed, and Tara had no one to play with. Furthermore, she kept thinking about her dancing school costume, which her mother had not yet had time to sew for her.

By the time Tara's mother came to pick her up, Tara was clearly feeling very sorry for herself. All she needed was the question, "What's wrong?" to explode, "I don't see why you have to be at work all the time. People shouldn't have kids if they don't want to take care of them."

Tara's outburst echoes comments that have resounded over most of this century. The anger pointedly directed at her mother (rather than her father) for working—and thus ne-glecting the duties of parenthood—is a familiar strain. For years mothers felt tied to their children's sides, reluctant to take paid employment for fear of igniting the sparks of emotional and psychological traumas that would explode in years to come.

Their fear was based on a barrage of advice founded not on facts but on the deep-seated prejudices and unsupported theories of an impressive lineup of "authorities"—usually men with wives who devoted all their time to home and family. Pediatricians, psychiatrists, psychologists, and philosophers told mothers that if they did not devote full-time to rearing their children, they were acting "contrary to human progress," that day care caused "permanent damage to the emotional health of a future generation," and that they should be away from their young children only in exceptional circumstances.

What, then, do these dire warnings mean for the 30 million American children today whose parents work outside the home? Are well over half of the children growing up today— those with employed parents—doomed to being maladjusted in school, at home, and in society? Fortunately, the outlook doesn't seem so bleak. It is, in fact, quite bright. British psychiatrist Michael Rutter let a healthy gust of fresh air into the nursery when he said, "Many of these statements imply that we understand what sort of upbringing a child needs and precisely which factors cause psychiatric disorder in children. But we do not, and it is our failure to recognize our ignorance which has led to these confident but contradictory claims. It is not the ignorance as such which is harmful but rather our 'knowing' so many things that are not true."

HOW ARE CHILDREN AFFECTED BY THEIR PARENTS' EMPLOYMENT?

What, then, do we know that *is* true? Those diagnoses of the past—the mother's-working-causes-all-sorts-of-problems type —had as much relation to science as the earlier pronouncements by the scientific "experts" that the world was flat. When scrutinized they just didn't hold up. In more recent years, with a surge of research on the children of working parents, social scientists have come up with very different—and very reassuring—findings.

After poring over nearly 300 studies involving thousands of children of working parents, for example, pediatrician Mary C. Howell concluded, "Almost every childhood behavior characteristic, and its opposite, can be found among the children of employed mothers. Put another way, there are almost no constant differences found between the children of employed and nonemployed mothers."

Both groups are equally likely to make friends easily or to have trouble getting along with other children, to shine or fail in school, to get into trouble or be models of good behavior, to be well adjusted and independent or be emotionally tied to their mothers' apron strings, to love and feel loved by their parents or to reject and feel rejected by them.

This does not, of course, mean that a mother's or a father's employment has no effect. Anything that affects parents' lives is bound to spill over to affect their children. The effects can be favorable, though, as well as unfavorable.

Most of the research we have on a father's work has focused on the nature of the work itself. It helps to shape children's values: Men whose work involves personal judgment in dealing with ideas, symbols, and other people are going to value self-direction and independence in their children, whereas men who are more closely supervised will encourage their children to be obedient and conforming. Work's psychological effects on the man affect his relations with his family: positively, in the case of men who meet their needs for a sense of accomplishment, fun, intellectual stimulation, morality, and self-esteem through their children rather than their work; or negatively, in men who take out their frustration at work by being hostile and severe with their children. And there have also been studies on how men's work schedules affect their closeness to their children—very little, according to wives' reports.

Most of the research on women's work, however, has focused not on the kind of work they do or its demands on them but on whether they work at all for pay. And the bulk of this research was conducted in earlier years or refers to those years when the working mother was the exception rather than the rule, as she is today.

How *does* a mother's outside employment affect her children? This depends on many things—mostly on how her job and life circumstances affect her and on how well her children are cared for when she is at work. But fifty years of research do not show an overall bad effect of the working itself. Most researchers today, in fact, stress the *positive* effects of the mother's employment on the entire family.

- A working woman's self-esteem tends to be higher than that of a full-time homemaker, whose work is generally undervalued in our society. And in general, the better a woman feels about herself, the better a parent she is.
- The husband of a working woman can relax more, knowing that he is not the only adult responsible for the family's financial support. Also, he can spend more time with his children because he is less likely to hold a second job.
- The division of labor between the parents is less traditional. Even though the wife still does more housework and child care and is responsible for thinking about what has to be done, her husband does more than husbands of homemakers. So the children are less likely to think in stereotyped ways.
- The children are likely to be closer to their father. Because husbands of working women tend to be more involved in their children's care than are husbands of homemakers, this care is likely to bring out their ability to nurture, a personality trait that doesn't often surface with men.
- For some insight into how children feel, see the box "What Kids Say About Their Working Parents."

WHAT CHILDREN OF DIFFERENT AGES NEED

Infants and Toddlers

When Sandra Metosky of Pittsburgh, Pennsylvania, went back to her job as a tax and corporate attorney, her daughter, Susan,

WHAT KIDS SAY ABOUT THEIR WORKING PARENTS

- Jon, five: on showing a drawing he made of his mother, a touring musician: "See—her hands are bandaged—now she can't play the piano."
- Cindy, nine: "I can't be sick Mondays, Tuesdays, and Fridays 'cause those are the days nobody's home."
- First words of the two-year-old son of two writers who work at home: "Quiet, I can't concentrate."
- Cliff, eleven: "My mom will say 'yes' to anything if I ask her when she's talking on the phone."
- David, nine: "Why can't you be home when I get home from school like Mark's mother? She always gives us milk and cookies."
- Mark, nine: "Why don't you get a job like David's mother? She always brings him home stuff when she has to go to a meeting."

was five months old. "I had no guilt feelings about leaving the baby," Sandy says, "because in many ways she was even better off than if I had been taking care of her at home. I was really fortunate in getting my former pediatrician's nurse to take care of Susan. This woman was not only a warm and loving person—she was able to diagnose things like an ear infection and give the baby better medical care than I could have!"

Baby-sitting perfection like this is hard to find, of course. But this example does illustrate the point that the very basic and important needs that babies have can often be met by people other than the parents. What *do* babies need? They need the security of knowing that they will have enough to eat, they will be kept warm and dry and comfortable, they will be protected from harm. They have to develop a sense of trust that the person or persons caring for them love them and will continue to nurture them.

Psychoanalytic thinkers, from Freud to Erikson through their many followers, have tended to stress the requirement of an exclusive relationship between mother and baby. This belief seemed to be borne out by studies of hospitalized children conducted during the 1940s and 1950s. René Spitz in the United States and John Bowlby in Great Britain found that infants in understaffed institutions, who were cut off from familiar people and places and who were cared for by a bewildering succession of different nurses, eventually suffered severe emotional problems. But—and this is a big BUT—this research tells us nothing about babies who are looked after by good baby-sitters or day-care workers during the day and are then reunited with their own loving parents come evening.

More recent studies have shown that babies in these situations do not, in fact, suffer. Most of the research suggests that a mother's working does not have harmful effects on her baby's social, emotional, or intellectual development—if the mother herself is warm, accepting, competent, and available when she is with the baby. These babies also do well when their fathers are very involved with them—and especially when their fathers are the ones who take care of them in their mothers' absence.

Babies of working parents who receive high-quality care from other caregivers don't suffer ill effects either. On the other hand, when they get unstable or poor-quality day care, there seems to be a risk of emotional and social problems later on. And when babies—especially boys—receive more than twenty hours of such care a week, the emotional risk does seem to rise. But as with so many aspects of bringing up children, it's hard to point to a single cause for such problems. The children who have them are likely to come from highly stressed families and to have mothers whose personalities don't mesh well with theirs. We cannot make a blanket statement about day care without looking at the kind of care, the kind of people involved, and the situation.

Even in families in which the mother does not go out to work, other people—especially the father—are important people in babies' lives. Milton Kotelchuck of Harvard University, for example, has found that one- and two-year-olds are just as attached to their fathers as their mothers. Furthermore, the typical baby in our society is cared for by several other people besides her parents—like grandparents, a teenage neighbor, a family friend, older siblings, and paid baby-sitters.

The late anthropologist Margaret Mead, who examined child-rearing patterns all around the world, hooted at the notion that a baby must not be separated from his mother. When I was lucky enough to speak with Dr. Mead in her office at the American Museum of Natural History in New York, we talked about the care of young children. "Babies are most likely to develop into well-adjusted human beings when they are cared for by many warm, friendly people," she said. "As long as most of these people remain in the babies' lives." Of course, here's the rub: It's hard to find warm, friendly people who come to stay. But more later about getting and keeping good child care.

Preschoolers

When four-year-old Melinda asked her mother why she wasn't there when the nursery school bus came to pick her up, her mother, New York television executive Ann Berk, told her, "Some mommies are mommies and other things, too, and they sometimes have to be other places. But when it's important, I'll be with you. You always come first. You're the most important." Melinda said, "Oh," and seemed content.

Children in the three- to six-year age range—like children of any age—need to feel they come first in their parents' lives. And young children still have a lot of basic physical needs to be taken care of. But they are so much more independent now that the age of three is one of the most comfortable times for a mother to take on a job outside the home. The three-year-old not only walks well—she hardly ever sits down! He not only talks—he hardly ever keeps quiet! Preschoolers are constantly testing the atmosphere in the outside world, moving away from their parents a little at a time, sticking a toe in the water and then running back to dry land and the arms of a loving adult.

More than half the children this age go to nursery school and then to kindergarten, whether their parents work or not. In preschool they learn how to get along with other children and other adults, how to use a wide range of materials not found in the average home, how to have a life of their own apart from Mommy and Daddy.

Because this age group accounts for most of the children in day care, it is the most studied. What do the studies show? That the average middle-class child in a good day-care program doesn't seem any different in most ways from children raised at home by their parents. These children don't do any better or worse in school later on, their social and emotional development doesn't suffer, and they are just as attached to their parents. One study even found that the preschoolers of working mothers have just as much one-to-one contact with their mothers as children of full-time homemakers.

A few differences have shown up between home-reared and center-reared children. One is that children from low-income homes who go to a good day-care center reap major benefits. They do better in school later on and do better on IQ tests than children who don't have the day-care experience. Another difference is that day-care children interact more intensely with other children, both in ways that make their parents and teachers smile—and ways that drive them crazy. They play and share more—but they fight more, too, and this difference lasts at least through the first few primary grades. Children who have been in day care a long time are sometimes less cooperative, less involved with schoolwork, and more aggressive than home-reared children. But this is truer in the United States than in other countries and may say more about the kinds of cultural values our society emphasizes—and that get passed on by child-care workers and other children—than anything having to do with group care itself.

We do have to take these findings with a healthy dose of caution, though. First of all, most of what we know about day care comes from studies of high-quality, well-funded, university-based centers, which can care for only about 10 percent of all children of working parents in this country. We know practically nothing about the effects of the most common form of child care, baby-sitting by either relatives or paid sitters. Then, these studies tell us only about short-term effects because there are hardly any follow-up studies. And practically none of the researchers have even raised such bigger issues as the significance and effect of day care for parents, for the family as a whole, and for society in general.

So we really know very little about day care. Early day care probably has some effect on children's development, but it's hard to say just what that effect is. The single most important factor in the effect of day care on a child boils down to the personality of the caregiver and how much she or he knows about children. And here parents' intuitive feelings about the person(s) who are taking care of their children are probably the best measure we have.

Professor Urie Bronfenbrenner of Cornell University has been a strong voice in favor of the needs both of children and working parents. When he was asked to help the federal government set standards for day care, he forcefully demurred and said that government should not be setting those standards—that parents should.

"We professionals don't know enough about what's good for kids," he told me, adding emphatically, "The people who do know are the parents." (In Chapters 5–11, we'll talk about the ways parents can get and keep the best kind of care for their children.)

More important than the fact of a parent's working or a child's being cared for by someone else are the answers to these questions posed by Lois Wladis Hoffman, professor of psychology at the University of Michigan, working mother of two children, and an eminent researcher on maternal employment:

- What is happening to the child while the mother is at work?
- Is the child in a stimulating, affectionate, and stable environment?
- In what way is that environment different from the way it would be if the mother were at home?
- Would the mother be resentful (about staying at home when she wants to be at work) or inattentive or less effective than the present caregiver?
- How do mother and child get along with each other when they are together?

Only when we have answers to questions like these can we judge the effects of a parent's working and of another person's caring for a small child. For one way to help children express their feelings about their parents' work, see the box "Family Talk About Parents' Work."

Schoolchildren

Tara's tearful outburst described at the beginning of this chapter highlights a common grievance. Children often feel that the sometime unavailability of their working mothers means that these mothers are not interested in or are rejecting them. (This complaint is still rarely voiced against fathers,

---

FAMILY TALK ABOUT PARENTS' WORK

Too often, in the crush of everyday life, parents and children don't talk about some of the things they feel most strongly about. One way to bring out both happy and sad feelings is to do a "whip" around the dinner table—to go around with one question to which everyone gives a quick answer. Sometimes these quick answers will spark conversations afterward; sometimes they serve their purpose just to let everyone else in the family know how you feel about a particular issue. Here are some questions that can elicit genuine feelings about combined parenting and working:

- What do you think is the best thing about our family?
- What is the best thing about Mother's job and the way it affects the family?
- What is the best thing about Father's job and the way it affects the family?
- What is one thing you'd like to change about the way we live?
- What is one thing you'd like to change about Mother's job?
- What is one thing you'd like to change about Father's job?

whose work children tend to take for granted.) Chuck, who was living with his mother after his parents' divorce, lamented, "She does not pay any attention to me. I want her to be a mom with an interest in what I am doing with my life, not just a machine that shells out money."

Judith Wallerstein, Ph.D., director of the Center for the Family in Transition in Corte Madera, California, and an authority on families affected by divorce, attributes much of this distress to children's preoccupation with "the idealized family of their fantasies." These "fantasy families" are often created by television sitcoms and storybooks, which don't represent current reality but are often more influential than the real-life situations children see all around them. As media portrayals catch up with what is happening in the real world, children's expectations are sure to follow.

They are already moving in this direction. For years the time after the youngest child goes to school all day was the most popular one for women to leave hearth and home for office or factory. Today, when most mothers are already at work by now, the first day of school still marks a new phase of a child's life—when Tara or Chuck takes one more step toward independence. With schools taking over children's supervision for a five- or six-hour stretch, at a time when most youngsters are eager and able to do more on their own, it's easier for parents to arrange for part-time child care.

The school-age children of working parents benefit from two conditions of family life. For one thing, they tend to live in more structured homes, with clear-cut rules. Necessity creates the framework, which then gives these youngsters guidance for running their lives. (More about setting up structure in Chapter 12.) For another, their parents usually encourage them to be independent. (The only exception to this encouragement of independence seems to come from mothers who feel guilty about working.)

And children usually love the independence. In fact, the parents usually fret more about problems than do the children. Brad, eleven, reassured his mother by saying, "Don't worry, Mom. You're a lot nicer to have around when you're involved in something besides us."

Of course, children—like adults—don't always *like* the obligations they have to assume. The reassuring Brad also said, "I wouldn't have so much to do in the house if Mom wasn't working." But they often relish the freedom of being on their own. One group of eleven-year-old "latchkey" children (children who are not supervised by adults for part of the day) told a researcher that they loved having and using their own keys and that they considered having the house to themselves after school a big plus.

Most children of working parents thrive in school, as well as at home. Research has shown, for example, that daughters of working mothers do better in school than daughters of homemakers; they also score higher on tests of self-esteem. These girls benefit from seeing their mothers as strong role models, by their closer relationships with their fathers, and by their own independence. The findings for boys are less clear-cut and more varied by social class. For example, some sons of middle-class working women score lower on intelligence tests and do more poorly in school. Lois Hoffman suggests that the superior showing of the sons of homemakers may not reflect the boys' ability as much as their conformity to adult standards; their superiority may not hold up over time. Then, sons of working mothers in lower-income families are more likely to have strained relations with their fathers, possibly because both father and son may see a mother's going to work as a sign that the father cannot provide for his family. As society adjusts to the fact that now the *typical* mother is a working mother, there should be fewer negative effects on boys.

Children of working parents often voice their complaints loud and clear. (Dorri, fourteen: "Nobody sews or cooks for me anymore—I feel like I have two fathers and no mother." Johnny, eight: "Why can't you ever be home when I get home from school?") But they express more positive thoughts, too. (Carla, ten: "I don't get bored of her, and she doesn't get bored of me." Marc, twelve: "If Mom wasn't working, we wouldn't be able to take such super vacations.")

Adolescents

When Flo told her three children that she had just been offered a good job and that she had decided to take it, her middle child, fourteen-year-old Tony, looked worried. "Andy told me that when his mother went back to work, she got so mean—she was always yelling at him. I hope you don't get that way." A few months after Flo took the job, Tony came up to her and said, "You know, Mom, it's good you took that job. You don't get on our backs so much."

By the time the youngest child is in her teens, almost all mothers are working out of the house, and this seems to suit both adolescents and parents. In a study conducted for General Mills, seven out of ten teenagers said that their mothers' working had either positive effects or no effects on them.

Teenagers want to be independent—to make their own decisions. They like being on their own. They hate the feeling that their parents are breathing down their necks, watching their every move, and they resent having to answer for the way they spend their time. Mothers who are at home are often sorely tempted to tell their teenagers what to do and how to do it; and when their well-meaning advice or questions are rejected, they often feel personally rebuffed. The working mother avoids some of this conflict.

At home, mothering abilities are needed less—and tested more—at this stage of children's lives. But on the job, a woman can use other abilities. Her response to this challenge shows up in the fact that the working mother of teenagers is apt to see herself as more competent, more attractive, and more fulfilled than does her counterpart at home. And again, the way a mother feels about herself sends ripples into her family circle to affect the lives of everyone in the home.

This may explain why adolescent children of working mothers are better adjusted socially, feel better about themselves, have more of a sense of belonging, and get along better with their families and with their friends at school than do other teenagers. They also hold less stereotyped ideas about men's and women's roles and abilities. Daughters of working women make a particularly strong showing. They are more outgoing, independent, active, and highly motivated to do well in school and in other activities.

Some observers in society worry, seeing the empty homes of teens whose parents are away at work as dens of temptation. But those young people whose parents show interest in them, are available by phone, and keep track of their children's whereabouts are no more likely to get into trouble with drugs, sex, or the law than are those whose mothers are at home. Teenagers are resourceful. The ones who want to do the forbidden have always managed to find a time and a place to do it.

HOW PARENTAL EMPLOYMENT AFFECTS THE FAMILY

Because a mother's working, in and of itself, is no longer considered a crucial factor in a child's development, what then *is* important? To find out, let's ask a different question. Instead of thinking in terms of working and at-home mothers, let's ask what the differences are in the families of women who enjoy what they're doing, whether they're working full- or part-time, or are at home.

The answer from study after study comes up the same: The more satisfied a woman is with her life, the more effective she is as a parent, and the better adjusted her children will be. This is true whether she goes out to work or stays in the home. We'll know our society is truly liberated when we can say the same thing about men—and have it be widely accepted.

It's important to remember the influence of parental attitude, especially now, when the working mother has indeed become the norm. In the minds of some observers, this is a good thing.

"Combining parenthood with paid employment is a more appropriate pattern for the time we live in," says psychologist Lois Hoffman. "Today's family is smaller, the modern home requires less upkeep, and the kinds of products that women used to make can now be bought more cheaply in the stores. As a result, the full-time homemaker often has time on her hands, which she sometimes uses to provide too much mothering."

Dr. Hoffman's statement illustrates a vast change in the way we now look at parental employment. In the past, those who cared about family life often stressed the negative aspects and tried to figure out how working mothers could compensate for the smaller amounts of time and attention they could give their children. Today we see the positive aspects that working holds for the entire family.

The mother often feels better about herself because she feels more competent, more economically secure, and more in charge of her life. The better she feels about her life, the better she functions as a parent. The father can relax a little, knowing he is not the sole financial support of his family. He sees more of his children and is more of a presence in the home, partly because he is less likely to be holding a second job, and partly because he assumes a larger share of child care.

And as we have seen, the children of working parents benefit in a number of ways. One of the greatest benefits may well be a new way of looking at family life, at the roles of mothers and fathers.

Yet even though the working-parent household may, in the long run, be the healthiest for both parents and children alike, it has, as every working parent knows, its own share of headaches. As one textbook editor with two small children said, "I cannot imagine doing without either my job or my children. I am, however, unsympathetic with those who imply that it is easy." When parents are pressured because of too little time, too little money, and too little energy, the entire family suffers. When children feel they take a backseat to their parents' careers, the entire family feels this unhappiness. When the small details of everyday life or the major decisions involving basic life-style crowd in on the working parent, it is hard to feel fulfilled or competent. And so the rest of this book is devoted to resolving the kinds of issues and problems that plague working parents the most.

3

You CAN Plan Your Life

―――

"When I was about to have my second child, I was finishing up the work for my Ph.D., teaching a couple of classes a week, and directing the human relations program for the City University of New York," social science professor Ved Kawatra told me. "I had such a full schedule that I told my husband, 'The only day I can have this baby is on the Friday before vacation.' She must have heard me because at seven o'clock on Friday evening, as I was coming down the elevator after my last class, I went into labor. By the time vacation was over, Anita and I were home from the hospital and both feeling well enough so that I didn't have to miss one class. This is the way I make appointments with my life!"

"Before Debbie and I got married, we knew we wanted three or four children. We also had professional goals for ourselves," says Matthew Klein of Stamford, Connecticut. "So we sat down and planned our careers and our family at the same time." Debbie, who entered medical school soon after their marriage, decided that their first child should be born the spring of her first year of school. "I knew my hours would be regular that first year," she told me. "I knew I'd be home every evening, and that summer would be the only one I'd have

33

off throughout my medical training. The second year I'd have regular hours half the time, so I could still spend a lot of time with the baby—not like the third year, when I would be on duty at the hospital every third night."

Joshua was born in March, the first spring of Debbie's medical school and Matthew's law school. "We were very lucky, of course, that we had a lot of financial help from our parents and from student loans, so we were able to hire full-time help right from the start," says Matt. "We were in debt for years, but we still figured it was better to have our children while we were both young than to wait until we were out of school and had a better economic base. Also, my being a student during part of this time let me spend a lot more time with Joshua than if I had been putting in the long hours required of a new lawyer. I missed some classes when I had to be with the baby, I put off my studying some weeks, and as a result I think I was with my baby much more than most fathers are."

When Matthew graduated from law school and Debbie was about to enter her fourth year of medical school, when her schedule was fairly regular, they conceived their second child. Rachel was born two-and-a-half years after Josh, and was followed three years later, as Matt and Debbie had planned—by Samantha.

At a time when both men and women expect to be working for most of their adult lives and when birth control technology has advanced enough to allow precise family planning, more and more couples are—like Matt and Debbie—carefully scheduling the timing and spacing of their children, with special consideration to coordinating their work and family lives.

WHEN TO HAVE CHILDREN

If you've made it this far in this book, it seems safe to assume that you have already made the really big decision—whether to have children at all—and that, like most people, you've opted for parenthood. If you haven't already had those children, you can think about whether you want to get an early start on adding to your family—or whether you want to wait for a few years. Early or late childbearing—which is better? Better for parents and better for children? Both patterns have their own sets of pluses and minuses, and only you can decide which one fits in better with your plans for your own life. (See "Advantages to Having Children Early and Late.")

Many women—especially working women—are choosing to have their babies later these days. Almost one in four white women are now having their first baby after the age of thirty. (Black women tend to become mothers earlier.)

According to Richard P. Leavitt, spokesman for the March of Dimes Birth Defects Foundation, "There is no universal, narrow time-window within which all women would be wisest to do their reproducing." The medical statistics favor women in the midrange—those past adolescence and not on the brink of menopause. But personal health factors and good prenatal care tend to be more important than age.

You may decide for biological reasons to have your children early. The major risk that parents over thirty-five or forty encounter is the increased possibility of bearing a child with a chromosomal disorder such as Down syndrome, which involves various physical problems, as well as mental retardation. The risk for this defect increases with age, from 1 such birth in 2000 among twenty-five-year-old mothers up to 1 in 40 for women over age forty-five. The risk also rises with the age of the father, especially among men over 50.

However, new technology and good prenatal care can do a lot to offset these higher risks. The availability of various prenatal diagnostic techniques—like amniocentesis, chorionic villus sampling, and new blood tests—means that Down syndrome and various other disorders can be detected before birth, early enough to terminate the pregnancy if you choose to. In addition, in recent years, a number of programs have been developed to help Down children improve their skills, and many of these youngsters have shown remarkable early gains. Other high-tech childbirth procedures, like fetal heart monitors and ultrasound, can help make delivery easier for older first-time mothers.

You also need to ask yourself how childbearing and child rearing fit in with your overall career aspirations. After

ADVANTAGES TO HAVING CHILDREN EARLY

- You are likely to have more physical energy. You can cope better with getting up in the middle of the night, staying up all night with a sick baby, keeping up with the heavy demands of job and family.
- You are likely to have fewer medical problems with pregnancy and childbirth. Women who conceive after age thirty-five or forty are statistically more likely to suffer from toxemia, high blood pressure, and kidney disorders, and they run a higher risk of bearing a child with a birth defect.
- You will be younger with your children—more energetic, and psychologically in tune with them later as they become teenagers and then young adults.
- You can use the children's early years to continue your education, work at a less demanding entry-level job, or work on a part-time schedule, and then when your children demand less time and attention, you will be free to concentrate more on your work.
- You will be giving yourself a cushion of time if you have trouble conceiving immediately. (Some older couples who do not conceive right away hear the clock ticking away. The more trouble they have, the more anxious they get, and this very anxiety may lead to further difficulty.)
- You will have had fewer years to engage in various activities that have been identified as risk factors in childbearing—such as alcohol intake, smoking and overeating. Hypertension and related circulatory problems, glucose intolerance, and diabetes are also more likely to develop in middle age.
- You will not be as apt to have built up an unrealistically high set of expectations for your children, as do many couples who have waited many years to have a family.

ADVANTAGES TO HAVING CHILDREN LATE

- You have had a chance to think more about your goals—what you want in life, both from your family and your career.
- You are more mature and can bring the benefits of your life experience to your role as parent.
- You will not have had to interrupt the course of your career between your schooling and starting to work.
- You will be better established in your career, so you won't have to press so hard on the job at the very time when your children's needs are likely to be greatest.
- You've already proved to yourself that you can make it on the job, so you won't feel as if your children are keeping you from attaining career success, and you can relax a little and enjoy them.
- You are likely to have more money that will make it easier to handle the expenses of children, buy time- and labor-saving services, and get more child care.
- You will be in a stronger position to negotiate a favorable maternity/paternity leave, a part-time work schedule, an arrangement whereby you can do some work at home, or some other benefit. Knowing your value to the organization, your employer will be more likely to make concessions to hold onto you.

studying the earnings differential between men and women and analyzing the reasons for it, Lester C. Thurow, professor of economics and management at the Massachusetts Institute of Technology, said, "Women who wish to have successful careers, compete with men, and achieve the same earnings should have their children either before twenty-five or after thirty-five."

After looking closely at the lifetime earnings profile of men, Thurow pointed out that it is very hard to predict which twenty-five-year-olds will become financially successful, but very easy to predict financial success for thirty-five-year-olds. These ten years, between ages twenty-five and thirty-five, are crucial ones in practically every occupation. And these are the very ones when women are most likely to stop working for pay, or to cut back to part-time work, to bear and raise children. "The current system of promotion and skill acquisition," says Thurow, "extracts an enormous lifetime price for those who do." It extracts just as big a price, of course, from men who put family concerns ahead of career ambitions during these years, and who—for the sake of their young families—cut back on their working hours and their availability for promotions, travel, or relocation.

These hard economic facts do not, of course, have to dictate the way you should plan your life. Although this trend may be true for many working people, it doesn't hold for all. If you already had your children between the ages twenty-five and thirty-five, or if you want to have them during these years, you don't have to give up any hope of success in work. Many parents who have had their children in this decisive decade have still gone on to career success—sometimes at a spectacular level—despite the call of colic or the demands of diapers at strategic times. Again, you need to weigh the arguments on all sides and do what makes sense for you and your life.

Looking back on their lives, working parents who shared their experiences with me had differing feelings about what they had done. Some were very happy that they had their children early and then had gone on to pursue their careers. (This was the route I took, which worked well for me.) Others agreed with editor Jamie Raab who told me, "I'm glad I became established in my career and waited until I was in my thirties to get married and have a child."

Then there's a third pattern, named after Arlene Rossen Cardozo's 1986 book, *Sequencing*. The sequencer (almost always a woman—at least up to now) establishes herself in her career, leaves it to raise children, and then picks up work in a way that doesn't put too much pressure on her or conflict with her role as mother.

Laurel Dutcher, who formerly served as office manager for The Hunger Project, is currently staying home with her twin sons, now fifteen months old. She says, "I had been working long hours at a job I loved before our babies were born, but since we had twins, both my husband and I felt it important to give them as much parent-time as possible so that each child has some individual time with us. I don't have the earning power or the career orientation that my husband does, and I like being able to keep the child-care job in the family instead of hiring it out, so I decided to stay home.

"Since our children are so young, I can't say anything decisive about our arrangement. But at fifteen months Josh and Ben are talking and walking ahead of schedule, while most twins typically do things later. I think the boys benefit from lots of attention, I love being the 'primary' parent, and my husband's career is blossoming. For right now I think we have an ideal arrangement. We have great resources—lots of support is available, our major personal needs and goals are satisfied, and the kids are flourishing. We're lucky to be able to have it pretty much the way we want it."

Probably the most famous sequencer in the country today is Associate Justice Sandra Day O'Connor of the United States Supreme Court. Justice O'Connor took five years out of her law career to take care of her three children, returned to full-time work as assistant attorney general of Arizona, and has said she is glad she spent that time at home. Unlike Justice O'Connor, however, many women—and men—who take time out slip off the fast track of their careers as a result. They don't make partner in their law firms, they don't become vice-presidents in their companies, and it takes them longer to make the same kind of money as their colleagues who worked right through. They do, however, reap other benefits, and for many the enriched quality of their personal lives is worth the career sacrifice.

By and large, the trend today—especially for people whose work is important to them—is to have their children later. When asked what they would have done differently, hardly any of the working parents who spoke to me or who answered my questionnaire regretted having waited to have children. But a number said that they would have had their children lat-

er, after they had gotten more education or established themselves more securely in a career. As one father said, "I would
have married later and had children later. I was not adequately prepared for either role." And a mother told me, "I think I
would have gotten more education before having my children. Now there are things I would like to do, and it's harder
when you've got the children."

HOW MANY CHILDREN AND HOW FAR APART?

"It's a whole different ball game with two children," one
mother told me. "I thought I was busy before—but now, with
juggling my job, my marriage, my toddler—and now the new
baby, there are just not enough hours in the day or days in the
week."

You don't have to be a mathematical genius to realize
that two children involve more time and effort from their
parents than one does, that three require more than two,
and even—if you're so inclined—that ten require more
than nine. These parental obligations are reflected in the
work patterns of one parent. (It's not too hard to guess
which one.) Yes, the more small children a woman has at
home, the less likely she is to be in the workforce. One recent report underscores the cost of raising children, however, in its finding that the more *older* children a woman
has, the more likely she is to look for work.

Yet by the time the mother of several children does find a
job, she is often at a serious disadvantage in the marketplace.
A mother of three children, spaced three years apart, earns 13
percent less on the average than a woman who has no children. The major reason for this disparity lies in the interrupted life pattern of the woman with several children. Women
with one child, for example, work two and a half years less
over their lifetime than do women with no children; those
with two youngsters stay out of the labor market for two more
years, and mothers of three are out for one additional year.

This decision is far from cut and dried because there are so many exceptions to the general rule. There are, for example, two-paycheck families that consist of eight or nine healthy children and two parents who are both active and successful in their careers. There are achieving single parents of three or four children. (Yes, Clark Kent, there *are* Supermen and Superwomen.) There are endless possibilities for planning a career around children or children around a career.

Northwestern University professor of psychology Niles Anne Newton, for example, who has devoted much of her professional life to research in breastfeeding and other aspects of parent–child relationships, carefully spaced her own four children seven years apart. "This way," she told me, "I've always been able to give my full attention to the newest infant. I've always had a helper close at hand, and I've been able to combine my family and professional lives for a longer period than most people."

On the other hand, parents of closely spaced children reap other benefits. Because the children have each other, they make fewer calls on their parents to play with them and keep them company. And because the intense parenting that very young children need is limited to a shorter time span, parents have a longer time to shift from child care to career care. (See "Things to Think About in Planning the Size and Spacing of Your Family.")

THE WORKER BECOMES A PARENT

"I never realized how much of a difference this baby would make in our lives," Tom, a telephone repairman, told me. "I was one of six kids, so I thought I knew what it was all about; but what I didn't take into account is that, with inflation the way it is, Margie was only planning to take three months off from her job—not like my mother, who was home full time.

"I like spending time with my son—not like my dad, who was never around us when we were little. But I never knew how much was involved in the care of a little baby. Darrin's

THINGS TO THINK ABOUT IN PLANNING THE SIZE AND SPACING OF YOUR FAMILY

- A Syracuse University study of housework found that the more children a woman has and the younger they are, the more time she spends at household chores.
- A mother is more likely to work outside the home the fewer children she has and the older they are.
- Children of different ages need different kinds of child care, often requiring parents to take them to two different places.
- Brothers and sisters who are less than three years apart in age develop closer, more intense relationships than those spaced more than three years from each other. They are more likely to feel rivalry toward each other, but are also more likely to be good friends.

four months old now, and he's still waking up in the middle of the night, so Margie and I both walk around half-dead most of the time. Then we thought maybe Margie should stay home longer, but the bills have been piling up. Only four months old, and he's costing a fortune, what with the doctors and the hospital and the baby furniture, so we need her pay.''

Tom and Margie's story is a common one. No matter how much you know about children in general, no one can know in advance the full impact of having one of your own. "It's as if this tiny little creature has taken over our whole house," said one young mother. "She fills every room of this apartment with her paraphernalia, and I always feel her presence even when she's sound asleep. I feel like the lady-in-waiting to an imperious queen!"

Because of this all-consuming attention that infants demand (usually very loudly), their new parents are becoming louder, too, in the demands they're making for maternity and paternity leave.

WORKING PARENTS SPEAK TO WORKERS THINKING ABOUT HAVING A BABY

- Go ahead and have the baby. Your job issues will work themselves out.
- Just remember, you don't go home at 5 PM, and you don't get weekends off anymore. It's a full-time job being a parent and you will never understand it until you do it yourself. But it's wonderful!
- Get a dog first—it gives you an idea of the demands that are going to be placed on you.
- Wait until you're financially secure enough to survive on one income for a while.
- It's hard to take care of a baby. You have to really want it.
- Having a baby is more of a commitment of time, energy, and money than most people can imagine.
- Children are the most wonderful precious gifts we will ever be given. But they are not for everyone. Be sure you really want the child and be ready to accept all the beauty it will bring—and all the changes you will need to make, along with the sacrifices.
- Think carefully about giving up sleeping late on weekends, candlelight dinners, and traveling. And now let me tell you about how beautiful and smart my little girl is.
- Do it! Go ahead! Having a child puts you in touch with the basics of life and love in a way that work does not. The joy that comes from it is like no other. You can work out a way to do it and still keep working if you want.

MATERNITY/PATERNITY LEAVE

Eileen got her Ph.D. at age twenty-three, her assistant professorship at a major midwestern university at age twenty-five, her wedding ring at age twenty-seven, and her baby at age twenty-nine. "The head of my department was horrified when I told her I was planning to take a semester off to care for my baby," says Eileen, holding six-month-old Jessica, a carbon copy of her blue-eyed, flaxen-haired mother. " 'What about all the gains women have made here? You'll ruin it for the rest of us," she warned me.

"You see, at my school the contest among us is to see who can take as little time out as possible. You dream about going into labor as you're lecturing, then rushing to the hospital, having your perfect natural childbirth, coming home the same day, and being back in front of your class for the next assigned lecture. I felt apologetic about wanting to stay home for the first four months, and I'm afraid it will really hurt my career—but I still think it was important for me as well as for Jessie."

Leave for New Mothers

Eileen was lucky that she could stay home for four months—that her employer held her job for her and that she didn't need the income she was giving up beyond her two weeks of paid leave. Among the women with whom I was in touch, leaves ranged from one week for an adoptive mother to one year, most of which was unpaid. For most women the materni-ty-leave picture is a crazy-quilt patchwork of official paid ma-ternity leave (which, when it exists, may be as little as two weeks or as much as six months), pieced out with disability or sick leave, vacation time, or unpaid leave. Fathers have fewer opportunities to take new-parent leave, and even when it is available, few men take it (see the next section).

The legal picture for maternity leave is better than it was and not as good as it should be. The United States is the only industrialized nation in the world (besides South Africa) that does not have a national maternity-leave policy. Only about 40 percent of American working women receive any salary while on pregnancy leave, and up to one-third of the nation's 49 million working women are not covered by any pregnancy-leave policy. Often this is because they work for small companies that are exempt from the 1978 Pregnancy Discrimination Act, passed as an amendment to Title VII of the Civil Rights Act. It requires that firms with fifteen or more employees treat pregnancy just as they do any other temporary disability. When a pregnant woman is able to work, she may not be fired, denied a job or promotion, forced to go on leave or to stay out a prescribed period of time. Furthermore, under the Equal Employment Opportunity Act, pregnant women cannot be required to use up vacation benefits before receiving sick-leave pay or disability benefits, unless other temporarily disabled workers have to do so, too.

The extent of legal coverage depends on a company's overall health policies. If your employer has no temporary disability plan, you do not have to be covered for pregnancy and childbirth. If it does, though, you have to be treated like any other worker with a temporary condition interfering with your ability to work.

You are entitled to the same benefits other workers are for disability, sick leave, and health insurance. Expenses for pregnancy-related conditions have to be covered on the same basis as expenses for other medical conditions. If other workers can get their old jobs back after taking disability leave, women who have taken maternity leave have to have the same privilege. If the man who works at the next desk is paid during the three months he is out recuperating from a heart attack and then comes back to his old job, you have to receive the same treatment.

This legislation does not go far enough, but it is important. Says Felice N. Schwartz, president of Catalyst and director of its Career and Family Center, "This act was significant because it acknowledged women as an important, permanent part of the work force, and it took the first step toward recognizing child care as a national priority."

A few states—eighteen as of this writing—have enacted their own laws granting some form of parental leave.* And sixteen others, including Washington, D.C., were studying or actively pursuing such legislation during 1987 and 1988. So

*California, Colorado, Connecticut, Hawaii, Illinois, Iowa, Kansas, Louisiana, Maine, Massachusetts, Minnesota, Montana, New Hampshire, Oregon, Rhode Island, Tennessee, Washington, and Wisconsin

this may be the wave of the future, but so far it is far from a tidal wave.

According to a 1986 Catalyst survey of 384 companies among the Fortune 1500 firms, 95 percent of the largest firms offer some kind of pregnancy disability leave. Some companies are shining examples, like Aetna Life & Casualty, which offers six months of unpaid leave to help workers balance the demands of career and personal life. And a small but growing number of companies offer unpaid leaves of twelve to seventeen weeks for birth, adoption, family illness, or care of elderly relatives.

But many corporate giants offer very little. Fewer than half of the firms in the Catalyst survey offer a comparable job after the leave, 6 percent offer "some job," and 13 percent offer no guarantees. Only 40 percent of these companies pay full salary during pregnancy leave, 58 percent pay something, and the rest pay nothing at all. Fewer than 40 percent provide for unpaid, job-protected paternity leave for new fathers.

Other studies—by Columbia University and the Bureau of Labor Statistics—show an even gloomier picture: fewer than half of all female full-time employees get any paid maternity leave at all. In one study, conducted by Columbia University professor Sheila B. Kamerman, only 16 women out of 119 who went back to work within eight months of the birth of their babies received *any* official maternity leave, with either full or partial payment for the time they took out for pregnancy and childbirth. Of those who did, a six-week leave was the most common. A more recent study, covering California and New York, found that the average pregnancy leave ran ten weeks.

As of this writing, a Congressional bill providing for parental leave to care for a newborn, newly adopted, or seriously ill child and other family medical situations died in both houses. It is sure to be reintroduced, and if support for it is powerful enough, parents may get legislative protection. (Watch for news of it—and take some of your precious time to write to your Congressional representatives.) Until then—and even if the law is enacted—you may improve your situation by using your smarts to negotiate the best new-parent leave you can.

Yes, you have some rights under the law, and the chances are that you will have more in the years to come. But you're likely to win an even better arrangement than you're legally guaranteed if you approach your employer the right way.

If your employer is typical, he or she is concerned much more about your work life than your home life and is less likely to see the birth or adoption of your baby as a blessed event, at least as far as the company is concerned. While you're out having or taking care of your baby, someone else will have to do the work that you ordinarily do, probably involving double pay for that time (if, in fact, you're being paid). Besides, whenever another person picks up the reins, the smooth flow of an operation is interrupted to a greater or lesser degree. The better you can put yourself in your employer's place and the more you can empathize with him or her, the more effective you can be at getting you both in a win–win situation. (See "Negotiating Maternity Leave.")

Leave for New Fathers

In 1981 a Catalyst survey found that fewer than 9 percent of a sample of the nation's biggest industrial, financial, and service companies offered any kind of paternity benefits. A scant five years later, the percentage had quadrupled; by 1986, 37 percent of such companies offered unpaid leave time to new fathers. Typically, the companies offered men shorter leaves than women—one to four weeks for the men, compared to one to three months for women. Men's legal rights to such leaves have been filed, but the issue has not been settled in court.

Even when these leaves are offered, though, few men follow the example of Boston attorney Jon Laramore, who took one month off from work to stay home with his baby daughter after his wife, Janet McCabe—also an attorney—had come to the end of her five-month maternity leave and gone back to work. The greeting cards produced by Hallmark Cards may exalt the father's role in infant care, but none of the company's own male employees have taken more than a week of its unpaid one-month paternity leave. Most men take a few days off from work at the birth or adoption of a baby and call the time off vacation, personal days, or family-crisis leave. There are a number of reasons why most men don't press for parenting leaves and don't take them when they are available (as indicated in "Overcoming Barriers to Paternity Leave").

NEGOTIATING MATERNITY LEAVE

Not all workers have the kind of success that graphic designer Alexandra Guzek-Hoffman did when she told her boss, "After eight years of service with the company, four months is the *least* amount of time I deserve." She was paid for two months, unpaid for the next two, and now that her son Peter is five months old, she is looking forward to taking the one month's vacation coming to her this year. The following suggestions for approaching your employer are based on the experiences of Alexandra and other parents:

- Fairly early in your pregnancy tell your employer about your pregnancy and your plans for continuing to work. You don't have to call work before you call your husband and mother, but your boss should not be the last to know. Before you give your co-workers the good news and before you show up at work in a maternity dress, ask for an appointment with your supervisor, at a time convenient for him or her, to discuss your future with the company.
- At this time tell him or her how long you expect to continue working, how much maternity leave you would like to take, and when you expect to be back on the job.
- Suggest that you tackle any upcoming major projects now; you can get them rolling well enough before you take your leave, thus enabling someone else to pick up where you left off.
- Suggest that you or someone else train one or more employees in the work that you are doing, so that

---

your work can be handled by other workers while
you are out.

- If you're not sure about your future plans, leave the
door open to work as long as possible. If you need to
stop sooner because of health or other reasons, you
always can. But if you give a definite end date and
then decide you want to work longer, you may
not be able to. Someone else may already have been
hired or promoted to your job, or your department
may have been reorganized so that you won't fit in
any more. Here, too, give your employer as much
notice as possible.

- Ask your immediate supervisor and the personnel
department about the particulars of your company's
policy toward maternity leave and illness and
temporary-disability leave, vacation time, and
unpaid time off. Get a clear statement about your
right to resume work at the same job, seniority, and
pay scale.

- Get confirmation in writing of your agreement.

- Come up with your own creative suggestions, like
the following:

   Keep in telephone touch even when you're not
"supposed" to be working. If you can accept calls
during your maternity leave, you can get a sense of
continuity, and your employer can feel reassured of
your continued interest. You'll have to see, of
course, whether the calls become excessive. You'll
also have to fit them into your schedule. Because a
new baby keeps erratic hours, you may want to let
an answering machine take the calls—and then
return them at a time that works for you.

   Work at home for a while, first part-time and
then full-time, before you return to the office. This
will give you a chance to be with your baby longer,
to ease into your child-care situation, and to make a
gradual transition back to work.

   After you go back to work, if you do the kind of
work that can be done at home, you may be able to
take one day a week at home. Some editors, for

example—even those without children—find they can do more work at home, away from telephones and drop-in colleagues, than they can in the office. One new mother told me of the "unofficial" agreement she has with her supervisor: she takes her one day a week to work at home—on a different day every week. This way, she can decide on her day at home depending on what is going on in the office. And her special arrangement is not too obvious to her co-workers.

You may be able to use accrued vacation and sick-leave time to receive a part-time salary for several months.

• If you and your employer cannot agree on an arrangement, make your points in a calm, rational way—always keeping your employer's viewpoint in mind.

Emphasize your value to the company, the years you have already been working there, the years you expect to continue to work.

Offer the facts about your legal rights. No firm wants to be subject to a suit or complaint.

Ask for a change of company policy.

• If none of these approaches succeeds, you have several avenues:

You can go to a different department within the organization—the personnel office or a supervisor at the next higher level (if you have reason to believe you'll get a friendly hearing).

You can go to your union.

You can file a complaint with government agencies: your city or state human rights commissions and the local office of the federal Equal Employment Opportunity Commission.

For help in filing complaints, you may want to contact a lawyer and/or a women's political action group, such as the National Organization for Women.

THE FIRST FEW MONTHS

The birth of your first baby marks a major transition in your life. Moving from a twosome to a threesome changes people, changes marriages, and changes careers. Social scientists see the advent of parenthood more as a time of transition than as a crisis, but they're not the ones getting up in the middle of the night—or the ones staying in a bathrobe till dinner time.

For both biological and cultural reasons, it is usually the mother who reacts most intensely to the birth of the baby. First, of course, there are the physiological demands of pregnancy, childbirth, and breastfeeding. Then, even today when the roles of men and women are undergoing great change, in most homes most of the responsibility for raising the children still falls to the mother. Some women become so wrapped up in the care of their new babies that they resent both their husbands and their jobs. Others resent the baby. The more highly educated and career-oriented a woman is, the more trouble she is likely to have adjusting to parenthood. The breastfeeding working mother has special concerns, as indicated in, "If You Are Nursing Your Baby."

What are women bothered by the most? According to one study, it's fatigue, interrupted sleep and rest, feeling "edgy," and worry about personal appearance. Men also groan about the interruptions of sleep and rest, but their other concerns are different. They are bothered by the need to change plans because of the baby, by the extra work and money problems the baby brings, and by in-laws who give advice. Sometimes the excitement of parenthood so outweighs its responsibilities that a "baby honeymoon" occurs for the first few months, and the most difficult period of adjustment doesn't come until the baby is about eight months old. Whenever the most trying time is, though, new parents have to remember that with time they can work out the problems special to their own situations and can develop a working routine. If you look around, you'll see that plenty of other families have done it who aren't nearly so smart, capable, and loving as you are. If they've been able to manage, so can you.

OVERCOMING BARRIERS TO PATERNITY LEAVE

While some of the same approaches listed under "Negotiating Maternity Leave" can also apply to a father, your situation is different—and not only in the biological sense. No, as you may have noticed, you're not having this baby. But yes, you and your family might well benefit from your taking a leave around the time of the birth or the adoption of a baby. Why, then, if you're a typical father, are you not likely to take such a leave?

In the book *Fatherhood Today: Men's Changing Role in the Family,* the staff of Catalyst took a close look at new options for fathers in the workplace and explored the reasons so few men take paternity leave. Based on their analyses and on the reports I received from working parents, here are the biggest barriers:

- *Money.* In most families, the husband earns twice as much as the wife. Because babies, bless them, come with their own price tags and because the mother is taking time off from her job—some or all of which is likely to be unpaid—the family needs the father's income even more. Therefore, the new father cannot afford to take off any substantial amount of time.
- *Not knowing paternity leave is available.* Hardly any companies use the labels "paternity" or "parental leave." Instead, 90 percent of the major companies in the 1986 Catalyst survey called such leaves "personal leaves" and made no effort to tell employees that new fathers are eligible for them. It is therefore up to the employee to find out from the personnel department whether his firm does offer such leaves.
- *Fear of career static.* Men are often afraid that asking for parental leave will hurt their careers. Unfortunately, this fear seems to be well founded. Almost two-thirds of the managers in the Catalyst survey thought that it was unreasonable for new fathers to

ask for any time off, and *even in the companies that offered paternity leaves,* four out of ten managers thought that men should not get any time off for this purpose! While the woman who takes off from work for a new baby is usually applauded for being a good mother, the man who takes off is more apt to be criticized for being a wimp who doesn't care about his work.

- *Not understanding the importance of a fatherly presence.* Many men cannot imagine what they could possibly do for their new baby. They haven't been raised to nurture, they've never thought of themselves in this way, and they feel inadequate and unprepared for taking care of an infant.
- *Lack of encouragement from their wives.* Many women, too, have these same ideas. They see themselves as the nurturers and caregivers and don't even picture their husbands' playing these roles—or they do consider it and are jealous of the possibility that a strong father–baby bond might make the mother less important. This fear is happily not well founded because babies who have close ties to both parents generally grow up better adjusted and more competent than those whose fathers are distant and uninvolved.

Fortunately, there are some steps that expectant parents and new parents can take to make the transition a little smoother. (See "Easing the Transition to Parenthood.")

THE PARENT BECOMES A (PAID) WORKER

When a parent who has been home full-time with a child (usually the mother) takes an outside job, this is another major family transition. Not a crisis, just a change. Recognizing it as a change that affects the entire family and not just the parent and child, you can do a number of things to smooth the crossover.

IF YOU ARE NURSING YOUR BABY

- Encourage the baby's father to be involved in her care right from the start. He can go to the baby in the middle of the night, change diapers, bring her to you in your bed, and, if the baby sleeps in a separate crib, take her back after the feeding.
- Do all that you can to get a maternity leave of at least four weeks, and if at all possible, shoot for one of four to six months.
- *While you are still on your maternity leave:*

Find a caregiver who will support your plans to breastfeed.

Introduce your baby to the bottle about two weeks before you go back to work. Have someone else give the baby one bottle a day, preferably starting at about six weeks of age. By giving bottles much earlier than this, you run the risk of causing "nipple confusion" in your baby; if you introduce bottles much later, your baby may absolutely refuse them.

Use a bottle nipple similar to the breast nipple— such as the Playtex™ or the Nuk™.

Learn to pump your milk or express it manually. This will help relieve your own discomfort when you go back to work and will help maintain your milk supply. If you plan to feed your baby your own expressed milk, this skill is, of course, essential. You may want to rent an electric pump for a few weeks.

If you plan to give your baby your own milk in bottles, stockpile a week's supply in your freezer. You can build this up by expressing small amounts (one-half to one ounce) before or after feedings for several weeks before you go back to work.

- *When you go back to work:*

Try to work part-time during the first six months, or rearrange your work schedule to accommodate your baby's feedings. Maybe you can skip coffee breaks to get a nursing break during the day, or come in later or leave earlier.

If you can, work part-time; fewer hours every day work out better than fewer days per week. Express milk during the middle of your working day (fifteen to twenty minutes during a coffee or lunch break should do it), put it in a sterile container, and refrigerate it or store it in a Thermos bottle until you leave work. It will stay fresh for twenty-four hours in the refrigerator and up to several weeks in the freezer.

Check ads in parenting magazines for kits for working nursing mothers that include the equipment you need for expressing and storing milk.

Over the weekends, keep up your weekly breast—bottle schedule so you and your baby won't have to keep readjusting.

Try out different nursing schedules. One might be nurse first thing in the morning, at lunchtime (if you can get to your baby or the baby can be brought to you), as soon as you get home (a great way to relax!), and then late at night.

For more suggestions on being a working nursing mother, consult *The Complete Book of Breastfeeding* by Marvin S. Eiger, M.D. and Sally Wendkos Olds (see the appendix "Recommended Reading" for details).

When to Take That Job

All other things being equal (which they rarely are), there are some "best" and "worst" times in a child's life for you to go to work for the first time. If you need to take a job at a time that is not optimal for your baby, your sensitivity to your child's special needs will help you help your child make the best adjustment possible. The following are generally considered the best times to make a change like this in a child's life.

EASING THE TRANSITION TO PARENTHOOD

Some of the new-parent jitters will go away if you take some of the following steps.

Before the Baby Arrives

- *Learn.* To find out what babies are like, attend classes for expectant parents, read books and magazines, and spend at least one weekend taking care of a friend's baby (if you can find friends who'll trust their baby to an amateur).
- *Talk.* Talk to your spouse about the roles each of you will play in the baby's care. What will you do, and what will he or she do? How can you both change your schedules to accommodate this new project—and new product? Try to anticipate the kinds of situations that might come up.
- *Decide.* What kind of child care will you get when you both go back to work? Talk it over and check it out before the baby comes. You have much more time now than you will later.
- *Arrange.* Set up your child-care plan to begin at least one month before both parents return to work.
- *Say "No."* Get ready to turn down overtime work assignments, unnecessary household duties, and most social engagements—at least for the first few months—or the first few years.
- *Reach out.* Look for support from a pediatrician who is sympathetic to, rather than critical of, working parents, from other working parents, from family and friends, from community resources.
- *Take parental leave.* If at all possible, arrange for at least one parent to be home for the first three or four months of the baby's life.

After the Baby Arrives

In a study of 120 couples whose babies were under one

year old, Dr. Brent C. Miller of Utah State University and Dr. Donna L. Sollie of Texas Tech University found that the couples who coped best reported having followed these guidelines:

- *Be adaptable.* Learn to accept the unpredictability of a baby's day and to be both patient and flexible.
- *Communicate.* Share your feelings with your spouse—both the ones that have you floating on air and the ones that have you ready to fall in a heap on the floor.
- *Share responsibility.* Break away from stereotyped roles in the household and negotiate new ones.
- *Pursue adult interests.* If you can possibly fit in one or two activities that you enjoyed before the baby was born, it's worth the effort. Your life will be more fulfilling if it includes more than just parenting and work.
- *Spend some time away from the baby.* Babies are wonderful, but if you can manage to spend some time alone, with your spouse, at work, or pursuing those adult interests, you'll go back to your baby with fresh vigor.
- *Look ahead.* Think about and talk about your career goals, plan to implement them, and remind yourself that your parenting responsibilities will ease up as your children grow.
- *Get all the help you can.* Use your friends, relatives, and neighbors as resources for information, advice, and help with child care.

- *After the baby is at least three months old.* If you can swing a three-month maternity/paternity leave, you will be better able to enjoy these first few weeks of parenthood, and you will also be more energetic when you do go back to work. You and your baby need some time to get used to your new relationship, to ease the transition from womb to outside world. Furthermore, you need to marshal your strength. Looking at a tiny newborn infant, you cannot imagine the mammoth amounts of physical energy that his delivery exacted from his mother and that his care requires from whoever is feeding, bathing, changing, and getting up in the middle of the night with him.

By three months of age, your baby may be sleeping through the night (allowing you to get a decent night's sleep) and may be on a fairly regular mealtime schedule (allowing you to plan more easily for feedings).

- *Between three and six months—or after two-and-a-half to three years.* Between seven or eight months and one year, and then again between one-and-a-half to two-and-a-half years of age, many babies experience two kinds of anxiety— "separation anxiety," when they cry after the person who takes care of them most of the time goes away, and "stranger anxiety," when they resist going to an unfamiliar person. Any change in child-care arrangements at these times is apt to trigger strong negative feelings in the child. One recent study found that eighteen-month-old boys whose mothers had gone to work in the first half of the babies' first year showed healthier emotional attachment to their mothers than were those whose mothers had gone to work in the second half.

Children may howl when their parents leave the room or when a new person approaches, may quiet down while the parents are away but then cling in terror on their return, and then not let them out of sight. Some children also react poorly to change at about the second birthday, when they are struggling to master the use of language.

By age two-and-a-half or three, most children are better able to cope with a major change in their lives. They can understand the meaning of words. They can remember that even though Mommy and Daddy leave, they always come back. And they are ready to enter into all sorts of activities outside the family nest—nursery school, day care, classes at the Y, visits with other three-year-olds.

- *When life is relatively tranquil.* A study on families' adjustment to divorce found that children whose mothers had worked all along suffer no more from divorce than the children of at-home mothers. Those whose mothers got their first full-time jobs right around the time of the divorce, though, had extra problems adjusting to this double change.

Of course, divorce or death may be the very reason why a parent who has been home full-time suddenly has to go to work. If it's at all possible, though, postpone the new job for a couple of months so it won't coincide with another major change in your child's life; it will be easier for the child. It's also better if you can arrange the beginning of your new job so it doesn't come at the same time as the move to a new home, the child's entrance into school, or recovery from illness or accident. Children have a much easier time of it if they are required to cope with only one big change at a time.

If You Have to Take the Job at a Less Than Optimal Time

If a family crisis or some other reason does mean that you have to go to work at a less than ideal time, the best you can do is to be sensitive to the double load of adjustment required of your child. You can be extra sure to lend an ear when your child wants to share a feeling, a hand when your child needs to be picked up, a shoulder when someone needs to lean on it. You can expect more tears than usual, more babyish behavior, more tantrums, more clinging or more of whatever way your own child says, "I need extra loving, even though I'm not acting very lovable!"

You also have to remember to take care of yourself during this transitional time. At a time of stress, which any major life change is, you need to take extra special care of your physical needs. You need to get enough sleep, to eat properly, to get enough exercise, and to meet your psychological needs, as well. (This may sound like the impossible dream, but see Chapter 12 for some helpful hints.)

Making the Change from At-Home Parent to Working Parent

- Start your new child-care arrangements while you are still at home—from a week to a month ahead of time. This

WORKING PARENTS SPEAK TO PARENTS PLANNING TO TAKE A JOB

- Make it a part-time job if possible. Find a caregiver you consider inspirational, if possible. Get ready for a weird mixture of guilt, fatigue, and happiness.
- Don't assume you'll be emotionally ready to leave your baby to go back to work. Don't assume it will be easy to find good child care. Get ready for the guilt and torn feelings you'll experience as a working parent.
- If I weren't forced by the economy to have to work, I would stay home until my child went to first grade and would get my fulfillment from him and from volunteer work.
- Be committed to each other and to your common goals (my husband and I are). Take off at least six months to acclimate (I didn't). Work part-time (I don't). Buy three smashing outfits to wear to work (I did).
- A job? Do it for the fun of it if money isn't the main burden. Try to get a job that will make you feel good about yourself and will bring out your special talents. Makes for a happier Mom.
- Go for it! It's great and a real experience for the whole family.

way you'll be able to spend a little extra time at the daycare center, or you'll be available while your child and the new baby-sitter gradually get used to each other.

- Cut back immediately on all nonessential activities. This includes having the Cousins' Club at your house, volunteering for community activities, painting the house from top to bottom. You need all the energy and time you can muster to oil the transition.
- Go back to work on a Thursday or Friday. This way you'll be away only a day or two at first, will be home over the weekend, and the change will be less abrupt.

- If your child is old enough, take her to visit your workplace, so she can see where you will be spending your days. If you don't feel comfortable going in, just show her the building from the outside.
- Talk casually about the upcoming change—no matter how young your child is—so that when it comes, he will be prepared for it, at least at some level.
- Stay in especially close touch with your child during the first few weeks of work. If possible, have lunch with her. If not, phone a couple of times a day. To what better use can you put a coffee break?
- Make as few other changes as possible in your child's life. This is not the time to move her from a crib to a big bed, to change the babysitter, to start her in a new nursery school, or to move to a new apartment.
- Minimize other separations as much as possible. Postpone that vacation without the children and do most of your socializing as a family, with other families.
- Tell your child's teacher about the change in your home life. If he or she knows your child is under extra stress, he or she may be able to offer extra understanding and help.
- Keep a low profile about your job. Talk about it, yes, but don't obsess over it. If you bring home work, do it at night after the children are in bed. Stay "Mommy" or "Daddy" first: Your children need to know they are more important to you than your job.

DECIDING WHERE TO LIVE

One Saturday in August Dan Miller came inside, covered with sweat after mowing the lawn of the half-acre property where he lived with his wife Carol and their two-year-old son Kevin. Carol, in the midst of her weekend house cleanup, was hot and tired herself. "What do you want?" she asked, impatient to finish before Kevin woke up from his nap. As rivulets of sweat ran down Dan's face, he said, "We never have any fun on weekends anymore. We don't go anywhere, we don't see anybody, we don't even get time with each other. We spend all our time taking care of this place."

"I'd love to be back in our little apartment," Carol said wistfully, brushing a wisp of hair back from her forehead. "Life was so easy then."

"Let's sell this whole place and move back to an apartment," Dan blurted out. "We need the time more than we need the space."

The Millers did sell their house and, with the proceeds, bought a co-op apartment. Carol and Dan found they were arguing less about chores because there were fewer chores to do. Dan took a larger role in Kevin's care because he wasn't feeling pressured by a weekly backlog of house repairs and yardwork. "Maybe we'll buy another house someday," Dan says, "but right now, with Carol and me both working long hours all week long, we both feel we're better off out of it."

Other couples have moved back into the center of town from the suburbs; or have never moved out in the first place; or have stayed in a modest neighborhood because it offered many conveniences for their children; or have moved to a specific city, neighborhood, or street to be near a network of family and friends.

Where you live affects *how* you live. If your children have to be driven everywhere they go, your working may mean that they will be deprived of after-school activities and playing with other children. Or you may have the extra job of finding—and often paying—someone to drive them. If you live in an isolated community, you'll be limited in the kind of child care you can obtain. If medical and other community resources are not close by, you will have to spend more of your precious time finding and getting to them. And if you have no friends or family nearby, you will be isolated at times of need.

To help you decide whether the home you're in—or the one you're thinking about—is the right one for you, ask yourself the questions in the next section; if the answers tell you to move, start packing.

Is the Living Good for Working Parents?

- Are you close to convenient public transportation? (Not only does this affect your own and your children's access

to activities and services, but it may limit you in finding baby-sitting help.)
- How long do you have to commute to work? The advantages of suburban or country living may not be worth the extra time you have to spend getting to and from work or the unease you may feel being far from your children in times of emergency.
- How close are you to relatives and friends? The availability of people who will pitch in at times of crisis (a sick child, a baby-sitter who doesn't show up, a sudden need to work late) may make it worthwhile to stay in—or to move to—a house that's just a little inconvenient in other respects.
- How available are child-care services? Are centers, baby-sitters, and after-school programs nearby? If you have to travel half an hour to take your child to a center or a baby-sitter, you're losing a precious hour out of your day. It might make sense to move to an area richer in child-care facilities.
- Can you, your children, and your baby-sitter walk to a grocery store, a drugstore, a hardware store? To dancing school, piano lessons, baseball practice, scout meetings? The doctor, the dentist?
- Can the children walk to school? If they take the school bus, you'll be under pressure to get them ready in time—and if they miss it, to drive them. If they need to be taken by an adult, you'll have to plan your work schedule around this requirement. But if they can walk, you have much more freedom. Even when they're too small to go alone, you can often make arrangements to have them go with an older child in the neighborhood.
- How much upkeep does your home require? You may have dreamed of a suburban ranch or a country farmhouse for years, but if that dream demands so much work that it robs you of the energy and time you could be spending on family and job, it may turn into a nightmare.
- What are the community attitudes toward working mothers, single parents, day-care centers, fathers who assume a large share of child care? If you will be subjected to constant criticism because of your life-style, neither you nor your children will be comfortable.
- What services do the public schools provide? Can your

children eat lunch in school, or do they have to go home? Is there a prekindergarten? A supervised after-school program? The existence of one or more of these services may make it well worth your while to move to the school district that offers them.

COORDINATING WORK AND FAMILY

The following are some of the ways two-parent families today are balancing family and job obligations:

1. Both husband and wife work full-time, with maternity–paternity leaves of less than three months. Children are cared for by other person(s).
2. Both parents work full-time or part-time, arranging their schedules so that one parent is always with the children.
3. One parent works full-time; one works part-time. Outside child care covers times when both parents are working.
4. Both parents work part-time, outside care used.
5. One or both parents work at home, carving out their working schedules around the needs of the children.
6. One parent works full-time; the other stays home with the children for the first year, the first three years (till nursery school), the first six years (till first grade), the first twelve years (till junior high), the first fifteen years (till high school), or the first eighteen years (till high school graduation).

This list of options may not apply to you. You may be a single parent, restricted by financial need and by the lack of a partner to serve as backup. Or—single or married—you may feel that your economic needs, or a tight job market, or the limited availability of child care has locked you into a particular situation. You may feel that even thinking about the possibility of doing things differently is a luxury you can't afford.

And yet no matter what your situation is, you may be able to modify it so that it works out better for you and your children. This modification may involve changing your schedule at work, starting a home-based business, or switching child-care arrangements.

Ronnie, for example, is a nurse; Jerry a linotype operator. When Jerry's mother became too ill to continue to take care of their two young children, he switched to the night shift, so that one parent would always be with the children. Ronnie has just received an okay from her supervisor at the hospital to take the night shift for a couple of months while Jerry goes back to working days.

Bill, a salesman for a small plastics manufacturer, needed to be more available to his four children after his wife took a job an hour away from home. Bill pointed out to his boss that he traveled one or two weeks out of every month, that most of his business was done by phone or mail, and that he could get just as much accomplished if he came into the plant only one day a week. Bill's boss said, "Okay, I'm willing to try it, but if sales fall off, or if we run into other problems, you'll have to come back to the plant." Ten years later, Bill is still doing his job from home.

As a single parent, Roseann was getting overwhelmed by the demands of spending two and a half to three hours every day traveling, between taking her four-year-old to the baby-sitter and then commuting to her secretarial job. In desperation she decided to start her own secretarial service from home, and she now has such a profitable business that she has had to employ two other typists, both of whom work from their homes in her neighborhood. All three of the women like being able to schedule their work around the time their children are playing or sleeping, enjoy not having to worry about outside child care, and also appreciate not having the expenses of commuting, work clothes, and lunching out.

STAYING LOOSE

The key to optimum organization of your life is flexibility. Because the needs of children are much more variable than are the demands of the typical job, working parents have to be adaptable. You have to be open to changing your systems when necessary and to taking advantage of opportunities that will help you maintain this adaptability. You need to remember that the only constant in life is constant change. In one survey of 200 working parents, for example, 2 out of 3 changed their child-care arrangements over a six-month period.

For example, you may have taken only four weeks' maternity leave after the birth of your first child, but after the second is born, you may feel the need for a breather of a few months. Or you may have decided to stay home full-time till your youngest is in nursery school but then find that when she's a year old, you're chomping at the bit to get out of the house. With will and ingenuity, you can change your original plans to the benefit of everyone in the family.

4

THE NOT-IMPOSSIBLE DREAM: THE FAMILY-ORIENTED JOB

The jobs most people hold do not encourage them to be good parents. To the contrary, they generally seem to be in direct conflict. The hours are often long and rigidly defined. There is pressure to complete the work in hand immediately, no matter what the home situation. No provision is made for taking time off for family-related reasons such as a child's illness or performance in a school play. Parents often feel guilty about spending time with their children. When they do feel they have to take time off from work, they often feel forced to lie about the reasons.

Eleanor and Dick, both junior high school teachers, take turns staying home when one of their two children is sick. "We take these as our own sick days," says Eleanor. "Fortunately, we're healthy, so we have enough leeway to take off for our kids' runs of colds and sore throats. What I can't understand, though, is why a school, which is concerned with the welfare of children, doesn't have an official policy of letting parents stay home to take care of their own children."

And Frank, a salesman for a radio station, says, "My boss doesn't mind my coming in a couple of hours late occasionally if I have a dentist's appointment, but I know he'd hit the ceiling if I told him I would be late so I could see Jennifer be the Yellow Fairy in the second-grade play. So he just thinks I have a mouthful of rotten teeth."

As Cornell University professor Dr. Urie Bronfenbrenner says, "American business today pits family and work against each other. They make it, 'Which one are you going to pick, baby? If you want work, these are our conditions. If you don't want those conditions, tough. We can always find people who do.'"

More and more people, however, are refusing to accept these conditions. Even career-committed people of both sexes who come from backgrounds in which the "work ethic" has been the "life ethic." More and more reports have emerged—from pollster Daniel Yankelovich and social critic Betty Friedan, as well as from publications as diverse as *Playboy* and *The Wall Street Journal*—of the growing numbers of young men who value self-fulfillment and family involvement over an unthinking climb up the corporate ladder. They are the workers who turn down promotions when they require relocation, extensive travel, or long working days that rob them of family time.

And more and more employers are learning that if they want to attract the brightest and the best of young workers today, they have to take into consideration the value by which these people are living. The trend is growing slowly in the direction, for example, of "cafeteria" benefits for employees. That is, instead of offering a fixed portion of benefits decreed by management, some companies let employees choose among optional holidays, flexible scheduling, insurance, and pensions.

When you first interview for a position then, your concern would be as much with whether you want these employers as with whether they want you. Without waving the flag about the importance to you of family and personal time, you can be alert to "code" words dropped by the interviewer. Does he say, for example, "This job is not for a nine-to-five—it's for someone who is really dedicated to the company"? Or, "We need someone who's not afraid of working under pressure and tight deadlines"? Or, "We don't operate by a time-clock mentality around here. If a job has to get done, and it runs into an evening or a weekend, we expect our people to pitch in"? Or, does the interviewer say something like, "We want to help our people integrate their work lives with their home lives"? Either way, you have a better idea of what to expect, and you are in a better position to decide whether this is the job—and the employer—for you.

"People need to get satisfaction from two parts of their lives—their families and their work," Dr. Bronfenbrenner told me. "And children need two kinds of care—the capital *C* Care that represents an irrational commitment from someone who deals with a child as if he or she were the most important creature in the world, and care with a small *c* from outside people who are more rational, objective, and fair.

"The present system in our society works against providing both these types of care. Because of the way we run our world of work, parents either have to be in it all the way or not at all—or suffer second-class citizenship for being part-time workers. If employers would offer flexible scheduling and part-time work and all sorts of other supports for workers' family obligations, and if government offered tax incentives to businesses that do this, people could hold jobs and be parents and do both with dignity and satisfaction. Right now we run American society in a way that pits these two parts of people's lives against each other. It's bad for individuals, it's bad for families, and it's bad for business, too."

FLEXIBILITY ON THE JOB

The two-paycheck families that run the smoothest often tend to be those in which at least one parent has a flexible or part-time job.

In one survey of parents who share child care almost equally, two-thirds indicate that this is possible for them only because one partner has a flexible working arrangement. Many of the working parents who spoke to me or answered my questionnaire took special pains to point out the backup they got from their husbands' or wives' ability to juggle their schedules to be home with sick children, to drive youngsters to softball practice, or to be on hand for other special family needs.

When flexibility is possible, situations often stop being problems and turn instead into challenging puzzles that, with ingenuity and perseverance, can be neatly solved. Karen Hemmigsen, for example, was the director of a methadone project in Hartford, Connecticut; her husband Martin Henner was teaching law at the University of Connecticut. During Karen's pregnancy, she made arrangements to cut her working week back to three days a week. Meanwhile, Martin arranged with his department chairman to cut his daytime classes to two a week, and he took on more evening classes. On the days Karen worked, Martin took care of Jake and the house, bringing the baby to Karen at lunchtime so she could nurse him. On the days he worked, she took care of Jake. On weekends they shared his care. The result: Both workers continued to work, and both parents parented.

Some kinds of work lend themselves to more flexibility than do others, of course. And some employers are more open to the notion of change than are others. But even large corporations with relatively rigid ways of doing things will often bend when the occasion calls for it.

Anne, for example, is an editor with a major New York publisher. She has been with the same company for fourteen years, through her marriage and the birth of two children. While life had been a continual juggling act for Anne and her husband Paul since the arrival of Niels and then Kirsten, it turned into constant crisis when three-month-old Kirsten became seriously ill.

Both parents took turns staying overnight with the baby during the eight days she was in the hospital, but then when it was time for her to be discharged, Anne and Paul decided that one of them absolutely needed to be home with her. Because of the critical nature of Kirsten's illness, they felt it was out of the question to leave her in the hands of a baby-sitter. Paul, who had just begun a new job that involved frequent traveling, felt that his future would be jeopardized with the company if he asked for significant amounts of time off at this point.

So Anne went in to speak to her immediate supervisor about the possibility of working from home for a period of six months, until Kirsten had recovered. "I had made up my mind that I would have to leave the company if I couldn't work at home, and since I had three books in production, the company said okay," says Anne, smiling down at a chubby two-year-old Kirsten, now the picture of rosy-cheeked health.

"My colleagues kept talking about what a good deal I had, but it turned out to be a good business decision for the company," Anne says, punctuating her comments with frequent laughter. "I was feeling so guilty about getting this special arrangement that I probably did twice as much work at home as I would have done in the office!"

Such special arrangements are probably more common than most people realize. It helps, of course, when the employee has worked for a company long enough to prove her worth, as did engineer Cynthia Fabian Mascone, who says, "It was good that I had been in my job for almost five years when my son was born. I had proved my value to my management, which made it easy for me to negotiate the terms of my leave and return to work part-time. I was the first in my department to go out on maternity leave and return to work."

GETTING THE JOB: THE INTERVIEW

As a new bride just out of college, I was being interviewed for my first full-time job, as a receptionist/"gopher"/would-be-copywriter. The president of that small advertising agency in Cleveland, Ohio, seemed just about to say, "You're hired," when he asked, "What are your plans for having children?" I may have been young and inexperienced, but I knew enough to say, "Oh we don't plan to have any for several years," even though my husband and I actually had not definitely decided when we would begin our family. (I did get the job.)

That was many years ago. Today, employers are not allowed to ask about a woman's birth control plans, about her plans for having children, about the number and ages of her children, or about her child-care arrangements—unless they routinely ask these questions of all applicants, male and female. An interviewer might legally ask, for example, "Is there anything in your personal life that might interfere with your ability to come to work?" If you have made your child-care arrangements carefully, you can answer this question quite honestly with a firm "no."

No matter what the Equal Opportunity Employment Commission says about this issue, however, in actual practice you have a better chance of being hired if you volunteer information before the interviewer even has a chance to worm it into the conversation. You'll be ahead if you stress the reliability of your child-care arrangements. If you act as if you're in control, as if you've planned ahead, and as if you're confident about the plans you've made, your prospective employer will be impressed not only with your prospects as a reliable worker but also with your ability to solve problems and handle details.

Although this problem is almost always a women's issue, another topic that sometimes comes up in interviews is pertinent for both sexes. One personnel interviewer told me, "I'm amazed at the number of times applicants will try to impress me by telling me about their spouses' high-powered jobs. They don't know, I guess, that that turns me off immediately because I start to think that the spouse's job is the really important one in the family and that this one doesn't matter as much. I'm probably being unfair in a lot of cases, but that's my gut reaction." So while you don't want to repress information about your spouse's job, you probably don't want to bring it front-and-center-stage either.

In the job interview, the questions don't all have to come from one side. This is the time to find out whether this is the job for you. If you don't already have enough information about the company in general and this job in particular, you'll want to ask, for example, whether you'll be expected to work overtime, whether regular night or weekend work is expected, and whether the job involves extensive travel. You'll want to know what benefits are offered and whether you have a choice of benefits so that you can pick the ones that are most important for your own family situation.

YOUR JOB AND YOUR LIFE

"The working world is not always lovely and wonderful and full of freedom. It can be as oppressive in its own way as being at home is. Each person has to find out what balance nourishes him or her best." This comment, by Cleveland, Ohio, abortion counselor Jean Dooley, sums up the way many working parents feel. Finding that balance is the key to success at home and on the job.

One important element in achieving your equilibrium is your performance on the job. The better you do while you're at work, the more reliable you are as an employee, the more satisfaction you get from your job, the more complete that part of your life will be. Also, the more convinced your employer is of your dedication and value as a worker, the more likely he is to be flexible and considerate of your family pulls. A few tips for success on the job, culled from working parents, are in the box "Doing Well on the Job."

Another way many workers counterbalance the pulls of work and family is through one of the flexible schedules described later in this chapter. Others work more traditional hours and manipulate conventional structures, sometimes in unconventional ways.

Adele, for example, a city planner for a Chicago suburb, reached the top of her salary scale a year ago. Her supervisor would like to pay her more money, but town regulations won't allow her to do so. So when Adele suggested an informal arrangement by which she comes in a little later in the mornings (allowing her to spend more time with her kindergartner) and is able to duck out occasionally during the day (for a doctor's appointment or the second-grade holiday pageant), her boss agreed. "When my children get a little older, I'll look for a better-paying job," Adele says. "But right now the extra time is more valuable to me."

DOING WELL ON THE JOB

- Learn to compartmentalize your life. Don't bring your home worries to work. As long as your child's caregiver can reach you at work, you'll know that you're available in case of emergency, and you can concentrate on your work instead of dwelling on what's happening at home.
- Bank your time by skipping coffee breaks and long lunch hours. By taking coffee and lunch at your desk, you'll have more time to do your work and will feel more justified when you occasionally need an extra hour or two to tend to family business.
- Prove your ability and your dedication *before* asking for that extra time off. First show your employer how responsible and capable you are; then he or she will be more likely to accommodate special requests.
- Save those special requests for times when they really matter. You won't be able to attend *every* school function, so ask your children to let you know which ones are really important to them.
- Be punctual about meeting your commitments to co-workers. If someone else's work progress depends on getting a report from you, get it in on time. If the person on the shift before you can't leave till you come in, get there on time. If you are expected at a meeting, show up—even if you come in to work just for the meeting and leave immediately afterward. By showing consideration for your colleagues, you'll be earning their respect and their willingness to help you out when you need them.
- Don't talk so much about your family that your co-workers and boss that your concerns at home overshadow your interest in your work.
- Take work home from time to time when the load piles up and you can't finish it during working hours. The important thing is not *where* the work gets done, but the fact that it *does* get done.

Other working parents maximize their flexibility within the system. Cathy and Alan Savolaine of Holmdel, New Jersey, both save up their vacation days from their respective jobs—from Cathy's post as a telephone company supervisor and from Alan's post as assistant headmaster in a private school. When their ten-month-old son Clark was sick and had to stay home from the infant playschool he usually attends, Cathy and Alan were able to alternate days staying home with him.

The working parent has become so familiar in the American marketplace that your employer is almost certain to have already faced issues revolving around the special needs of workers with children. Chances are strong, of course, that your boss is a working parent too. So not only does she understand, as a supervisor of other workers, what kinds of situations and conflicts can arise, she may well have the same problems in her own life.

For these reasons, more and more places of employment are building flexibility into their jobs, even if it is on an unspoken basis, not to be made explicit until you *ask* for the kinds of variations from traditional policy that you need. Many workers are finding that when their requests are reasonable and when they have already proved their value to their employers, they can obtain the kind of understanding that allows them to weave the strands of their working lives with those of their family lives to create a happy design for living.

Sometimes you can build the flexibility into your work by the basic structure that you choose. What are some of the options?

PART-TIME WORK

At a small factory in St. Paul, Minnesota, seventy-five women go in every morning to work the "mother's shift." During the school year they work from 8:30 AM–2:00 PM, with one fifteen-minute break, and in the summer from 7:00 AM–noon. When they go home, fifty-six students take over in the afternoons. "Using part-time workers is efficient, and it is sorely needed," says Richard Mangram, manager of the Control Data Corporations' Selby bindery, which has been using part-timers since 1970.

Many other organizations have followed Control Data's lead and have been hiring part-time workers in ever-increasing numbers. In Texas, for example, The Arlington Bank and Trust turned 30 percent of its full-time positions into thirty-hour-a-week jobs for employees with school-age children, who leave work at 2:30 PM daily and enjoy the same fringe benefits as full-time workers. All over the country, in all sorts of fields, and in jobs ranging from the menial to the executive suite, part-time work is booming.

In the United States, part-time work has been growing about twice as fast as full-time work since 1980. One in every five workers is employed for less than the traditional work year, or week, or day—compared to one in eight in 1970, and only one in ten back in the early 1960s. And more people would like to be working less than full-time.

While most of the people now in or looking for part-time jobs are married women, the number of men looking for part-time work is also on the rise. Both sexes want to have more room in their lives for parenting, going to school, and pursuing creative endeavors and leisure-time interests. A growing emphasis on the quality of life has pushed the percentage of out-of-work people looking for part-time work up to 20 percent from its 1950 level of only 5 percent.

The dramatic rise in part-time work reflects the entrance of more women into the labor force. About two-thirds of the growing army of part-timers are adult women, most of whom are married. Many women want to enter the working world as part-timers and to continue on a part-time schedule, while others use this as a way to ease their transition from full-time homemaker to full-time worker. Other workers—both male and female—work part-time because they cannot find full-time work and will take on full-time jobs as soon as they can find them.

For parents who can afford to work part-time, the arrangement often provides the best of both worlds. Women working part-time tend to be happier at work and at home than either full-time workers or homemakers. They also see their children in a more positive light. And, according to psychologist Lois W. Hoffman, "Part-time jobs always look best in all the studies that look at the effects on children of their mothers' working. The children seem to do better than children of either nonemployed or full-time working mothers.

"However, this is the way it's been in the past," Dr. Hoffman told me. "I think that the advantages that part-time work holds for women will diminish somewhat as it becomes easier for them to handle both family life and full-time work. This is happening now, with fathers taking a bigger role in child care, with fewer children to take care of, and with more stream-lined houses that require less upkeep."

This may be the prognosis for the future, but for the present, many parents will agree with me when I say, I've worked part-time and I've worked full-time, and with kids at home, part-time is better. It doesn't pay as well, it doesn't offer as many fringe benefits, and it's not the quickest route to advancement. What it does do is offer a wonderful balance of work, family, and personal time. (It was while I was working part-time that I was able to develop my career as a free-lance writer. In fact, my job and my writing complemented each other. My job gave me material to write about, and getting published upped my value to my employer.)

Even the benefits being granted to part-time workers seem to be increasing. They are closely related to the number of hours a person works per week, with one survey of 484 companies showing that 73 percent of the firms gave medical benefits to part-timers working thirty or more hours a week, but only 13 percent covered those working fewer than twenty hours. The same kinds of patterns showed up for dental benefits and for the most popular part-time benefit, time off for pay.

Most working parents don't have to be convinced of the benefits of part-time employment. When I asked people how they would change their work schedules if they could, parent after parent of both sexes told me they wanted to work three or four days a week rather than the five days that most were now putting in. As one mother confessed yearningly, "I would like to work four days a week and ten to five o'clock instead of nine to 5 o'clock, so I wouldn't feel guilty and disorganized and irresponsible when I slink into work late.''

Many employers, though, resist hiring part-timers for responsible positions. After Catalyst president Felice N. Schwartz urged an audience of 1000 corporate executives to follow the lead of the Continental Bank of Chicago, which lets women executives return to work part-time after they have had babies, she said—to loud applause from the half-male, half-female audience—''The next step will be to offer the same opportunity to men.''

At the same meeting, Barbara Scott Preiskel, at that time senior vice-president and general attorney of the Motion Picture Association of America and member of the boards of several corporations, referred to the seven years when she worked part-time while her two children were small. ''A woman who can only work part-time today may be a leader of industry in later years,'' she said. ''It is essential that such talented women be able to maintain their skills and continue to develop their careers during those years when they also have family responsibilities.''

Some employers seem to have heard—and heeded—this message because a report by the Association of Part-time Professionals, Inc., announced that the number of voluntary part-time professional jobs rose to 3 million in 1987, a gain of 14 percent from 1983. The jobs with the biggest percentage gains were engineers, math and computer scientists, health-diagnosing occupations, and such other jobs as librarians and accountants. Workers in health assessment and treatment (mostly nurses) and in teaching accounted for 60 percent of all professional part-timers in 1987.

Another report, by the Congressional Caucus for Workers' Issues, showed that the greatest increase in part-time work was in the retail and personal trade industries, with service, sales, and clerical occupations accounting for 75 percent of all female part-time employment.

GETTING THE JOB

One day I spotted this classified ad in my local suburban weekly:

                    Part Time Writer
                  Employee Publication
                   Publicity Releases
Prior public relations, advertising or magazine writing/editing experience desired. Flexible hrs., convenient North Shore location.
For further information call J. Ritter, 272-3700
                General Binding Corporation
1101 Skokie Boulevard   Northbrook

The ad was so perfect it seemed to have my name on it. I
rushed to the phone, spoke briefly to the personnel assistant
named in the ad, found we had interests in common, sent in
my resumé, went in for an interview, and landed the job. I
worked from 9:00 AM–3:00 PM three days a week, less than
ten minutes from my home, doing exactly the kind of work I
wanted to do—writing, editing, and public relations.

I reproduce the ad here just to show that occasionally a miracle happens. You just might find a job as ideally suited to
your background and present interests as this one was to mine
offered through traditional channels. This is rare, though.
Good part-time jobs hardly ever surface in the help-wanted
pages or in employment agency files.

The most exciting part-time jobs are usually created by the
worker. Even this ad would never have appeared if a woman
had not already broken ground for me in this very company.
Mary Ellen Hirsh of Deerfield, Illinois, had created her own
slot, sold the company on the merits of part-time employees,
and done so well in her work that the company was interested
in finding another part-timer. (I'll come back to Mary Ellen
soon.)

Part-time jobs are easiest to find in fields with a shortage of
qualified personnel, like accounting, market research, and
sales. They are in demand in businesses that serve the public
for a long business day or week, like hospitals, department
stores, real estate agencies, and restaurants.

The best part-time jobs are often custom-designed to retain
a highly valued employee who, in a full-time job, has proved
his worth to the company. When one editor, for example, was
told that her employer, a small publisher, could not afford to
raise her pay, she came back with a counterproposal: "Okay,
but how about letting me work only four days a week for the

same money?'' Her boss agreed, and the new arrangement is working out well.

Often an organization doesn't know that it needs a part-time employee until someone comes along to show how a particular job can be done in a nontraditional way. This is how Mary Ellen Hirsh created the first part-time job at General Binding Corporation. A writer, she had a rich background in producing advertising copy, especially the kind sent out by mail. Mary Ellen went to her local library, where she found a reference book that listed major corporations in Illinois. Zeroing in on those that were large enough to benefit from her skills and close enough so that it would take her no longer than twenty-five minutes to drive to work, Mary Ellen sent out fifteen letters like the one reproduced here (with her permission). She received four calls inviting her to come in for an interview.

SAMPLE JOB-HUNTING LETTER

Dear Mr. ———————————————————— :

I've never seen a want ad for the type of position I'm looking for, yet I may be just the employee your company needs. I'm not looking for a "9 to 5 job"—I'm looking for one that lasts from 9 AM to 3 PM. To compensate for the shortened hours, however, I can offer both experience and diversity.

For instance,

. . . if your company would like to do more direct-mail advertising, but there's not enough volume to justify hiring another full-time employee, or . . .

. . . if your advertising department could use some additional help in writing brochures, catalogs, and the like, or . . .

. . . if you could use some editorial assistance on monthly newsletters or other publications, or . . .

. . . if you'd like a writer on your staff who can tackle anything from handling correspondence to ghostwriting speeches . . .

then I'd like to serve as that extra hand in whatever department there's a need.

[Paragraph on experience.]

[Paragraph on education.]

I am married and have three children, all of whom will be in school full-time this year. Because of the children, I am looking for a position near my home. So— if you have need for a writer on your staff, I'd certainly like to discuss the possibilities with you. My home address is shown on the first page, and my home telephone number is . . . .

Sincerely,

One interviewer who had never hired a part-timer before asked Mary Ellen, "Why should I hire you? How can I be sure you'll be able to produce results for me?" Mary Ellen answered by pointing out the results she had already achieved for herself. "My letter to you was a form of direct mail," she said, "and you answered that. So I guess I can get people to answer my mailers."

For suggestions that might work for you, see the box "Designing Your Part-time Job."

FLEX-TIME

A simple request to register a child for public school can pose a major problem for working parents. The parent has to be at the child's school during working hours, and the school is

DESIGNING YOUR PART-TIME JOB

- *What do you need?* First, you have to look at the here
  and now. How much money will you need, and will
  a part-time job provide it? Besides the lower pay,
  you'll also be getting fewer benefits and lower job
  security. To balance this, you may have fewer expenses for commuting and child care. How do the
  figures add up for you?

  What about your future needs? Are you willing to
  work on the "slow track" for a few months or years,
  or would you lose too much momentum in your career? How will the loss of such benefits as a pension
  influence your decision?
- *What does your employer need?* Are there projects that
  are going undone because there's not enough time
  for present staff to handle them—but not enough
  work to justify hiring additional workers? Are there
  needs that you can address better than anyone else
  because of your unique experience and abilities?
  Does the firm have peak needs at certain hours of
  the day or days of the week that you as a part-timer
  could meet? Can you offer flexibility by changing
  your days or hours to meet shifting work demands?
  How can the company benefit from your working
  part-time?
- *What's in your future?* How long do you plan to work
  part-time? Do you see this as a one- or two-year
  option? Something you will want to do for five or
  ten years? Or a permanent arrangement? You may
  not want to make a long-term commitment now, but
  your chances of going on a part-time schedule now
  may be better if your employer can look forward to
  your coming back full-time at some set time in the
  future.
- *What are the facts?* Is anyone else working part-time
  at your firm? Is the kind of work they do similar to
  the kind you are looking for? How did they get the
  job? How is it working out? What benefits are they

getting? What can you learn from their experience? Do other firms in your field hire part-timers? How is the arrangement working out for both employers and employees? Can you cite success stories that will bolster your presentation?

- *Can you negotiate?* When you go in for your interview, keep the needs of your employer in mind and go in as someone who has something special to offer. Stress the ways in which the company will gain by hiring you or changing your hours to part-time work. Be prepared to make some concessions. If you ask for more than you expect to receive, you'll have a cushion of concessions you can make. Are you willing to give up a benefit or some pay to "buy" flexibility on the job? After the interview, put your proposal in writing, based on what you have agreed. If you have not been successful at this level, find out whether you can take your request higher up. Sometimes, changing company policy requires an okay from the top. Or, you may have to take your proposal somewhere else. Or, figure out a way to turn your experience and abilities to work that you can do as an independent consultant.

often located far enough from the workplace that it would be impossible to handle the job during a normal lunch hour.

When Pat and Cary Campbell received notice from the school where they were planning to send six-year-old Kelly, neither parent was fazed—even though both were holding down full-time jobs. Cary, the personnel manager for the colors and chemicals division of Sandoz of Hanover, New Jersey, spoke to me the morning he was planning to go over to Kelly's school. "When you're not tied to a rigid schedule, so many things are easier. I'm going over to the school during the midday 'glidetime' between noon and two o'clock. Then I'll work late to make up the time."

Sandoz, a Swiss-owned manufacturer of pharmaceuticals, dyestuffs, and chemicals, brought the concept of flex-time over from Europe and was a pioneer in this country when it instituted the policy back in 1972. The policy has been enormously popular with workers and has caught on with a growing number of American businesses. Its use doubled between 1977 and 1987, and now some 30 percent of 384 companies surveyed by the Administrative Management Society offer it to workers. Companies that offer flex-time have seen morale and productivity go up, while absenteeism, lateness, and turnover went down.

The Sandoz program, like the programs at many of the other companies, uses "core" periods when everyone is required to be at work: 9:30 AM–noon and then 2:00–4:00 PM. Then there are a series of "gliding" hours, from 7:30–9:30 AM, from noon–2:00 PM, and from 4:00–6:00 PM, which workers can juggle around to fit their own schedules or their own biological clocks.

Parents are especially appreciative of the ability flex-time gives then to make baby-sitting arrangements, to take children to the doctor, to meet with teachers, and to do all the other things that often pose conflicts. (Christmas shoppers and exercisers are also enthusiastic.)

"People at the managerial level have always had flexibility in their schedules," says Patricia Campbell, a district manager for American Telephone and Telegraph and wife of Sandoz's Cary Campbell. "What an official company policy allowing for flex-time for *all* employees does is take away that sharp distinction between professional and nonprofessional workers."

Then there are the variations on flex-time, like the following:

- *Flexibility over the work year.* Some companies have experimented with letting employees vary their schedules over the year by planning the year's work and receiving pay prorated over twelve months. A schedule like this would let parents work longer hours during the school year and take more time off when their children are on vacation from school. Another variant lets workers reduce their schedules and salaries to take a shorter workday or work week, take off blocks of time, or take time off on an occasional basis. Several employees of the accounting firm Touche Ross & Co., for example, work full-time during the tax season, and on an as-needed or as-available schedule the rest of the year.

- *Compressed Work Schedules.* Using these, full-time workers do their week's work in less than five full days—usually in four, but occasionally in three. In May 1985 almost 3 million workers reported doing their work in weeks that run from three to four-and-a-half days. The advantage of this kind of schedule? Ask Amy Messing, manager of corporate relations for MONY Financial Services in Purchase, New York, who works Monday through Thursday, 9 to 5—or as late as she has to get the job done.

  Her son hugged her one morning and said, "Mommy, if I were you I would stay home with my children." When Amy was able to say, "I do stay home with you three days a week," she said, "It felt a lot better than saying I stayed home only two days, only on the weekend. After all, three days is almost half the week."

Flex-time practices are a good example of, as Stanley Nollen, associate professor at Georgetown University's business school, puts it, "the recognition on the part of some companies that work life and home life conflict sometimes, and it shouldn't always be the home life that has to adjust."

JOB SHARING

In Coronado, California, Joanna Klinker and Karol McClelland share the teaching of one first-grade classroom. One of them teaches Mondays and Tuesdays for a year, while the other teaches Thursdays and Fridays; they alternate Wednesdays. The following year they reverse their workday schedules. Both women enjoy their work and appreciate having more time for their families; and the children they teach benefit from the talents of two enthusiastic teachers.

The idea of two people each working part-time to share one full-time job grew in popularity during the early 1980s, and by 1987 about 10 percent of the companies surveyed by the Administrative Management Society were offering it—although a report by the Women's Bureau of the United States Department of Labor says that fewer than 1 percent of the work force are believed to work this way.

JOB SHARING: PLUSES AND MINUSES

Pluses

- Less time consuming than full-time work.
- Flexibility of hours can often be worked out with partner.
- Shared jobs are often more interesting and responsible than those usually offered to part-timers.
- Stimulation of working with and learning from another person.

Minuses

- Less pay than full-time work.
- Lower fringe benefits than those offered to full-timers.
- Personal performance may become blurred in the team effort, putting a sharer at a disadvantage in terms of salary and advancement.
- The closeness of the relationship may give rise to competitiveness and personality conflicts.
- Job requirements and jurisdiction may be ambiguous, leaving the partners unsure just what they are responsible for.

In families that can afford to live on one income, sometimes a husband and wife share one job between them, each working part-time, each spending his or her nonpaid time with their children. This kind of arrangement lets both partners stretch their professional horizons, spend more time with their children, and make less use of outside child care. While this type of arrangement is rare, it is in effect in some situations, including some college campuses where two people may share one faculty position.

Jobs can also be shared by friends or strangers. At New York Life Insurance Company, 240 people fill 120 clerical jobs. Partners alternate, one week on and one week off, splitting wages and benefits. The jobs involved—typing, filing, and stenography—lend themselves well to this arrangement because they do not demand continuity. When some kind of follow-up does have to be made, sharers often leave notes for each other. Pat Ingram, who works in the group underwriting division at New York Life, finds the week-on, week-off schedule perfect. The mother of three hearing-impaired children, Pat's volunteer activities on a district committee that places disabled children in schools play an important part in her life.

Job sharing has been widely used by teachers, librarians, receptionists, and health-care professionals. Other jobs shared by two different workers include those of physician, administrator, lab technician, secretary, speech therapist, computer specialist, personnel representative, attorney, assembly-line worker, microbiologist, senatorial staff member, engineer, researcher, bank teller, auditor, and food-service worker.

According to one survey of 238 job sharers, most work in teams of two women, with the next most common arrangement consisting of a man and a woman. Partners are usually fairly similar to each other in age, marital status, education, income needs, previous employment, and division of responsibilities. The jobs are rarely unionized, and employers are generally small institutions. Job sharers tend to be young (three-fourths were under forty) and not in financial need (only 6 percent said their earnings were the only source of family income). About one-half had one or two children between ages one and eleven.

For more information about job sharing, you might want to consult the booklet, *Working Less but Enjoying It More: A Guide to Splitting or Sharing Your Job* ($4.75 from New Ways to Work, 457 Kingsley Avenue, Palo Alto, CA 94301). Or, contact one of the organizations listed below:

- The Professional Roster
  5 Ivy Lane
  Princeton, NJ 08540
  (609) 921-9561
- New Ways to Work (NWW)
  457 Kingsley Avenue   or   149 Ninth Street
  Palo Alto, CA 94301   San Francisco, CA 94103
  (415) 552-1000   (415) 321-9675

- Options, Inc.
  215 South Broad Street
  Philadelphia, PA 19107
  (215)735-2205

- Catalyst Library
  250 Park Avenue South
  New York, NY 10003
  (212)777-8900

WORKING FROM HOME

Even before Ralph deLeon founded his own business a few
years ago, he worked from his home in Berlin, New York,
some 200 miles from the offices and factory of his employer.
He had joined the Long Island–based firm twelve years earlier as an installer and factory worker at about the same time he
was moving his family from the New York City suburbs to a
rural area in New York's Rensselaer County. Soon after the
move, Ralph made a novel proposal to his employer: first, that
he move from doing the physical work of installing the company's products (movable office partitions) to selling them.
Second, that he base his selling operations not from the firm's
Long Island headquarters but from his own home. Because he
would be on the road about half the time anyway, he couldn't
see any reason why this arrangement, which would include
regular visits to headquarters, wouldn't work. "It's okay with
me," his boss said. "As long as you produce." Twelve years
later, Ralph was appointed vice-president of marketing for the
company—and he is still operating out of an office in his
home.

Because Joan deLeon was working a half-hour away as
nurse and office manager for a busy three-doctor practice, the
five deLeon children were, over the years, driven to doctors'
appointments, wrestling practice, and other after-school
events by their father more often than their mother. The flexibility offered by this arrangement makes parenting easier
than if *both* parents work at some distance from the home and
their children's school.

In the United States today, some 17 million people do some work at home, and more than 2 million work exclusively from their homes. Most of the full-time at-home workers are women. There are two kinds of homeworkers: those who are in business for themselves and those who work for others, either as salaried employees or as independent contractors. Estimates of the number of people who will be working mostly or totally from home in the near future vary widely, from 5 to 15 million, but most experts agree that the numbers are rising fast.

Futurist Alvin Toffler writes about the impact of new modes of production in his book *The Third Wave,* in which he talks about the civilization that follows the first wave of change (caused by the development of agriculture) and the second wave (touched off by the Industrial Revolution). We will have, Toffler says, "a return to cottage industry on a new, higher, electronic basis, and with it a new emphasis on the home as the center of society."

The "electronic cottage" will serve as the workplace for keypunch operators, computer programmers, and other workers who can use sophisticated technology to plug into a headquarters operation—basically, for anyone who handles information rather than things. Toffler sees families working at designing new products, handling the "electronic paperwork" for a hospital, doing the data processing for an insurance company, setting up schedules for a commuter airline, or preparing catalogs.

While some home-based workers are already on the beaches of this futuristic movement, most work done in the home today is much more of an extension of traditional ways of doing things. It may involve working as an independent consultant, a sales representative for several different manufacturers, a public relations representative, a free-lance artist, writer, or editor, a caterer, a producer of an item sold by mail order, and so forth. The possibilities are endless.

For many people, working at home represents a transitional stage in their lives, says Kathleen Christensen, director of the National Project on Home-Based Work at the City University of New York Graduate School and author of *Women and Home-Based Work* (see the appendix "Recommended Reading").

Some people go into it when their children are young and then move out into the business world afterward. Others (like me) become addicted to the independence and flexibility—and never go back to a structured job.

For some parents, like Helen Rosengren Freedman, author and publisher of *The Big Apple Parents Paper,* a monthly publication for New York City parents, working at home is the ideal arrangement. "I'm able to do work that I love, which keeps me happy and pleases my husband, and I'm there for my five-year-old daughter—who is very aware of my work and what I do."

But as "ideal" as it may be, working at home poses its own problems. "Paperwork intrudes everywhere," groans Helen. An even more insistent intrusion are the constant thoughts about work, which she, like many at-home workers, doesn't *bring* home with her; they're already home. Another major complaint by at-home workers is voiced by one professor who arranged her schedule to teach two days a week and work at home the other three so she can spend more time with her four-year-old: "When I'm home," she says, "everybody—including my husband—assumes I don't have professional tasks and expects me to do laundry, buy groceries, and take care of a million other odds and ends." Not surprisingly, Thomas A. Miller, director of research for the Home Office Research Program at Link Resources Corporation in New York, who works from home himself, says, "The Number One problem for people with home offices is overworking. The Number Two problem is separating work and home life. With children, especially young children, it's a superhuman exercise."

While many parents opt to work from home to have more time with their young children, it's impossible to work seriously and take care of a small child at the same time. Yes, you are *there.* If a child is sick or a baby-sitter doesn't show up, you have an ordinary run-of-the-mill crisis instead of a catastrophic one. But parents who are most successful with this arrangement either pay for child care or have school-age or older children. And even with this, some people feel that the problems outweigh the benefits.

To find out whether working at home is the answer for you, you need to take a hard look at the pro's and con's. You also need to ask yourself whether you have a service or product that you can offer from home—and whether you have the kind of personality and home situation that would support a home-based workload. For some help in making up your mind, look at the box "Is Working at Home the Answer for You?" If you finish reading it all fired up and ready to open shop, here are some suggestions for getting started.

IS WORKING AT HOME THE ANSWER FOR YOU?

Pluses

- You can be more flexible in your hours, letting you schedule personal and family appointments without asking for special permission.
- You are less dependent on baby-sitters. Even if you use child care to get your work done, a sudden illness of either your child or your baby-sitter poses fewer problems.
- Your children can see you as a role model of an achieving person and can get a concrete idea of the kind of work you do.
- When your children are old enough, they may be able to help you in some way and thus feel part of a working team.
- Because you don't have to commute, you save time, money and energy.
- You don't need as large a working wardrobe.
- You are more independent.
- You can benefit from some tax advantages.
- Because you do not work side-by-side with other people, you can avoid personality conflicts.

Minuses

- Your home is no longer your refuge from work, making it harder to establish boundaries between the two. You may have trouble concentrating on your work at one time and focusing on your family at another.
- Undone housework or home repairs may feel like rebukes to your ability to balance.
- You are isolated from fellow workers, deprived of the opportunity to be trained in additional skills, and away from the normal working network. You are also deprived of adult companionship and of the give-and-take of creative ideas.
- Some clients or customers may not respect your professionalism if they know you work at home.
- Children, spouse, and others may consider you available for social or homemaking activities because you are in your house.
- You may miss the imposed structure of a regular job and have trouble forcing yourself to get going.
- If you are starting your own business, you will incur considerable expenses at first, with no income to pay the bills.
- Because you are self-employed, your employer does not offer paid vacation, sick leave, or a retirement pension.
- If your children are small, you will probably need some child care during your working day.
- You will need to reorganize your home to set up a separate work area where your materials or papers cannot get covered with strawberry jam, eaten by the dog, or otherwise disturbed.

GETTING STARTED
WORKING FROM HOME

- Write out a detailed description of the product or service you want to sell. To clarify it in your own mind, write a brief history: When did you first demonstrate the ability to do this? What made you think you should offer it to the public? Have you ever sold it? What has the response been? If you have never actually done this, why do you think you can?
- Who are your potential customers? Make a list of all the people or businesses who might buy from you. Check with your friends, your business associates, your friends' business associates, the Yellow Pages, the research librarian of your local library, and appropriate local and national organizations (see the *Directory of Associations* in the reference room of your local library).
- Set your fees. Decide what your time is worth besides your costs for raw materials or other expenses. Research the prices charged for similar products or services.
- Draw up a marketing plan. How will you offer your product or service? Decide how you will contact potential customers—direct mail, advertising in newspapers or magazines, a publicity campaign, and always, of course, word of mouth.
- For helpful reading material, see the appendix "Recommended Reading."

STOPPING OUT

Barbara Kane, age thirty-nine, left her job with a prestigious San Francisco law firm to stay at home with her nine-year-old son and her eleven-year-old daughter. Her decision was not easy to make. In fact, "Barbara" asked me not to use her real name, for fear that her decision to take even a short time out from her career will be a black mark against her when she decides to go back to it.

TIPS FOR MAKING WORKING AT HOME WORK FOR YOU

- Treat your job seriously. Once you have set up your work schedule, you are not available for social chit-chat, tennis games, PTA meetings, and the like during working hours.
- Ask friends and family to phone only at specified times except for emergencies.
- Get a telephone answering machine. It will ensure your not missing important calls and can also be used to screen calls until it's convenient for you to answer or return them.
- Think about getting a separate business telephone number.
- Get a baby-sitter to take small children out of the house part of the day or care for them out of your earshot.
- Set aside a separate room, if possible, to work in. At the very least, you should have a corner of a room that is not used for anything else. Keep your work equipment here, all together.
- Set up your work space far away from the kitchen—on another floor, if possible. Eat only at specified times, as you would if you were in an office.
- Figure out your best time of day to work and do not make any nonbusiness appointments during those hours. (If you're best in the morning, for example, have your teeth fixed and your hair cut in the afternoon.)
- Cluster errands and do them on your self-set lunch hour or on a midafternoon break.
- Make a sign that says "Do Not Disturb" on one side and "Do Disturb" on the other. Teach your school-age children to respect the signs when they are home for minor illnesses or school vacation days.
- As your own boss, treat your employee well. Reward yourself after completing a project by doing something outside your usual routine—taking a bike ride, lunching out, phoning a friend.

- Meet with clients and colleagues at restaurants or their offices rather than your home.
- Join a professional organization to keep in touch with developments in your field, make business contacts, and make up for the isolation of working at home.

Why, then, did she decide to leave the practice of law at a time when her career is on the rise and her children are out of babyhood?

"I'm staying home now partly for the children and partly for me *because* of the children," says Barbara. "They need me now more than they need the baby-sitter—need the kind of intellectual stimulation I can give them that she can't, need the firmness with which I insist they live up to our household rules, need the values I think are important for them to learn.

"But I want something for myself, too. These past ten years have been real hard for me. My husband's been a good parent, but *I'm* the one who finds the piano teacher, signs the children up for tennis lessons, takes them shopping for clothes.

"Night after night, my husband and I would come home, help them with their homework, listen to them practice, work on projects with them. On weekends it was going to their tennis matches, taking them shopping, fitting in errands and chores around the house. Neither of us ever had any time for ourselves. And I never had time just to enjoy the kids' company."

Barbara looks wistful. "Jennifer is about to become a teenager. Maybe I'll have just one summer before she leaves me— if not physically, then spiritually and emotionally. And David is not far behind. I've worked hard as a mother all these years, and I'd like to have some of the rewards. I'd like to get out on a tennis court with them, take them to museums, sit down and talk while they still want to share their lives with me. I'll still have plenty of years to practice law full-time."

During Barbara's stopping-out time, she plans to explore branches of law other than the corporate work she has been doing so far. She has already lined up a consultant's job to a local bank, is interested in working with women who want to start their own businesses, and is open to other possibilities.

Academic life has traditionally supported the concept of the "sabbatical year," which professors are encouraged to take every few years. They receive either full or partial pay, then return to their teaching and research with renewed vigor. In recent years, colleges have encouraged students to take a year off during their studies for personal exploration and growth.

This concept is often a useful one for working parents too. When finances permit, it sometimes makes sense to take a year or two away from the career track. This stopping-out period can serve as a breather, when you can not only enjoy the luxury of time to spend with your children, but can also use this time to rethink your career goals and the path you're taking to fulfill them.

Many voices are being raised in American society to make the world of work more responsive to the needs of families. In the years ahead, we will no doubt see the emergence of many innovations that will enable adults to fulfill their roles as workers and as family members without feeling that doing their best in one role means stealing from the other. As workers continue to press for flexible, family-oriented work, employers will have to provide it.

5

WHAT ABOUT CHILD CARE?

During the week, while Rick Williams is on his job as parts department manager at a car dealership in Albany, New York, his wife, Renee, cares for their two children, Rachel, age five, and Richard, age four. On the weekend, when Renee works as a licensed practical nurse at Bennington Hospital in Bennington, Vermont, Rick takes over at home. He cooks for himself and the children, bathes them, plays with them, and puts them to bed. "This kind of arrangement makes my working more worthwhile financially," says Renee. "Besides, Rick enjoys the time he gets to spend alone with the children."

Nery Bartell, a hospital housekeeper in Glen Cove, New York, says, "I wouldn't leave Simon (age five) and Christopher (age three) with anyone but my sister. I know she loves them as much as I do, so it's not like having an outsider take care of them. Children need so much understanding and affection, and I know my sister gives them that."

K. C. Cole, a newspaper reporter, told me, when her son Peter was seventeen months old, "I'm really divided. It's good for a baby to be with other children, but it's also important for a child to spend time with one adult. Besides, a center wouldn't work for me because my working hours change, and

---

PARENTAL CARE (STAGGERED HOURS)

Pluses

- Children are cared for by people closest to them, their own parents.
- No outlay of money is necessary.
- Child stays in familiar environment of own home.
- Parents stay in charge of home situations, using their own child-rearing practices, imparting their own values.

Minuses

- Parents are under great pressures of time.
- Parents have very little time with each other, and the marriage sometimes suffers.
- One parent often has to work an inconvenient shift and sleep at inconvenient hours.
- Impossible for single parents.

---

sometimes I have to work late. So I've evolved a combined system of child care for Peter. Three days a week a young woman comes to the house so that Peter can stay home with his own toys. On the other two days I take him to the house of a woman who looks after several children he can play with.''

Carol Bryant, a social worker in Portland, Oregon, told me, "Family day care is much more *real* than center care. At the home where I take my three-and-a-half-year-old son Mark, there's a mix of different ages—from an infant to an eight-year-old—just like a real family. The father works a swing shift, so he's there during the day with the children. And my little boy can take a nap whenever he feels like it. Furthermore, there's more flexibility. If I have a late-night meeting, Mark can stay longer. And one of the best things is that this family lives only half a block from my home.''

CARE BY A RELATIVE

Pluses

- Children are cared for by people who love them.
- Closest situation to care by own parents.
- Money outlay is usually modest. Services are often "paid for" by performing equivalent services for relative.
- Child is in familiar environment.
- Caregiver holds a stable place in the child's life.

Minuses

- Conflicts sometimes arise over child-rearing practices, and it is difficult for the parents to tell their own mothers, sisters, or other relatives that they do not approve of what they are doing.
- Conflicts sometimes arise over arrangements— hours, duties, and payment, causing bad feelings in the family.
- Care-giving relatives often give advice that the parents resent.
- Grandparents are sometimes physically limited in their ability to care for children and to give them enough activity.

Rosemarie Trentacoste, a receptionist, is the mother of John and Melanie, both of whom attended the CIAO (Congress of Italian–American Organizations) Child Care Center in Brooklyn, New York, before they went to public school: "I like the center much better than I do a baby-sitter. My son used to be very nervous. He threw temper tantrums all the time. But from the minute he started in the child-care center, he became calmer. The teachers have more time than someone who has her own children to take care of, too. And they're patient and affectionate."

FAMILY DAY CARE

Pluses

- Caregivers are often very close to the child's home, making it convenient for both parent and child.
- It's the closest thing to the home situation.
- Children of different ages can be cared for.
- Mother and caregiver often develop a close relationship.
- Hours tend to be flexible, allowing for unexpected transportation delays or work crises.
- Fees are usually lower than those for group care.
- Financial subsidies are sometimes available.

Minuses

- Because of the home-based situation, it is often hard to know what kind of care a child is getting. There is little or no official supervision.
- Caregivers rarely have training in child development.
- Caregivers are often hard to locate.
- Some caregivers spread themselves too thin by taking in too many children.
- In some homes, children are not offered stimulating activities but are instead plunked in front of a TV.
- If the caregiver gets sick, no care is available.
- If the child gets sick, a caregiver who cares for other children, too, may refuse to have him or her come.
- Children cannot invite their friends over to play.

Then there is the "dump system." Says one mother who runs a financial consultation service from her home and generally manages without baby-sitters, "When I'm very busy and the kids are home from school, I dump them with someone they like."

FULL-TIME BABY-SITTER/HOUSEKEEPER

Pluses

- Child remains in familiar environment of own home.
- Children of various ages can be cared for.
- When child is sick, care is still available.
- Caregiver often cooks, does light housework and errands, so when parents are home they have more time to be with their children.
- Hours are usually relatively flexible and can accommodate late work or other delays.
- If parents' work involves travel, baby-sitter can often stay in the home full-time while they are gone.
- The caregiver often becomes like a member of the family, developing a very close attachment to the children.
- Children can invite friends home to play.

Minuses

- Expensive—beyond the reach of most working parents.
- Scarce—very difficult to find competent people.
- Family privacy has to be sacrificed, especially if baby-sitter sleeps in.
- People doing this work rarely have any training in child development and are not able to offer the kind of educationally stimulating program available at a good center.
- It is often hard to know just what kind of care a young child is getting.
- Under the pressure to cook and do housework, some workers tend to put the children's needs last.
- Conflicts can arise over child-rearing practices.
- Workers have other priorities in their lives and may leave suddenly, causing instability in the child's life and uncertainty in the parents'.

GROUP CARE

Pluses

- Children learn to get along with other children and adults.
- Children are exposed to stimulating experiences and materials that they might not get even at home.
- Even if one caregiver gets sick, the center remains open.
- Centers often provide educational and social services for parents.
- Center personnel often have training in child development and can thus offer children richer experiences than they would get from home or from an untrained baby-sitter.
- Financial subsidies are often available for low-income families.
- Children from disadvantaged backgrounds who go to a good day-care center do better in school than comparable home-reared children. So do some middle-class children.
- Centers are usually government regulated, ensuring minimal standards of safety, sanitation, and supervision.

Minuses

- Opening and closing hours often do not allow for the commuting that working parents must do, so additional child-care arrangements may have to be made to cover an hour or so in the morning and/or evening.
- No provisions are made for times when a parent must work late or is delayed for some other reason.
- Location is often inconvenient to reach from home and/or work.
- Usually does not cover care for children who are too young or too old for main program—generally

suitable only for three- to five-year-olds. If there are other children, separate arrangements must be made for them.

- No provisions are made for care of a sick child.
- Often too expensive for parents in the middle economic range, those who earn too much to qualify for government subsidy but not enough to afford full tuition.
- Some children do not do well in a group situation and need more solitude.
- Turnover of center personnel can result in a great deal of instability in a child's life.

These parents are using some of the most common ways children of different ages are cared for, according to a 1987 report issued by the United States Bureau of the Census on child-care arrangements used by employed mothers.

Children under age three, whose mothers constitute one of the fastest-growing segments of the work force today, are most often cared for in their own or in other people's homes, either by their own parents on staggered shifts, by relatives, or by paid baby-sitters. Only 17 percent go to group care.

For older children, on the other hand—three- and four-year-olds—only about one child in four (27 percent) is cared for at home. About 8 percent are cared for by their mothers at the mother's workplace (either at home or away from home), and the rest are fairly evenly divided between group programs (day care, nursery school, and preschool account for 32 percent) and care in another person's home (31 percent). This other person is either a nonrelative who is paid for caring for the child or a family member—a grandmother, an aunt, or another relative who may or may not be paid. The primary caregiver is almost always a woman.

The public schools in this country serve as the single biggest source of child care for children six years old and up, who are supervised for some six hours a day or longer if they ride the school bus. Yet there's often an hour or two in the morning and two or three hours after school when they are on their own because the school day is shorter than the working and commuting day of most workers. So these children are looked after by neighbors, relatives, paid baby-sitters, personnel at after-school centers, or themselves.

Most parents do not confine themselves to only one form of care but instead use what Dr. Sheila B. Kamerman calls "packaging"—a combination of two, three, four, or more different arrangements. For example, Colin Lee Carrihill, age seven, goes to a Manhasset (New York) public school, while his sister, Laura, age three, attends nursery school in the next town. At 3 PM a college student picks up both children, brings them home, and stays until 6:30 PM until one of the children's parents gets home.

Charleene and Victor Weeden of Berlin, New York, have had to use a more complicated arrangement to care for six-year-old Scott while Vic is at his job for the Rensselaer County Department of Highways and Charleene is at hers, driving a school bus. Because Charleene has to take the bus out at 6 AM and Vic leaves soon afterward, Scotty needs care for those early morning hours until he climbs on his own kindergarten bus. So Charleene takes the little towhead to the home of a woman who watches other children along with her own. By the time Scott gets home from school, his mother is home, and by the time she has to make her afternoon run, his older sister, Charla, is home from school and able to watch him. Scott's grandmother, who lives five miles away, is close enough to pitch in in emergencies.

CHOOSING CHILD CARE THAT'S RIGHT FOR YOU

"Good child care is the single factor that makes working and parenting feasible and tolerable," says attorney Jeanne Smith. The trick, of course, is finding—and keeping—that good child care. Although options for care may seem many and varied, in specific cases the choice is usually much more limited. If your mother is holding a full-time job herself and your sister lives 300 miles away, you may have no relatives to call on.

MOST STABLE CHILD-CARE ARRANGEMENTS FOR INFANTS AND TODDLERS

- Two parents who can dovetail their work schedules, so one or the other looks after the baby.
- A grandmother, other relative, friend, or neighbor who cares for a child in either the caretaker's home or the child's home.
- Family day care—care in the home of a person who cares for other children and gets paid for the service.
- A full-time baby-sitter who comes to the child's home five days a week and may perform house-keeping chores, too.
- A well-run, well-staffed day-care center with special facilities for very young children.

If you are a single parent or if you and your spouse both have the kinds of jobs that do not permit flexibility of hours, there is no way you can provide all your child's care. If your budget is tight, a full-time "Mary Poppins" is no more possible than a voyage to the moon.

Your own work schedule also affects the availability of help. If you have to be at work at 5 AM or if your schedule changes from week to week, a day-care center may be out of the question, and other kinds of care may be so hard to find that you take what you can get, no matter what your preference is.

The number and ages of your children are a major factor in the kind of care you use. You might prefer a day-care center, but find that there is none in your community that will take a child under age three. If you have three children two or three years apart, you may need a different kind of care for each one.

Your child's personality must be considered, too. Is she outgoing and sociable, comfortable in large groups? Or, is she quiet and shy, happier with just one or two other people? Does he have a high level of energy, or does he need a lot of rest?

Finally, what you want for your children also plays an important role. Single working parents, for example, are much more likely to enroll their children in day-care centers than to use any other kind of care. Part of the explanation for this may lie in the fact that being single their lower financial circumstances tend to make them eligible for government subsidies. Another important reason, however, is the stimulation offered by the adults and children at the center. Marianne, a social service aide, told me, "With just the two of us in the house together, I think it's important for Tommy to be with other people as much as possible, to form his own little world. And the fact that the center uses male teachers is great for him. He never sees his father, so it's good that he has some men he can look up to."

Unfortunately, the demand for child care is outstripping the supply these days. Julia Kristeller, director of the Commonwealth Children's Center in Boston, told me, "The need for child care is much greater than it was just a few years ago—and the supply is much less. Many more mothers of babies are out working, and there's just not enough child care to go around. I'm seeing a lot of very upset, scared parents of young children who just don't know what to do."

What will you do? You may not have a problem deciding on the kind of care you want for your child. You may have a relative who's ready and eager to help out—and whose help you warmly welcome. Or, your employer may be among the few who sponsor superior on-site child care. Or, you may have nothing available but a neighbor who takes in other children along with her own.

But if you do have a choice, it can be bewildering to think about each of the different kinds of child care and which is best for your own child. This chapter and the four that follow (through Chapter 9) describe the most common kinds of care, giving the pluses and minuses of each, along with some suggestions for making each kind work. Chapter 9 also presents a few innovative variations.

Every child is different, of course, as is every parent, every family, and every work situation. No one else can prescribe the best solution for your particular problem. The box "Child-care Alternatives" summarizes the kinds of child care that seem to work best for most people in a range of situations.

CHILD-CARE ALTERNATIVES

Your Situation	Recommended Child Care
Child under 3 years	At-home caregiver, either in your home or hers
3- to 5-year-old	
• If you have regular work hours	Day-care center
• If you have a long or hard commute	Day-care center near your home
• If you have an easy commute	Day-care center at or near your workplace
• If your work hours are irregular	At-home caregiver, either in your home or hers, in combination with pre-school or day–care center
Young school-age child	After-school center or adult who can monitor out-of-school hours
Older school-age child	As above, or self-care, with adult monitoring by phone and an adult nearby to call on for help
Two or more children of different ages	At-home caregiver or combination of several options
Teenager	Self-care, with adult monitoring by phone

GETTING INFORMATION ON CHILD CARE

Because so many parents are not sure what kind of care would be best for their children or how to find care in their communities, a new kind of agency has been sprouting up around the country. Information and referral services (*I & R*s, sometimes called *R & R*s, for "resource and referral") provide parents with reliable information about people and places in their areas that offer good child care. They also counsel parents and help them decide what kind of care would be best in their own unique family circumstances.

Besides giving out information about child care that already exists, many of these agencies develop new resources. Staff workers at the Day Care and Child Development Council in Ithaca, New York, for example, found they were getting more and more requests for care for infants and that they couldn't help callers because there were so few facilities. So June Rogers, at that time the director of the Council, worked with Cornell University to set up what became a model infant-care and resource center. After knocking on doors in a Portland, Oregon, working-class neighborhood to learn the needs of the community, volunteers with the American Friends Service Committee founded Neighborhood Options in Child Care, which operates an association for family day-care mothers, a baby-sitting cooperative, a baby-sitters' referral service, and several play groups. In some areas, branches of the city or state government, usually under the Department of Social Services, offer information and referral services.

If you don't know where to begin looking for child-care information, you might start by contacting your city, county, or state department of child development, social services, or human resources. Or, call the United Fund, the Community Chest, a local day-care committee or council, or a family-service agency. A local chapter of the Young Women's Christian Association, National Council of Jewish Women, Junior League, National Council of Negro Women, League of Women Voters, or the National Organization for Women might be helpful. Look in the Yellow Pages under "Day Nurseries and Day-Care Centers," "Human Service Organizations," "Nursery Schools and Kindergartens," " Sitting Services," or "Social Service Organizations." Or, you could contact the National Association of Child Care Resource and Referral Agencies (see the appendix "Helpful Organizations") for the name of the nearest local agency.

COST OF CHILD CARE

One of the best things in life that is not free is good child care. For most employed parents of small children, child care gouges a gaping hole in their paychecks. All too often, the child-care choice that parents make has less to do with what they want than with what they can afford.

Still, surveys show that anywhere from one-fourth to one-half of all working parents pay nothing at all for child care. These are the families that are so poor that they qualify for total subsidization of child-care expenses, the ones so fortunate that they can rely on a relative or good friend, or those so ingenious that they have managed to schedule their working hours around their child-care needs. The rest, though, pay heavily.

The most expensive kind of care is that found in a good center, where there is a high adult-to-child ratio, an educational program, health care, and other services. Such a center may spend between $1000 and 5000 a year per child. Government and nonprofit agencies fund much of this expense themselves, with parents sometimes paying what they can afford, on a sliding scale. Few parents who do not receive any subsidy can afford the full fees for center care. A 1985 survey of child-care costs in four major cities (Boston, St. Louis, Dallas, and San Francisco) found that center care ranged from $60–150 per week for children under two years of age, and from $50–110 per week for two- to five-year-olds. More recently, parents have told me of paying up to $182 per week for under-two-year-olds at a good center.

Parents who *can* afford high fees for child care often prefer to pay their money to a single caregiver who comes to the home to take care of the children—and do some of the housekeeping tasks. If you can find someone you like (a big "if" these days), you have to be prepared to pay steeply—up to well over $350 per week in big cities like New York. The 1985 survey on child-care costs in four cities found a range from $165–340 for such caregivers.

Family day care—which ranges from $35–160 a week in the child-care survey—is usually the least expensive alternative, which helps explain its wide usage, despite the fact that more parents express dissatisfaction with this kind of care than with any of the others.

Fees vary, of course, in every community. What's more, they keep changing in response to local conditions—the number of working parents willing to pay for care, the number of available caregivers, the general economic climate of the area, the current rate of inflation, and so forth.

So you need to be a good researcher when you look for child care. How do you find the going rates where you live and work? Ask what your friends pay, check newspaper ads, call employment agencies, and interview caregivers in person, either at your own home or at the place where your child will be cared for.

Then, when you find out what different caregivers charge, you need to weigh the fee with the service being offered. If you can afford it, you may feel that it's worth going well above the going rate to get the kind of care you want. Ellen, a copywriter with an advertising agency, justifies the high salary she pays her live-in housekeeper by saying, "Even though I have practically nothing left for myself by the time I've paid for my baby-sitter, my commuting, my clothes, and my lunches, I figure my outlay as an investment in my future. I know I couldn't concentrate on my job if I were worried about what was happening to my children. This way I know they're well taken care of, and I can concentrate on getting better at what I do.

"Someday this will all pay off—in two ways. First of all, Melanie and Jason won't be little and needing child care forever, and secondly, the fact that I'm out working now means that I can work myself up to a higher-paying job in a few years. So both ways, I'll be ahead. Some day."

FINANCIAL ASSISTANCE FOR CHILD CARE

When Angie Goldman separated from her husband and retained custody of their two sons, Tony, age eight, and Marc, age four, she went out to work for the first time since Tony's birth. She found a job right away as a secretary in the orders department of a small ice cream–distributing company, and she found a baby-sitter right away, too, a neighbor who took care of Angie's children, along with her own. The problem was that after Angie had paid the baby-sitter, she barely had enough to make ends meet.

Fortunately, after applying to the Department of Social Services, Angie learned that she qualified for financial assistance for child care. At about the same time she was informed she would get the subsidy she had requested, she heard about a day-care center in her neighborhood, which she felt would be even better for her sons than the baby-sitter she had been using. So Marc attends the center all day; Tony goes after school; and Angie doesn't pay anything. If she gets the raise she is expecting, she will be paying $10 a week to the center— and will be glad to do it.

Financial subsidies for child care are available under several state and federal programs, not only for recipients of welfare but also for people well within middle-income ranges who need child care in order to work. Because the situation varies from state to state and because regulations on eligibility and amounts of assistance granted are constantly changing, it is impossible to set any definitive guidelines here.

If you require funds to help pay for child care and think you might be eligible for a subsidy, contact the closest Child Care Information and Referral Service. If you don't know of one, contact the social services department of your city, county, or state. The day-care center where you want to enroll your child may also be able to supply information and help in applying for the subsidy.

TAX CREDIT FOR CHILD CARE

Finally, child care has begun to catch up with chauffeurs and limousines and country club memberships as a tax-deductible expense of doing business. There are two basic kinds of tax relief for child care.

1. The major kind of tax break, and the one that will be
   more beneficial if your family's gross income is about
   $20,000–24,000, is in the form of a tax credit. This is
   not a tax deduction. A *deduction* is an amount of money
   that is subtracted from your gross income before you
   figure out how much tax you owe, whereas a *credit* is
   subtracted directly from the amount of taxes you owe.
   It is not refundable as a cash payment but is limited to
   your tax liability.

   If you pay someone to care for your child under the
   age of thirteen (or a disabled spouse, older child, or other dependent who needs special care) so that you can
   work or look for work, you may be able to take a tax
   credit of up to 30 percent of the amount you paid. For
   one child, the credit can be as much as $720; for two or
   more, it can go up to $1440, depending on what your
   family income is and on how much you paid for child
   care. (You are reimbursed only up to $2400 of ex-
   penses for one child or $4800 for two or more.) If your
   family income exceeds $28,000 annually, however, the
   maximum credits you can take are $480 and $960,
   respectively.

   For highlights of the way this credit works, see the
   box "Claiming the Tax Credit for Child Care." For the
   most complete and up-to-date information, however,
   consult your local IRS office or your tax accountant.
   IRS Publication 503 (revised November 1987) gives
   detailed information on claiming the tax credit and on
   the required procedures you have to follow if you pay a
   household worker $50 or more in a calendar quarter
   (see Chapter 6).

2. The second kind of tax benefit is an exclusion provided
   by your employer; this is of greater benefit if your
   household income is over $24,000. When this employ-
   er-sponsored assistance program is available, it is offered as part of a "cafeteria" benefit plan that offers
   workers a "menu" of different benefits. Other possible
   choices include extra medical insurance coverage or extra vacation days. According to one recent survey, only
   21 percent of 800 large companies offer such plans,

and only 4 percent of their employees use them.

If yours does and if you choose such child-care assistance, you agree to have your salary reduced by up to $5000 a year; that money goes into a "spending account." Your employer takes the money from this account to reimburse you for your expenses for care for children under age thirteen. Thus, your child-care costs come out of your pretax salary, letting you pay lower federal and state taxes. You may also pay a lower Social Security tax, and you may also receive lower Social Security benefits in the future.

The Family Support Act of 1988 added new provisions to both these plans. One is that if you claim either the credit or the exclusion, you must report your caregiver's Social Security number to the IRS. Since this went into effect, some parents have dropped out of plans because they refuse to report their caregivers, who may be illegal aliens, relatives, or friends who do not report their income. Another provision that made many parents ineligible is the drop in the cutoff age from fifteen to thirteen years of age. And a third major change is that you may no longer claim both the tax credit and the tax exclusion, which had enabled a number of families to make their child-care dollars stretch further.

The next five chapters offer more concrete details about different kinds of child care and how to make them work for you.

CLAIMING THE TAX CREDIT FOR CHILD CARE

You Are Eligible If:

- You have one or more dependent children under the age of thirteen, or a spouse, older child, or other dependent, who requires care.
- You are a single working parent, or a married parent working either part-time or full-time, or actively looking for work, or a full-time student whose spouse is employed.

You are a divorced or separated parent with custody of a child under age thirteen for a longer time during the calendar year than your spouse, even if he or she claims the child as a dependent.

- You pay for child care in your home, in a day-care center or nursery school, in a day camp or residential camp, or in another person's home, even if the caregiver you pay is a relative and even if that relative lives with you (but *not* if you claim that relative as a dependent). Transportation is not considered a child-care expense. Neither is tuition paid to a private school for the first grade on up.

To Obtain the Credit, You Must:

- File Form 1040 (not the short form, 1040A). A line about the child-care credit appears here. You can take the credit whether you take the standard deduction or itemize your deductions.
- If you are married, you must file a joint return (unless you are married and your spouse did not live in your home for the last six months of the tax year, you paid more than half the cost of keeping up your home, and you had custody of your child for more than half the year).
- Add up what you spent for the entire year for child care, including any taxes that you paid as an employer of a household worker. Save all proofs of payments (canceled checks or receipts from a sitter or day-care center) for three years in case your return is challenged or audited.
- Fill out IRS Form 2441 to figure out the amount of credit due you. Attach it to Form 1040.
- Be sure to check with your local IRS office or your accountant for further information on your own situation.

6

CARE IN YOUR OWN HOME: WHERE IS MARY POPPINS?

At some time or another, virtually all working parents fantasize themselves into the Banks house on Cherry Tree Lane where Mrs. Brill cooks, Ellen lays the tables, Robertson Ay cuts the lawn, and the children are cared for by none other than the incredible Mary Poppins. Mary Poppins, the perfect nanny, who always gets the children to take their medicine and pick up their toys, who amuses them, and who takes the very best care of them. But even Mary Poppins takes off one day, sailing into the air as she holds on tightly to the parrot-shaped handle of her umbrella. And if Mrs. Banks had been employed, as Mr. Banks was, they would have been in the same dither the rest of us are in when we try to make good child-care arrangements.

As with most things in life, the fantasy solution rarely materializes. Yet many working parents *have* come close enough so that parents, children, and caregiver are all happy.

115

GRANDMA, GRANDPA, AUNT TILLIE, OR COUSIN JAKE

If you have a close relative who loves you and loves your children and isn't pursuing her* own career, she may be happy—or at least willing—to look out for your children while you are at work. The most enthusiastic family caregivers are generally grandmothers, who relish bringing up baby's baby, and sisters who are home with their own children and can find room for one (or two or three) more.

If you do have such a loving relative—or a friend or neighbor who knows you and knows your children and agrees to care for them while you are working—count your blessings. As the late anthropologist Margaret Mead told me emphatically, "Nobody wants a day-care center if they've got a proper relative or a friend or neighbor with whom they're on close terms—nobody in the whole world would want one!"

But even if you are lucky enough to have someone like this to care for your children, don't make the mistake of thinking that just because you know this relative well you don't have to iron out both practical and psychological wrinkles. The clearer you are about all aspects of the arrangement, the better it will work out for your child, yourself, and your caregiver.

Should You Pay Your Relatives for Child Care?

"At first my sister didn't want to be paid for baby-sitting," says author and publisher Helen Rosengren Freedman, "but I insisted because I knew she needed the money, and besides I didn't want to take advantage of her. She and my daughter love each other, so the arrangement is wonderful for all of us." An argument for paying grandparents for child care was cited by one father, who told me that this eliminated "hassles" with his sister, who had felt that her parents were doing more

*Because these relatives are almost always female, I'll refer to them as *she.*

for her brother than they were for her (even though she lived farther away and had other child-care options).

Whether money changes hands in this kind of arrangement depends usually on how well you can afford to pay and how badly your caregiver needs the income. It may also hinge on such other considerations as what she would be doing if she weren't cooing over your little darling. Would she be working at a paying job? Would she be caring for someone else's child for a fee instead of as a favor? Does tradition in your family dictate that you feel more comfortable paying for services?

One working mother who was very close to her single sister made her a proposition the sister couldn't refuse: "When my son was born and I decided not to go right back to work, my former supervisor offered me a great deal—that I return to work one day a week as a consultant instead of an employee. For this to work I asked my sister—who was earning less than I was—if she would be willing to change her job to four days a week and stay with my son the other day, for six months. At that time my son would be eligible to enter the day-care center near my job. In return I paid her her day's pay, plus an additional percentage. It let me take the job, and my sister thinks it was wonderful, too, because that early experience has made her and my son very close, also."

If you do pay, you'll want to know the going charges for this kind of service. Even if you don't approach the market rate, it will help you to appreciate just how much your relative is offering you. You'll want to keep records and get receipts if you plan to apply for the child care tax credit (described in Chapter 5), which you're entitled to even if your caregiver is a close relative who lives with you, as long as you don't claim her as a dependent.

If you don't pay your caregiver in money, you'll want to reciprocate in some other way. You don't want to feel guilty, as one mother told me she does, for "taking an 'ex-mother's' free time away." Even the most loving, giving mother or sister does not want to be taken for granted.

A good time to discuss holding up your end of the arrangement is at the very beginning. Ask your caregiver what you can do that will be helpful to her, then do it. If she says, "Nothing," do something anyway. You don't want to feel you're exploiting another person's freely offered services. Depending on her needs and wants, you might want to take her out for an elegant dinner (one she'd never treat herself to ordinarily), drive her around on several of her errands, or present her with surprise gifts when it isn't even her birthday.

Becky Ramirez of Riverside, California, for example, took care of Scott Richard, age seven, and his sister, Wendy, age six, every afternoon after school for a year until their mother, Becky's friend, Janet, got home from work. Janet tried to press money on her, but Becky would never accept a penny's pay. "I treasure our friendship," Becky told me, "and I would be insulted if money changed hands." So when Becky was expecting her second child, Janet bought her a beautiful new crib for the baby.

Making the Family Connection Work

One scientist, whose mother and mother-in-law's help made it possible for her to get her graduate degree, credits the success of the arrangement to three major factors: "We always made sure to let them know how much we appreciated what they were doing for us—how important the emotional attachment is to our child, how much money we were able to save, and how we were able to do things with our lives that would not have been possible without their help. We always respected their right to a life of their own. And we always remembered that we were still the boss."

The beginning of the arrangement is the best time to get clear about such practical details as the days and hours you will need care, whether there is a chance of your sometimes working late and how to handle this, how many meals you expect your child to receive, and so forth. While you cannot, of course, make the same demands of a relative who's doing you a favor as you would of a paid baby-sitter, you can and should express what you would like so the two of you can work things out.

You always have to remember, though, that this is not an employer–employee relationship; in fact, remember that relationships among relatives are usually the most sensitive of all.

So you need to summon all your reserves of tactfulness and to put yourself in the other person's shoes as much as possible. How would you feel, for example, if you had raised three children (and done a pretty fine job of it, thank you), and then had to put up with hearing your "baby" tell you how to dress a toddler?

Generally, the fewer instructions you give your relative, the better off you are. Chances are that you and she have fairly similar values and opinions about important issues and that those you disagree about won't matter that much to your children. As Meg, an insurance company secretary, told me, "When my cousin offered to keep my kids for me while I work, I made up my mind to let her do things her way. I don't agree with everything she does, but I know she loves my kids and they love her, and so I just made up my mind that it isn't all that important that *everything* be done my way."

Sometimes, however, there are serious differences of opinion between you and your caregiver. Your sister admonishes Kathy for playing in the mud, saying, "Only boys do that." Your mother scolds Bobby for masturbating, telling him it's a "dirty" thing to do. You feel your caregiver is transmitting values absolutely opposed to the ones you believe in, and that she is thus harming your child. What do you do?

First, ask yourself how important the issue really is. Sexist attitudes, for example, are everywhere—on television, in school, in children's books, and in the minds of many people in your child's life. You can tell Kathy that some people have the old-fashioned idea that boys and girls should behave very differently, but that you know that this isn't so. Meanwhile, you can bring the issue up calmly with your sister. Point out to her that this is an important value you are trying to get across to your children, and ask for her cooperation. (You might even raise her consciousness in the process.)

One father told me, "When I start to react to something my mother-in-law is doing, I force myself to focus on the benefits to my children of extended-family relationships—and I think twice or more before I say anything. Usually the whole thing stops being so important."

When you absolutely cannot accept your caregiver's way of doing things, however, you have to meet the issue squarely.

Pick a convenient time to talk about it—when you're not dashing between work and home, when other people (including your child) are not around, and when your caregiver has some free time.

Let's take the example of Bobby's masturbation. Raise the issue without anger but from a sense of concern about him, a concern you know your mother shares. Let her know why you feel that his normal development could be affected if he is made to feel that his sexual impulses are bad and that his genitals are dirty. Tell her that you tell him you know it feels good when he touches himself, but that that is something to be done in private, not in front of other people. Point out how confusing it can be to a child when two people he loves handle him in two very different ways. Emphasize the importance of your mother's following your wishes in this regard—even if she doesn't agree with you. Sometimes a heart-to-heart talk like this can solve the problem.

When it can't—when despite your expressing your wishes clearly, your caregiver continues to say or do things you don't approve of, you're caught between a rock and a hard place. You have a choice between putting up with a poor situation or giving up what in other respects may be a perfect child-care arrangement. Only you can make this choice.

You may decide that your disagreements run so deeply that you have to make some other provisions for your child's care. If you do decide to make a change, though, don't do it in a blaming atmosphere. You have every right to make the best provisions you can for your children, but this doesn't mean that your caregiver is wrong. Just remember all the good things she has done for you and your children—and also remember that in her mind she is doing the best she can. It's just that her best isn't your best.

THE FULL-TIME BABYSITTER/ HOUSEKEEPER/NANNY

The person who comes to your home to look after your children and also does some amount of household tasks can unsnarl many of the tangles in the family life of working parents. These people do exist, even though their numbers are few, their salaries high, and their capabilities range from abominable to awesome. If you do decide to look for the superhousekeeper, here is some advice distilled from the experiences of others who have made the search—and sometimes even been successful.

Both parents should be involved in the search—in the basic decision about the kind of worker you want, in the process of finding and hiring her, and in the continuing relationship with her. Too often, a husband's only role is to allocate funds for the housekeeper and then to criticize her to his wife. But choosing a person who will have so much impact on your children's lives and, indeed, on your entire household is an important decision that you should share.

What Kind of Helper Do You Want?

Both of you, for example, should decide exactly which of the two basic categories of helper that you want.

1. *Do you want a housekeeper who will cook, do laundry, and clean for the entire family, as well as take care of the children?* This kind of worker may live with you, working a twelve-hour day, or may come in on a daily basis, usually with shorter hours. She is usually not specially trained in child care. You can expect to pay from $150 to well over $300 a week, depending on where you live and how much experience she has had. The biggest danger with hiring someone like this lies in expecting her to do too much. As one mother told me, "I gave up trying to find someone who could do *everything.* You just can't expect a spotless house *and* well-cared-for children. It's hard enough when both the house and children are your own, and you have that much more motivation. I'd rather see dust balls under the bed than feel she was cleaning at the expense of playing ball with my daughter."

2. *Or, do you want someone whose duties will be confined to the care of the children?* This kind of helper usually lives in

her own room in your home and takes her meals either with you or with the children. She usually works a twelve-hour day, prepares the children's meals, cleans their rooms, and does the laundry. If you want her to do anything else—even wash one dish that she or her charges have not dirtied—you need to make special arrangements. These arrangements may involve extra pay or extra time off or some other compensation. Who are these people? Briefly, they fall into the following categories.

THE PROFESSIONALLY TRAINED NANNY.   In recent years, the nanny has lost her British or European accent. This profession, fairly new on American soil, has blossomed over the past several years, in response to a demand created by increased numbers of women in high-level jobs who want—and can afford—excellent in-home child care. The more than two dozen nanny schools around the United States offer specialized courses that run for several weeks or several months; their graduates treat their work as a profession. For young women, it's often a temporary profession—a stepping stone to some other child-oriented work, but for more mature women it may be a lifetime career. Professionally trained nannies are still scarce—and expensive (earning from $200 to more than $400 a week plus room, board, and benefits). But parents who can afford them often swear by them. For a listing of nanny schools, refer to the book, *Live-in Child Care* by Barbara Binswanger and Betsy Ryan (see the appendix "Recommended Reading"), or contact The American Council of Nanny Schools, a nonprofit coalition of state-accredited schools (see the appendix "Helpful Organizations").

AN UNTRAINED "NANNY" OR MOTHER'S HELPER.   Many young women—usually high school graduates (occasionally college grads) from eighteen to twenty-four years of age—from rural communities, often in the West or Midwest, seek child-care positions for a year. They see the experience as an opportunity to live for a while in a metropolitan center, to gain a measure of independence from their families, to save some money, and to get a little perspective on their lives. Generally, they are not professionally trained in child care, but they tend to come from large families or to have done a lot of baby-sitting. They earn from $125 to $175 a week, plus room and board. They can be found through ads in rural and small-town newspapers and through a number of agencies that specialize in such jobs (for one list, see *Live-in Child Care*—in the appendix "Recommended Reading").

THE "AU PAIR." The name for this kind of helper—from the French *on a par with*—gives two clues: First, the au pair is usually British or European (more or less English-speaking), and second, she or he is usually treated as a guest of the family. These are people aged eighteen to twenty-five years, who have completed secondary school, have some experience in child care, and come to the United States for one year, to work up to forty-five hours a week over five and one-half days. The host family includes them in family outings, holiday celebrations, and other events and gives them the opportunity to attend courses for up to four hours per week (the family pays tuition up to $300). This program is quite expensive: While the young person gets only $100 a week, other costs add up to about $4000, making it beyond the reach of most working families. For those who can afford it, however, it can provide an interesting cultural experience, along with good child care.

The two agencies that legally bring American families together with au pairs are:

- Au Pair in America, American Institute for Foreign Study Scholarship Foundation, 100 Greenwich Avenue, Greenwich, CT 06830 (203) 869–9090
- Au Pair Homestay USA (800) 328–7247

A Note About Foreign-Born Workers

One category of caregivers that used to be a mainstay for working parents is much less available today. This included women who had come to the United States illegally but wanted to remain to work here; at one time employers could spon-

workers for a "green card," allowing them to work
...ly. Since the passage of the Immigration Reform and
Control Act (IRCA) of 1986, however, it is illegal for any employer to hire anyone who is not already authorized to work in
this country. It is up to the employer to verify the worker's
documents, which prove both identity and employment eligibility. "There is no doubt that the law applies to household
workers," says New York attorney Susan Leboff, "but the fact
is that while the Immigration and Naturalization Service may
make examples of some people, it is going to be impossible
(and arguably unconstitutional) to reach down into individual
homes to enforce this law."

What Kind of Person Do You Want?

Whichever route you go, there are certain qualities you'll look
for in an applicant. You want someone who

- Loves to be with children your children's age.
- Has realistic expectations of them.
- Is kind to them—and yet is firm in setting limits.
- Is sensitive to children's feelings—won't tease or ridicule
  them or be cruel or indifferent.
- Has a cheerful disposition and a sense of humor.
- Is intelligent enough to handle the details of day-to-day
  life and deal with any emergency that might arise.
- Is flexible and can adapt to the thousand and one unpre-
  dictable events that make family life a constant challenge.
- Is honest, sober, healthy, and clean.
- Is dependable—shows up on time and can be counted on
  to do what she is supposed to do.
- Can get along reasonably well with the adults in the family.

Your precise needs, of course, depend on the number and
age(s) of your child or children. An older person who could
give gentle, tender care to an infant may not be lively or ar-
ticulate enough for an active toddler. If the person you hire
cannot adapt, you may need to change caregivers as your child
grows. If someone fits your present needs, though, don't refuse to hire her because she might not be the person you need

in a year or two. If she stays a year or two, you'll be ahead (the game!

You may also have special needs revolving around your own situation. Does your caregiver need to know how to drive, for example? Do you want her to cook for the family? Is it important that she be able to take accurate telephone messages?

What about the ability to speak English? You may get an applicant who speaks little or no English. How would this fit into your life-style? If you speak a foreign language yourself and can communicate with her, this may work out well for you. Your children might improve their language skills, and you might avail yourself of a wonderful worker. You do have to ask yourself a few questions about the importance of speaking English, though. In an emergency, would your housekeeper be able to get the right kind of help? Would your children be frustrated by their inability to communicate with her? Do you receive important telephone calls that a non-English-speaking person could not handle?

Sometimes two or more families can share a full-time baby-sitter. One case that I heard about was a perfect solution for two couples, both of whom had three-year-old boys. The boys had a full-time friend, and the parents had forty hours of child care a week—at half what it would have cost otherwise.

HOW TO FIND A FULL-TIME CAREGIVER

Sometimes parents are lucky and they find an ideal person right away. More often, though, they need to invest considerable amounts of three scarce commodities—time, effort, and money—to find someone with whom they feel comfortable leaving their child. As college administrator Jane Hoffman, the mother of one-year-old Rachel, says, however, "Caring, responsible caregivers looking for work *are* out there. I know of many parents besides myself who are very pleased with the care their children are receiving. So if you're persistent and thorough, your chances are good for finding someone good." How to do it? The following routes have worked well.

WORD OF MOUTH. Tell everyone you know that you're looking—especially friends and neighbors who employ people themselves. Very often someone's caregiver has a sister or a cousin or a friend who's looking for work and who will be just right for you. Other parents—in the playground or in the pediatrician's office—may also be good sources, as can the local clergy. Try calling the financial aid office of local colleges or a community information-and-referral service.

ADVERTISING.   Newspaper ads often yield good results. Some avenues that have been successful are the following:

- If you live in or near a big city and are looking for a baby-sitter who will live in her own home, you may be able to reach people by advertising in the biggest nearby metro-politan daily paper.
- If you're looking for someone to live in your home, you may get better results by placing ads in rural newspapers because young women from farms and small towns some-times see this kind of work as a way to experience a differ-ent kind of life while making more money than they could in their own community.
- Other good resources are newspapers aimed toward a spe-cial readership (*The Irish Echo,* for example, in New York).

Be sure to say in your ad that you're a working parent be-cause many workers are savvy enough to prefer working for people like you. (They know that you need them so much that you'll overlook a lot; they also know they'll have more auton-omy because you won't be breathing down their necks all day.) Also specify in the ad the number and ages of your children (better to scare people off now instead of later), the hours and days you'll need help, and whether you want someone to sleep in or out. Be sure to add "Recent references required." Salary is usually not given in the ad: If "Ms. Right" comes along, you may be willing to up it a bit.

Wherever you advertise, be specific and clear. Avoid news-paper abbreviations because longer and easy-to-read ads are more likely to be read.

SITUATIONS WANTED ADS. Sometimes a well-qualified person will place her own ad in the paper, showing a certain level of initiative and self-confidence. At other times, an employer who is moving out of town or who no longer needs child care will place an ad on behalf of the caregiver she hates to lose and wants to help. In this kind of situation, a reference comes with the ad.

BULLETIN BOARD NOTICES. A three-by-five-inch card on a supermarket bulletin board giving basically the same information you'd put in a newspaper ad sometimes produces results.

STATE EMPLOYMENT AGENCY. This service, free to both employer and employee, made the best marriage between housekeeper and family that I have ever heard of. The housekeeper stayed with the family for years, providing a strong measure of stability for the family's three daughters during the parents' divorce, and has since retired on a pension plan set up by her employers.

PRIVATE HOUSEHOLD-HELP OR NANNY AGENCY. This is the most expensive way to find caregivers, with fees ranging from 18 percent of the first month's salary up to 150 percent. A good agency earns its hefty fee by locating and screening applicants, and it also usually guarantees satisfaction or replacement of the worker within a set period (usually from one to three months). Busy parents who can afford these agencies and have had good experiences with them often swear by them. Others complain that they are not worth the money—and that you can do as well or better by yourself.

If you do use an agency—and even if the agency prescreens any applicants it sends to you, you should still interview everyone and check her references yourself. First, you may have special questions to ask. And second, you need to check your own intuitive response to the applicant. In a matter as important as the person who'll be taking care of your children, you can't afford to take anyone else's word.

SCREENING APPLICANTS

The screening process is time consuming, but when you look at it as an investment in your child's well-being, you can look more kindly on the three-step process: preliminary screening by telephone, a personal interview, and the checking of references. Before you do any of this, it's a good idea to take out pencil and paper and sit down with your spouse (or, if you are single, with a good friend). Get straight in your mind—and then write down—all duties that you absolutely require of a caregiver, including the hours you want her to work. Also write down the pay and benefits that you can offer. Then you're ready to talk.

Screening Step One: The Telephone

The first step in the interviewing process takes place as you speak to the person who's answering your ad or the employment agency listing. You can find out basics such as the following:

- Her ability to reach you by phone. An elementary skill, to be sure, but one that some applicants don't have! Their sisters, boyfriends, or friends sometimes make the calls for them.
- Her command of English. You're not checking for grammar and elocution, but you do want to be able to understand her.
- Some basic information like her name, availability, and general level of experience. Meanwhile, you can repeat your basic requirements, just to be sure she knows that you want someone to live in during the work week, that you have three children under the age of six, that you need her from Tuesday through Saturday, not Monday through Friday. Even though all this information may have been in your ad, it's remarkable how often an applicant will act as if she never heard it before.
- Don't be too quick to judge an applicant's personality by her telephone voice. Some people who sound remote or

slow-witted are just shy. It often pays to give them a chance in person.

- Although you might be tempted to prescreen with your telephone-answering machine, you run the risk of losing out on a good applicant who, because she has not had much experience with an electronic message taker, may leave an awkward message or none at all. At the very least, you should call back anyone who sounds remotely possible; you may be pleasantly surprised.

Screening Step Two: The Personal Interview

"We feel that if a potential housekeeper gets on the right bus, gets off at the right stop, and then walks the couple of blocks to our house that by just finding us she's passed the first obstacle," says one experienced father. Other good reasons for interviewing applicants in your home revolve around their ability to see the setting in which they'll be working and your ability to see how they respond to the place and to you and your children.

What else can you tell from the personal interview? Her dependability, for one thing. Did she come on time? If not, did she phone to say she'd be late? Her common sense, for another. If she had trouble with the directions, did she flounder for two hours or call you for help?

What does her appearance tell about her? Says public relations consultant Therese Williams, the mother of three daughters, "A slovenly applicant will keep a slovenly house; a neatly dressed person will keep a neat home; and a gorgeously dressed applicant will be afraid of breaking her fingernails." You're looking, of course, not for beauty and high fashion, but for neatness, cleanliness, a presentable appearance.

As you talk to an applicant (see the sample interview questions), you can tell a great deal about her personality. Does she have a pleasant manner with a ready smile? Does she sound intelligent, with thoughts of her own, without spouting imperious theories about the proper way to bring up children? Could you imagine her in *your* home with *your* children?

The most important interviewers of all are, of course, your children. Be sure to have any applicant come at a time when

INTERVIEW QUESTIONS

- What experience have you had doing this kind of work?
- What do you enjoy most about it?
- What are your best qualities for the job?
- What was your last job like?
- Why did you leave it?
- What are your long-term goals?
- Would you like to stay on this job for the next few years?
- How many days did you have to take off from work over the past year for sickness? For personal reasons?
- Could you stay late occasionally if an emergency comes up and I can't get home on time?
- How would you get to work? (You have to consider how she would be affected by winter snowstorms, train delays, or transit strikes.)
- Do you drive?
- What do you like to do with children?
- Do you have children of your own?
- Who's taking care of them?
- What would you do if my little boy got an earache? What if he fell and cut his head and it was bleeding a lot?
- What would you do if my little girl didn't want to stay in her crib when it was time for her nap?
- What would you do if you came back from a walk with the children and realized you'd locked your key inside the house?
- What do you like to cook?
- How do you feel about having the children's friends come over sometimes for lunch and to play?
- What would you do with the children on a rainy day?
- Do you like to spend time outdoors?

they'll be awake and you can see their reactions to one another. This is a summit meeting of the interview. Does she show a friendly interest in them, or does she ignore their entrance into the room? Does she respond to them when they talk to her, or does she turn a vacant expression toward them? Some people who are quite shy with adults—who may be terrified to look you straight in the eye—come alive with children. Your chances of finding someone who shines equally well in every possible way are extremely remote, and if you have to make some choices, you'll be wise to do what most successful working parents do—find someone who likes and is liked by the children. This makes up for a great many shortcomings in other areas.

What can you do to make the interview go more smoothly? You can put an applicant at her ease by offering her basic courtesies: hanging up her coat, offering her a glass of cold soda or a cup of hot tea, asking her whether she wants to use the bathroom, addressing her as "Mrs. Jones" rather than "Mary." You *want* to give her a chance to be at her best, so you won't try to trip her up with your questions, but ask them only to draw her out as much as possible. Some suggested questions are in the box "Interview Questions." You won't want to overwhelm her by asking *all* of them, and you may have others related to your own special situation.

Your applicant may have questions, too, and you'll be doing both of you a favor by encouraging her to ask them now instead of a week or two into the job. This is the time for you to spell out conditions of her employment: hours, duties, salary, sick days and holidays, vacation time, Social Security arrangements, and so forth. (See the boxes "Your Tax Obligation as an Employer" and "Code of Standards for Household Employment.")

Be as specific as possible when spelling out her duties. It's better to scare off an applicant at the beginning than to hire someone who will become increasingly resentful over being asked to perform additional duties, and who may take her resentment out on your children. If walking your child half a mile to school in all kinds of weather is required or if you have to work late one or two nights a week and will want her to stay late those evenings, now is the time to say so.

YOUR TAX OBLIGATION
AS AN EMPLOYER

- You have to pay Social Security tax if you pay a worker at least $50 in cash wages in a three-month period. Within one month after the calendar quarter, you have to file Form 942 with the IRS, accompanied by your payment. Obtain the form from your local IRS office.
- You will need an employer-identification number. If you do not have one, write "none" in the space provided for the number. The IRS will give you a number and send you a Form 942 every three months.
- If your employee asks you to withhold income tax, you may agree to do this, too.
- When you hire a household worker, make a record of her name and Social Security number exactly as they appear on her card. If she doesn't have a number, she can apply for one by using Form SS–5 (available from Social Security and IRS offices and from the post office).
- Both you and your employee are expected to contribute equally to the Social Security tax, which in 1988 amounted to a total of 15 percent of her wages.

Even if she refuses to have half of this amount deducted from her pay, however, you are responsible for the total payment. There is no statute of limitations for this requirement, and the government can charge you penalties of nearly 50 percent on back Social Security taxes. Many employers pay the entire amount of the tax, and feel it is well worth it. These tax payments may be computed in figuring out your child-care tax credit (see Chapter 5).

- You have to give a completed copy of Form W–2 to your employee by January 31 of the following year, and file the form with the Social Security Administration by February 28. (You'll also need to file Form W–3, which serves as a transmittal form for W–2.)

- If you paid $1000 or more for household work in a calendar quarter, you are required to pay federal unemployment tax (FUTA). You as employer are solely responsible for this tax, which in 1988 was 6.2 percent* on the first $7000 of cash wages paid during the calendar year. You need to file Form 940 for this tax.
- For more detailed information on your tax obligations, see IRS Publications 15 (Circular E) and 503, as well as the instructions for Form 942.

If you really like an applicant, tell her so. Tell her she's hired if her references check out. Don't wait to see whether someone better might call you. Good caregivers get snapped up quickly, and employers who hesitate often lose them.

If you find that a high proportion of your job applicants lose their enthusiasm for working for you after this initial interview, you have to ask yourself why. Are you expecting too much? Paying too little? No matter how capable a person you hire, she is no more of a superwoman than you are. She can only do what one person can do, and she has to feel that it's worthwhile for her to do it.

One issue has been troubling many women in recent years. The spirit of sisterhood engendered by the women's movement has spurred pangs of guilt among many working women about exploiting the labor of other women who make it possible for them to succeed on the job. But there is no need to feel this way. If you respect the work of caring for children and home and do not consider it demeaning and unworthy of effort, you will respect the person who does it. And if, out of that respect, you have realistic expectations, pay a fair wage, treat your employee with dignity, and offer appropriate working conditions, you have no reason to feel guilty.

Screening Step Three: Checking References

I once fell in love at first sight with a woman an agency sent out to me. During the interview she was warm and loving to

*If you took the 5.4 percent tax credit, this is reduced to 0.8 percent.

CODE OF STANDARDS FOR HOUSEHOLD EMPLOYMENT*

Wages and Hours

The hourly wage should be no lower than the federal minimum specified by the Fair Labor Standards Act (1988: $3.35). Where the cost of living is higher than the average, wages should be raised accordingly.

Some states have minimum wages higher than the federal minimum. Information about your state is available from your State Department of Labor (or from NCHE).

Higher wages should be paid for jobs requiring previously required training or special skills.

Wages and paydays should be discussed and agreed upon in advance.

Gifts of clothing and/or food should not be considered part of payment.

Hours for live-in workers: Any hours exceeding 44 hrs/week should be paid at 1½ times the hourly rate. Hours exceeding 52 hrs/week should be paid at double the hourly rate.

Hours for live-out workers: Day workers should receive overtime for hours in excess of 8 hrs/day. Day workers employed on a full-time weekly basis by one employer should be paid 1½ times the hourly rate for hours exceeding 40 per week.

Benefits

Social Security: Earnings should be reported and payments made in accordance with the law for Social Security credit toward old age, survivors', and disability insurance. Records of payment should be furnished annually in compliance with Social Security legisla-

*Reprinted with permission from the National Committee on Household Employment, National Urban League, Inc.; 500 E. 62nd Street; New York, NY 10021.

tion. Further information about Social Security can be obtained without charge from your local Social Security office.

Sick Leave: Employees working one day a week in one home should receive a minimum of one-day paid sick leave a year. Full-time employees should receive a minimum of six days paid sick leave a year.

Vacations: Full-time day or live-in workers should receive two weeks' paid vacation after one year of service. Employees working one day a week in one home should receive one day paid vacation for each six-month period worked.

For longer service, there should be an agreed-upon increase in vacation time.

Holidays: Live-in workers should receive at least eight paid legal holidays/year.

Full-time live-out employees should receive six legal holidays with pay/year.

A day worker working one day/week in one home should receive one paid legal holiday/year.

Working Relationships

A written agreement between employer and employee should clearly define the duties of the position, including specific tasks and frequency.

Time schedules should be agreed upon in advance of employment.

If an employer does not require the services of a day worker for the agreed-upon time, the employee must be notified at least a week in advance or else be compensated in full.

The employee has the responsibility for notifying the employer as soon as possible if she or he is unable to report to work.

Rest periods, mealtimes, phone privileges, and time out for private activities (such as church or recreation times for live-in employees) should be agreed upon in advance.

ing appliances should be efficient and safe,
uld be used carefully.

k and work relationships should be discussed
ically with the intent to improve efficiency and
understanding.

A professional working relationship should be maintained by both parties.

my three-year-old, friendly to me, and absolutely oozing competence. Just to make sure, though, I placed a long-distance call to the former employer whose name "Hattie Smith" had given me. In a charming southern drawl, the former employer told me, "Hattie? I haven't heard from her in ten years—not since I had to let her go because of her drinking problem." I had to ask myself: Why hadn't Hattie Smith given me a recent reference? And one who hadn't fired her for drinking? What had she been doing in the meantime? With a reluctant sigh I fell out of love and went on looking. As one mother told me, "Trust your instincts—but check her references."

QUESTIONS TO ASK A REFERENCE

- When did Ms. X work for you? For how long?
- What were her duties? How well did she perform them?
- Why did she leave your employ?
- How old were your children at the time? What was she like with them?
- Did you find her honest? Neat? Dependable? Sober?
- Do you have any reservations about her ability to do this job?
- Did your children like her?
- Would you hire her again?

Your own intuition and powers of judgment can tell you a great deal about an applicant, but first impressions are sometimes deceiving. Checking references provides an extra measure of safety. Be alert for the voice of a reference who sounds suspiciously like the sister or best friend of the applicant. If you suspect that you have been given a phony name, ask some very specific questions of the reference. See suggestions in the box "Questions to Ask a Reference." And listen carefully to the answers. You might also call back at an unexpected time, with another question you "forgot" to ask the first time, or ask the applicant for an additional name you can contact.

MAKING IT WORK

Now that the first big hurdle is over—finding someone you feel will be your support at home while you are at work—you enter into the second phase. This involves making the arrangement work out well for all concerned: you, your children, and your housekeeper. You can do a great deal to avoid the revolving-door situation so common between housekeepers and their employers. The following are some suggestions gleaned from those experienced in employing workers at home.

Prepare for The Big Day: Her Arrival

The most important groundwork involves your children. By talking about the new person who will be taking care of them while you are at work, you can lay the foundation for a happy reception and a smooth transition. The younger the child, the closer to the date of arrival you should begin talking about the new caregiver. (Younger children need a smaller window of preparation time.) Even if your children are too young to fully comprehend your words, some of the message (including the new caregiver's name) may well make an impression. And if your children are older, this is the time to encourage them to bring up any questions they may have.

The other preparation, for a live-in person, involves setting up the room where she will be staying. Besides the usual furnishings, which should include as much to make her comfortable and at home as you can think of, most helpers appreciate having their own television sets and clock radios.

Treat Your Caregiver with Respect

Ask her how she likes to be addressed and follow her preference. Accord her the dignity that the importance of her job demands. She is not your personal maid; do not treat her as such. Show confidence in her judgment, allowing her the right to do things her way even if they are not the way you would do them, unless an important issue is involved. Do not undermine her authority with your children: If you cannot back her up in most of her decisions, you need to start looking for someone else.

Cooperation and open communication are essential. For a live-in person, you need to strike an especially delicate balance: sharing a close relationship while respecting each other's needs for privacy.

Be Very Clear About Your Expectations

Not only should you spell out, in your initial interview, the range of duties you expect, you should also go over them carefully as soon as your helper comes to work for you. You would do well to write down everything you can think of that you consider important to the care of your children and the running of your household. Even if your housekeeper is not given to reading, writing down your policies will help fix them in your own mind and will provide a backstop for her if she is ever in doubt about what to do. (Keep your typed original set of instructions and give a photocopy to your helper. Should she leave, you'll have your copy, which you can then update for her successor.)

Be Clear from the Start
About Her Hours and Duties

Do not indulge in creeping chore dumping. Try to anticipate any possible situation so that each of you knows what to expect. Says Washington, D.C., environmental planner Sheryl Sturges, "Be very careful not to overreach the boundaries you've set in terms of your helper's time, so she won't get burned out and feel taken advantage of."

Invest extra time at the beginning to introduce routines and other information gradually; it will pay off in the end. If you can, hire a new person two weeks before you actually need her to take over. During her first week she can watch you or your present caregiver to learn how you do things. Then during the second week, she takes her turn—and you watch her. If you can't take off this much time, try at least to take off a couple of days to be with her at the beginning.

If, after she has been working for you, you have new requirements that you had not anticipated, discuss them with your helper without taking for granted that she will do them. Even if she lives with you during her work week, she is not available to you twenty-four hours a day. All of you should have a clear understanding of the extent of her free time. She should have an hour or two off during the day, if possible—maybe in the early morning while you have breakfast with the children. After dinner, she should not be expected to answer the phone, help you entertain, or go to a child who awakens in the night—unless these requirements are spelled out from the beginning, or special provisions (like extra pay or time off) are made.

Be Generous

As writer Shirley Sloan Fader told me, "I always pay about a dollar an hour above going rates for cleaning help; fifty cents above for baby-sitting. What it buys in loyalty is amazing. People will go out of their way to find transportation to you; to rearrange their personal schedules; to do everything they possibly can to *keep* a job that pays more than the going rate. Not only that, they will feel good about themselves for having found a job that pays 'top wages.' This in turn makes for a good attitude toward their work.

"In short, for a relatively nominal sum (if it's just cleaning for a few hours a week, it might be only two dollars to five dollars more), you usually are able to eliminate most of the turnover in help that makes being a two-paycheck family so difficult." As Ms. Fader, who brought up two children and ran a big house while maintaining a busy writing career, says, "I can't think of anything else I could buy with those dollars each week that would be as valuable to me."

Generosity also extends to granting extra time off when you can afford to, to letting your helper go home earlier than usual when your schedule permits, to assiduously avoiding pressing for every last ounce of flesh for your wages. While an unexpected occasional small gift is often appreciated, too many employers think that giving their housekeepers outworn, out-of-style clothing or leftover food that has lost its bloom are marks of generosity. Most employees would rather forego such "Lady Bountiful" largesse in favor of fair wages and a businesslike arrangement.

Your Attitude Toward Discipline

Even if you occasionally swat your child's fanny yourself, you are on dangerous ground when you grant this privilege to someone else. You do not know what another person considers a mild spanking and whether she will hit your child too hard and too often. Furthermore, a small child is defenseless against the superior strength and power over his life held by an adult in charge. He should not be put in a position whereby any adult has the right to hit him at will. Tell your housekeeper very firmly that she is *never* to hit your child, no matter what the provocation. Threats ("I'll tell the policeman on you") and frightening stories about bogeymen and other carriers of justice should also be forbidden.

Instead, suggest some alternate ways of handling obstreperousness, such as distracting the child, bodily lifting her and carrying her where she needs to go, sending him to another room for a time-out-period, withdrawing some privilege (like television or a story), and using logical consequences (such as not giving her any jelly beans after she deliberately spills a whole bag on the floor).

Television-Viewing Policy

Are there certain shows you do not want your child to watch? Do you want to place limits on the amount of time spent watching television? What about rainy days, school holidays, sick days? Let your caregiver know how you feel about these right at the beginning, to avoid misunderstandings later on.

Vital Telephone Numbers

Leave these on a card posted by the telephone. See the list in the Box "Important Telephone Numbers."

Safety

Instruct your caregiver on the rules for safety:

- Put all medicines, poisons, and caustic cleaning products in locked cabinets.
- Put breakable items where a toddler cannot reach them.
- Cover all exposed electrical sockets.
- Be sure tap water is not hot enough to scald a child.
- Get rid of all poisonous plants from house and yard.
- Put safety gates at the tops and/or bottoms of stairways.
- Pad the edges of or remove furniture with sharp corners.
- Do not wax floors to too slippery a finish.
- Do not leave small throw rugs around where people can slip.
- Pick up all items from stairs.
- Never leave a child alone in the bathtub.
- Never leave an infant on a surface she can fall from.

IMPORTANT TELEPHONE NUMBERS

This house: phone no.: _____

address: _____

Mother's number at work: _____

Father's number at work: _____

Close neighbors (three you could call on for help):

_____

_____

Grandparents (mother's parents): _____

_____

Grandparents (father's parents): _____

_____

Other close relative: _____

Fire: _____

Police: _____

Pediatrician: _____

Family doctor: _____

Dentist: _____

Drugstore: _____

Taxi: _____

Hospital: _____

Ambulance service: _____

Poison Control Center: _____

Child's school: _____

- Get a copy of a first-aid book and encourage your helper to become familiar with it.
- Teach her the Heimlich maneuver to help a person who is choking.
- Take her with you to a class where you can both learn CPR (cardiopulmonary resuscitation) for children and infants.

(A videocassette demonstrating this is good to have as a refresher.)

- Keep a well-stocked first-aid kit handy.
- Always know where the children are and what they are doing.
- Point out to your helper that the phone numbers of fire and police departments and your nearest poison control center are on the list kept by your phone.
- Teach her to follow the safety precautions listed for self-care children in the box "Keeping Your Home and Your Child Safe from Burglars" in Chapter 10.

Your Special Wishes About Food

- Child's favorite lunch foods.
- Foods your child doesn't like, is allergic to, or should not have.
- When he is allowed to have between-meal snacks.
- What such snacks should consist of.
- Name(s) of store(s) where you like to market.
- Specific preferences for brands and sizes.
- For person who prepares family meals: special likes and dislikes, general quantities (are you big or small eaters), and type of food (highly spiced or bland, exotic or familiar, and so on).

Schedule Time for Ongoing Communication

In the typical working household, parents and caregivers are like ships that pass in the morning and evening. As she arrives in the morning, you are rushing out to get to work on time; and as you come home in the evening, she is eager to get to her own home. When she calls you at work, your heart sinks because you know something has gone wrong. When you call her, it's usually to give instructions you forgot to write down or transmit in passing. This kind of split-shift scheduling leaves no time for you to get any sense of the texture of your children's lives during those hours when you are not with them. Nor does it give you the chance to tell your caregiver about anything special in your children's lives that she should be especially sensitive to.

There are several ways you can get around this impasse. Perhaps you can arrange to have your caregiver come a half-hour early every morning, so that she can sit down with a cup of coffee (or follow you around, cup in hand), giving the two of you time to catch up with what happened yesterday and what the plans are for today. Or, you might be able to schedule an overlapping half-hour in the evenings. Or, plan for a regular telephone conversation during the day, possibly during your coffee break. You may find that you don't need to make this a daily routine, that two or three conversations a week will keep the lines of communication flowing freely.

Trouble on the Horizon

One problem for some working parents, which is only a problem if you make it one, is jealousy of your caregiver. When Susie runs to Mrs. Burnett with a scraped knee rather than to you, or asks *her* to read a story, or turns to *her* with questions, it's only natural for you to get that sinking sensation inside that makes you wonder whether you've signed away your child's love for a paycheck. But even though there may be times when Susie seems to prefer Mrs. Burnett over you, deep down Susie knows that you're the one who's there for the long haul. As you and Susie will probably find, *you* are permanent, whereas Mrs. Burnett is likely to have other priorities in her life that will take her out of your household eventually.

For the time she is with you, however, you should count your blessings that Susie has formed such a close relationship with another person in her life. Susie is fortunate because intimacy feeds the capacity for intimacy, and the attachment Susie is forming now is likely to bear fruit later in her life. You, of course, are fortunate because your knowledge that your child is happy with the person taking care of her frees you from the biggest worry working parents have, uneasiness about their children's well-being.

Other problems that come up between employers and care-givers often have much more substance. What do you do, for example, when your children complain bitterly that Mrs. Brown is mean to them or doesn't talk to them? When they become so rambunctious at night that you wonder what they've been doing all day? What do you do when she is habitually late, making you late for work? When, even by your relaxed housekeeping standards, the house gets so dirty you expect to be cited by the Board of Health? When she walks around the house with a sullen expression much of the time?

What you do is take some kind of action the minute you suspect that things are not going as well as they should be. The action may involve nothing more than talk—asking your children very specific questions, for example, to find out in what way Mrs. Brown is so mean. (You may find she's no meaner than you would be in a similar situation.) It may involve talking to Mrs. Brown, pointing out the importance of her being on time for work, because you can't leave until she arrives.

If you suspect that all is not well, you might want to come home unexpectedly in the middle of the day. If you can't do this yourself, you could ask a neighbor, a friend, or a relative to pop in to check out your home front. I've heard horror stories from parents who did just this. One found a baby-sitter asleep, with a toddler propped up with pillows watching television. Another discovered a cooperative arrangement among several neighborhood baby-sitters, who would take turns watching three or four children while the other sitters went shopping. Then there was the father who went to the playground, saw that his baby-sitter was not paying any attention to his child and took the three-year-old home with him. It took half an hour for the sitter to notice that the little boy was missing! Fortunately, such serious lapses seem relatively rare, but because they're possible, parents have to stay on top of a situation, especially with a new caregiver.

If the problem is a misunderstanding between you and your caregiver or a mechanical problem like overreliance on the electronic baby-sitter, the television set, a straightforward talk may straighten things out. But if the difficulty runs deeper than that, involving your employee's basic personality, there may be nothing you can do short of firing this woman who may be the best cook this side of Cordon Bleu but the worst person for your children this side of Simon Legree.

If you do feel you have to fire, do it quickly. Probably the biggest mistake parents make is keeping a caregiver for too long, after they've come to the conclusion that she's not right for them and their children. It's hard to let someone go. And it's especially hard for working parents because you become so dependent on the person taking care of your child. Your job, your daily life, your peace of mind—all hinge on your child-care arrangements working out. This feeling of dependency can make it hard for you to manage your caregiver as effectively as you would like. So you have to keep reappraising the situation: Is your caregiver doing what you and she agreed on? Is your child doing well? Can you go off to work with an easy mind? If not, you need to talk. And if talking doesn't change the situation, you may need to fire.

If you do fire your caregiver, pay her the equivalent of one or two weeks' wages, but ask her to leave immediately. You do not want a resentful person in charge of your children. If you don't have some sort of emergency backup arrangement (which you should have—more about this in Chapter 9), you can usually get a temporary worker from a reliable household-help agency. Expensive, yes, but on a short-term basis it might be the best solution.

This is the worst. You might also have a situation that's the best. When you ask your children pointed questions about their caregiver (a good idea, even when there are no complaints)—such as "What do you like best about Ms. Lopez? What don't you like about her? What special things do you do together?"—you may find that their answers make you purr. If so, you should feel not only lucky but proud because you have found this paragon, you have recognized her good qualities, and you have provided the kind of atmosphere in which she can shine.

After She's Gone

The day comes when even Mary Poppins leaves your home. Your child may be ready for preschool, and you don't need a full-time caregiver any more. Or, you may move out of town. Or, your situation may change in some other way. Or, you may desperately want that caregiver to stay—but her needs or wants change. Or, you may have signed up for a nanny or au pair who has right from the start planned to leave after one year.

The departure may be hard for both you and your children. As one working mother told me, "Aside from the fact that I know I'll have to start making new arrangements nine to ten months after each nanny comes, the major problem is that Jeb, who's only two, doesn't understand why someone he's been very close to for a year suddenly disappears and he won't be seeing her any more. He adjusted to Mary, the new nanny, and likes her. But the other day when he heard me mention Terry in conversation, he came over and piped up, 'Terry? Terry come?' And then he led me to her room, which, of course, is now Mary's room. My heart broke for him."

Saying goodbye to someone who's been an important part of your life is always hard. But the eminent child psychiatrist Stella Chess, M.D., coauthor of *Know Your Child,* recommends turning it into a learning experience. "This is something that happens to all of us throughout life," Dr. Chess says. "Nice people come into our lives, and they become very close to us; and then things come up, and they have to go away. And life goes on."

Parents, then, need not feel too alarmed or guilty when this happens with their children. They can, however, help their children adjust to the change. First they can talk about "Terry's" leaving, starting a couple of weeks or so ahead of time (longer for an older child). Although a two-year-old may not understand all the words, Jeb can absorb the fact that there is some explanation for this event, that it is not a secret, and that the door is open for talking about it.

Then you can help your children make transitions by keeping a photo of the beloved sitter, by encouraging her to drop them a note or card occasionally, and by telephoning her, especially in the period soon after she leaves. Meanwhile, if your new caregiver works out well, chances are that your children will be able to store their thoughts of the previous one back in the recesses of memory. And, of course, the most important thing to remember is that you remain the most important person in your children's lives. If you children know that even though baby-sitters may come and go, you and your love remain constant, they will be better able to handle the many other changes they will undergo throughout life.

7

CARE IN SOMEONE ELSE'S HOME

When three-and-a-half-year-old Jenny, fair-haired and apple-cheeked, looks up and asks, "Mrs. Hayes, may I please be excused?" those simple words gladden the heart of Margaret Hayes of Dryden, New York. When Jenny first came to Mrs. Hayes a few months before, to be cared for three mornings a week while her mother was working as a researcher at nearby Cornell University, Jenny couldn't say a word. Jenny was born with Down syndrome, a chromosomal condition that causes mental retardation. Although she had attended a special program for such children, she had never learned how to talk. Until Mrs. Hayes, a warm and loving family day-care mother, made up her mind to teach Jenny some communication basics.

Family day care—paid care in the home of a person (almost always a woman) who cares for small groups of children—can be very good indeed, as it is for Margaret Hayes's young charges.

When I spoke with anthropologist Margaret Mead, we talked about the care of young children. "When we talk about babies up to the age of two, whose mothers don't have a relative or neighbor they can call on, family-based care in the

149

home of a woman who takes in three or four children and enjoys it is far better than the big institution," Dr. Mead told me.

"The essential thing with an infant and a child who's just learning to talk and to understand the world is somebody who remembers what happened yesterday," she said emphatically. "This woman is there every day. There's not the turnover in personnel that you find in a large institution. You see, you have a baby who's just discovered—or thinks he's discovered—that 'boo-boo' means bedroom slippers. A great discovery! But if he says 'boo-boo' to someone new, nothing would happen. And he would feel uncertain and distrustful. Trust is the basic point in infants and little children."

Unfortunately, of course, not all family day-care homes foster trust, as Sandra Noyes, a Burlington, Vermont, administrative assistant, found out, to her distress. Sandra was leaving her daughter, Stacy, with a woman we'll call "Mrs. Smith."

"One day," says Sandra, "I was picking up Stacy after work and Mrs. Smith said, 'Oh, I thought Stacy had already gone home.' When I looked surprised, she explained how she was on the phone and thought it was Stacy who had left instead of somebody else." Mrs. Smith's lack of involvement with the children showed up in other ways too—such as sending the children outdoors to play without adequate supervision and not bothering to provide toys for them to play with, but instead just sitting them in front of the television set. While Sandra quickly moved Stacy to a different family day-care home, other children remained with Mrs. Smith, continuing to receive care marked by indifference and lack of involvement.

Family day care in private homes has been characterized as "the mainstay for working parents" by John C. Moore, Jr., project director of the 1975 National Child Care Consumer Study conducted by the United States Department of Health, Education and Welfare, which surveyed 4600 American families.

Even today, with increases in the use of group care for infants and preschoolers, about one in five working mothers pays a nonrelative to take care of her child in the other person's home, and more than 2 million children receive their primary care from these caregivers. However, family day care is the least popular child-care method. About a third of the parents who use it would like to change. Parents talk about caregivers who are nice people but take in more children than they can give individual attention to and about facilities that don't provide enough room for play or resting. And about a third of the people giving care would prefer to be doing some other kind of work. Caregivers talk about the low pay and low prestige of the work. Why then is this kind of care used so frequently?

It's usually the easiest to find and the least expensive; furthermore, the hours are flexible. And when it's good, it's very good—the closest thing to a home away from home. Given the wide use of family day care, it makes sense for both government and private organizations to do all they can to make it better instead of focusing their efforts, as has been done so far, primarily on group day care. Some of this emphasis has been shifting in recent years as more and more state and local governments and community groups have been focusing on ways to improve family day care. In many communities around the country, efforts have been made to train family day-care providers, to set up a network so that they could learn from each other, to help them bring their homes into compliance with licensing requirements, and to put parents in touch with them. Such efforts support both parents and caregivers.

If you decide on this kind of care for your child, what can you do to make it the best possible?

FINDING A FAMILY DAY-CARE HOME

Strictly speaking, a relative or friend who offers, for a fee, to care for your child in her home meets the definition of family day care. In a situation like this, you'd want to pay attention to the same basic ground rules, spelled out in Chapter 6, for dealing with a relative who takes care of your child. In addition, some of the following suggestions will apply no matter who the caregiver is, whether it's your mother or a stranger.

...STIONS TO ASK A FAMILY
...-CARE MOTHER

General Information

- How many children do you take care of?
- How old are they?
- What hours and days do you offer care?
- Do you plan to continue caring for children for the next year? Longer?
- What areas of your house are used by the children? (Ask to see them.)
- Where do children take naps? (Ask to see the place.)
- Do you have a place where children can play outdoors? Is it fenced in? Does it have play equipment? (Ask to see it.) If you don't have a place at your home, do you take children to the park or the playground? How often?
- What activities do you plan for the children?
- What pets do you have?
- How long have you been taking care of children? What made you go into this kind of work? Tell me about your experience.
- Have you had any special training in child care? What was it?
- Have you and your family had medical checkups, including chest X rays, within the past year? (Ask to see the reports.)
- Are you licensed or registered?

Money Matters

- What fee do you charge? (Family day-care fees usually run between $50 and $150 per child per week, depending on the community. Hourly rates for children cared for part-time range between $3 and $6.)
- Do you offer a special rate for two or more children from the same family?
- Suppose we go on vacation for a week or two, would you still expect to be paid?

Suppose I have to work overtime or get stuck in traffic and am late picking up my child, is there an extra charge?

- How do you like to be paid, at the beginning or end of the week? Or, by the month?
- Do you give receipts so that I can receive a tax credit?

Special Situations

- What happens if my child gets sick? Will you still take care of him? Do you have a special room he can stay in? Will you give him his medicine?
- What happens if you get sick? Do you have someone who can substitute for you?
- Would you ever have to be away from the home while the children are there? If so, who would take care of them?
- Will you be driving the children anywhere in your car?

Health and Safety

- Where do you keep medicines and household-cleaning agents?
- What fire precautions have you taken? Do you hold fire drills with the children?
- Does your insurance cover the children you take care of?
- Do you keep handy the numbers of the fire and police departments, the poison control center, hospital, doctor, parents, someone who could come in a hurry to stay with the other children in case you have to take one to the emergency room?
- Do you keep medical information on the children?
- Will you give a child the medicine she's supposed to take?
- Have you ever had an emergency with a child? What happened, and what did you do?

HOW TO EVALUATE A FAMILY DAY-CARE HOME

The Person

- Is she friendly to both you and your child?
- Is she interested in what you have to say about your child?
- Does she devote individual attention to each of the children?
- Does she structure an interesting day for the children?
- Is she flexible and able to adapt to special situations?
- Is she in tune with your feelings about discipline, toilet training, eating habits, and so forth?
- Does she enjoy working with children all day?
- Does she seem levelheaded and able to deal with an emergency?

The Place

- Is there enough space for the number of children?
- Is it clean and sanitary—but not so spotless that you'd never know children were present?
- Have adequate safety precautions been taken? Are electrical outlets covered? Are potentially dangerous objects kept inaccessible?
- Is there a place where children can nap or be alone?
- Is there a place for children to play outdoors?
- Are there toys, equipment, and books suitable for children of your child's age?

If you don't have a willing relative, friend, or neighbor, you need to look beyond your immediate horizon. Word of mouth is always a good method; others are ads in your local "Pennysaver" or community newspaper (both following up ads you see and placing your own), supermarket and laundromat bulletin boards, and local contacts such as clergy and nursery

school teachers. In some communities, you may have other resources, either a broad-based information and referral service
(as described in Chapter 5) or a service especially designed to
bring together parents who need care for their children and
people who want to take care of youngsters in their homes.
Try calling your local or state Department of Social Services
or Department of Human Resources, a local day-care or child-
care council, or any of the organizations listed in the appendix
"Helpful Organizations."

CHOOSING A FAMILY DAY-CARE HOME

Before you leave your child in another person's home, it's absolutely imperative that you check out both the person and
the home. If possible, go the first time without your child, so
you'll be free to talk, observe, and evaluate without being distracted. And try to schedule your visit either near the beginning or the end of the day. This way you can see how the
caregiver acts with children, and you'll also have some time to
talk to her when she won't be distracted by her charges. If she
passes this first interview, you'll want to go once more with
your child to see how they get along.

Check the list of suggested questions and bases for evaluation. While you may be willing to compromise on some of the
points covered, be sure that you're satisfied on the most important ones.

DOES YOUR CAREGIVER
NEED TO BE LICENSED?

"I almost sent my daughter to an unlicensed day-care center.
And then it turned out that the husband and son in the house
where the day-care center was were arrested for sodomizing
children! Now I would only go to licensed, state-certified
places," says copywriter Hilary Markoe.

On the other hand, Sandra Noyes told me, "The baby-sitter who's taking care of my little girl now is licensed herself, but she says there is so much paperwork and red tape involved that she feels this is a major factor in preventing people from taking care of children in their homes. She also feels that this paperwork keeps her from spending more time with the children. Besides, Mrs. Smith was licensed, too, and she should not have been baby-sitting at all. Even though I wrote to the licensing agencies about her, nothing changed."

Some nine out of ten family day-care mothers across the country are "underground" workers. They are unlicensed and unknown to government officials. Some of them don't apply for licenses because they don't want government inspectors "snooping" in their own homes; others don't want to go to the expense of putting in child-size toilets or widening a doorway by an inch or two to meet the state code; others just don't want to get tangled up in bureaucratic red tape; and others don't want to report—and pay taxes on—their earnings.

Licensing assures that a day-care home or center has at least met a state's minimum health, fire, and safety standards—at the time of inspection. But because inspectors make few (if any) repeat visits and because they do not check out a program's quality above this basic minimum, you cannot depend on a program's license to assure you that this is the place for your child.

One study of sixty licensed day-care centers in Hartford, Connecticut, for example, found so many deficiencies that only 20 percent of the centers had passing overall scores of 80 percent or over. The problems included inadequate shock-absorbing material around playground equipment (97 percent), unsafe storage of toxic materials (38 percent), no barrier to keep autos from entering the outdoor play area (38 percent), no emergency plan (30 percent), and no functioning smoke detectors (17 percent).

One major disadvantage to unlicensed caregivers and the children they care for is that the caregivers are isolated from each other and from government resources that could help them offer better care. To remedy this isolation and to increase the number of family day-care homes, a number of communities have turned to voluntary registration. Under this system, caregivers list their names with a state or local agency and agree to meet local health and safety requirements and to inform parents of those requirements. The agency gives out the list of registered caregivers to parents but cautions parents that they themselves are responsible for seeing that the homes meet state standards.

"Licensing does not protect standards," said Peter Sauer, former director of the Consultation for Community Development and Self-Reliance of Bank Street State College of Education in New York City. "It lulls people into accepting dangerous situations because, once caregivers are licensed, they sometimes become complacent; and even if officials find a facility in violation, they are often reluctant to take away a license."

Evidence that registration can provide as much protection as licensing comes from the state of Texas, where the ratio of parent complaints is no higher now under a system of registration than it had been when Texas required licensing of family day-care homes. Spot checks have shown few violations of state regulations. Furthermore, in the first two years after Texas switched to registration in 1976, the number of official caregivers soared from 1950 to over 6000. The state offers a battery of services for these caregivers: ideas for play activities; tips for low-cost, high-quality nutrition; basic health and first-aid training; business management training; and courses in child development.

Ultimately, what registration does is treat both parents and caregivers as responsible, intelligent adults. Says David Beard, director of day-care licensing in Texas, "Registration places on the parent and the provider a lot of the responsibility that the state had previously assumed."

In the end, whether a caregiver is registered, licensed, or underground, she is taking care of *your* child. No inspector or official agency can take your place in determining whether you child will be safe, happy, and well cared for.

HELPING YOUR BABY OR TODDLER ADJUST TO SEPARATION FROM YOU*

- Play peek-a-boo games so your baby gets used to the idea that you go away—and that you always return.
- Hire a baby-sitter to come play with and take care of your child while you remain at home. Pursue an activity in a different room rather than hovering over your child and the sitter.
- Leave the room for increasing periods of time until your child seems comfortable with the caregiver. Then leave the house briefly, then for longer periods of time.
- Take your child to places where she will get used to being with other people—parks, playgrounds, other people's homes, and so forth. If she seems uncomfortable at first, hold her and stay close to her until she feels more secure.
- When you leave your child at the baby-sitter's home, leave one or more familiar objects—a favorite toy, blanket, pacifier, or bottle. Tell the caregiver how your child likes to use it.
- The first time (and maybe the first few times) you leave your child at a new baby-sitter's home, stay with him for part or all of the day.
- Tell the caregiver about any special preferences or anxieties your child may have and the kinds of comforting she responds to.
- Try to be available by telephone to the caregiver the first few times your child stays without you. If possible, be prepared to come in response to a phone call.
- Do not try to scold or shame your child into separating from you. His difficulty in separating is perfectly normal and a possible sign of a strong attachment to you. You can help him most by being patient and reassuring.

*Based on suggestions offered by the Parent Resource Center, Port Washington, New York.

HELPING YOUR CHILD
TO BE COMFORTABLE

Pamela Stern couldn't understand why three-year-old Max cried so bitterly the first day she left him with Mrs. Edwards. Max had warmed up to her immediately when he had first visited with his mother, and he was used to staying at home with baby-sitters. That night, as Pam was putting Max to bed, she found out what was troubling him. "I don't want to live over there—I want to live with you," Max said, between sobs. And then Pamela understood.

"I felt like such a simp," she told me. "Poor little Max was sure I was getting ready to turn him over completely to Mrs. Edwards. *I* knew I was leaving him with her just while I was at work, but I hadn't made it clear to him. Once I did, and once he got over that initial shock, he became happy as a clam about going there."

No matter how young your child is, be sure to tell her that this arrangement will be only during the hours while you are at work. Babies often understand much more than they are given credit for, and they can be reassured by your words.

Prepare your child for separation from you. One way is to leave him with your baby-sitter for short periods of time at first, gradually increasing them until he is there for the full day. Another way is to stay close by her for the first couple of days she is at your baby-sitter's home. Other suggestions, especially geared for infants and toddlers, are given in the box "Helping Your Baby or Toddler Adjust to Separation from You."

MAKING IT WORK
WITH YOUR CAREGIVER

Chances are that the person taking care of your child is doing this kind of work because she really likes children. (She's certainly not doing this to get rich: most family day-care mothers are not the sole support of their families and use their earnings from minding children to augment the basic family income.) She wants to do the best she can for your child. And you can help her do this in a number of ways.

One way is by staying in close touch. Instead of just dropping Johnny off or picking him up with a hasty greeting, allow a few minutes occasionally to chat with the caregiver. You want to tell her about what's going on in Johnny's life, and you want to hear what she has to tell you about him. If something unusual comes up in your child's world—if you and your husband just separated, for example, and four-year-old Annie has been waking up every night with nightmares—let your caregiver know. She may be able to offer that extra dollop of comfort and stability that Annie needs right now. If you need to talk to her privately or at length, call to make an appointment, either to talk by phone or in person.

Be responsible for holding up your end: Be on time to deliver and pick up your child; pay promptly; meet any other terms of your agreement. Your family day-care giver will also appreciate it if you send your child clean, in clean clothes with a clean diaper, and if you send along a change of clothing and the proper outdoor clothes for the weather.

Some of the same issues that can come up with a person who cares for your children in your own home can also come up with your child's "other" family at the day-care home: Like your child's unhappiness on weekends and holidays when she "has to" stay home with you, which may lead to jealousy of the family day-care mother. (Remember, be grateful that your child is happy there.) Like conflicts caused by differences in values between you and your caregiver, and differences in handling children (which it may be possible to resolve in a talk, scheduled for a time when you are both free from distractions). Like indications that all is not well (which must be pursued, through talk, personal investigation, or even official intervention).

If trouble does loom, deal with it right away. If you signed a contract stipulating what each of you expects from the other, you can refer to it if you believe that your caregiver is not upholding her end. Most family day-care arrangements are informal, with nothing being signed. If you do sign something, however, read it carefully, advises Maryland publicist Robin Latham Olsen. The pregnant caregiver taking care of Robin's son Nick gave him excellent care before she had her own baby.

"But after her baby was born, in spite of the fact that she wasn't capable of giving Nick adequate care, she desperately needed the money and insisted she was 'in good enough shape' to watch him," Robin told me. "I didn't want to be unkind to her, but I didn't want my son to suffer from neglect. I ended up having to pay through the nose to honor a contract I had signed stating that she was owed either two weeks' severance pay or two weeks' notice if I were to withdraw my child from her care. Around here, family day-care providers all have these kinds of contracts that protect *them* but offer absolutely no recourse to the parent for bad or neglectful care. I honored my commitment to her, even though I felt she hadn't honored her commitment to me and my child." Fortunately, after this experience the Olsens were able to find a place for Nick with the president of the family day-care association in their community, where he is getting excellent care.

Sometimes if you catch a problem early, you can turn it around. But if you wait, hoping that it will go away, it just gets worse. The tendency for working parents, who need their jobs and who need their children cared for so they can keep their jobs, is often to overlook the flies in the sugar bowl. But sometimes those flies are too obvious to ignore. Only you can decide how to deal with them.

Just because one family day-care situation doesn't work out, of course, doesn't mean that you might not find another that's perfect for you and your child. Like the one found by a graphic designer and audio engineer whose baby is being cared for by a couple in their late thirties. They have been in business for ten years, are licensed, and care for five children in their apartment. "Tony and Joy are great!" says Alexandra Guzek-Hoffman. "They remind me of myself and my husband. And we think it's a fabulous plus that Peter is with a male role model as well as a female." Many other parents have also found warm, stable, family day-care homes. Once again, the key ingredient to the success of this kind of arrangement lies in the personality and conscientiousness of the person to whom you are entrusting your precious charges. And once again, although luck is always a factor in bringing people together, your role in checking out the family day-care providers you meet is the crucial element that will make it possible for you to offer your child a "home away from home."

8

GROUP CARE: DAY-CARE CENTERS AND NURSERY SCHOOLS

Like many other towns, the Long Island suburb of Port Washington, New York, responded to lower birth rates by closing some of its elementary schools. Because of another major social change, local parents reap the benefits. A building that once housed an elementary school is now home to the Port Washington Children's Center, which cares all day for three- to five-year-olds in the afternoons and also for young elementary school children during school vacations.

Light streams in through the wide windows, brightening cheerful rooms with their various activity centers and their colorful decorations. The center's most beautiful aspect, however, is its sense of caring. This comes through in the gentleness with which I saw teacher Ellen Gaudioso draw an unhappy three-year-old, sucking his thumb and holding his blanket, onto her lap as the other children were eating their breakfast. ("Not everybody can work in day care," Ellen told me later. "You're a parent, a doctor, a nurse, a teacher, a playmate. And you have to like being all these things to the

163

children.'') It also shows in the center's concern for the families it serves. As director Marlene Selig told me, "Some of our parents have good backup—either a spouse or their own parents who can help them out. But some don't have anyone but us. So we try to get them together with the other parents, so they can give each other mutual support."

The parents respond to this concern, both for themselves and for their children. As copywriter Hilary Markoe said, "Cassandra used to go to another place where she wasn't stretched enough, so she'd come home and have all this energy she'd have to use up. Now she comes home tired, dirty—and happy. She's in a very caring and healthy environment, and I think we're both really lucky."

This center is quite a contrast to another center, whose establishment was trumpeted as a major community achievement and whose board was achieving great success in raising funds. "On paper the center sounded great, but the trouble was that the people running it had gotten in over their heads," an attorney for an activist community agency told me after she had visited the center to offer some requested legal advice. "The day I walked in, I saw kids lying all over the floor, with people stepping over them and around them and not making any effort to organize a program. This went on all morning, so it wasn't just rest time. At first these people started the center for the kids, but then politics took over, and the kids became an incidental concern.

What can you do to find a center like this first one and scrupulously avoid placing your child in one like the second? A lot, as we'll see in this chapter.

WHAT DO YOU CALL THEM?

First, let's talk about terminology. What's the difference between a nursery school, a preschool, a day-care center, and a kindergarten?

A *nursery school* is the same thing as a *preschool*. It is usually licensed by a state board of education and is designed to offer an educational experience to children ages three to five. Traditionally, it runs for two or three hours in the morning or afternoon.

A *day-care center* is licensed by a state's Department of Social Services, Human Resources, or Welfare. Because it is designed to provide physical care and supervision to children of parents who are at school or at work, it runs for a full day, usually from about 7:30 or 8:00 AM to 5:00 or 6:00 PM. Its children may range from infants (who are in a special program), through preschoolers (who are there all day), up to school-age children (who come to the center after school and during school vacations).

A *kindergarten* is the traditional introduction to school for five-year-olds, providing a year's transition between the relative freedom of home or preschool and the structure of formal schooling. Publicly supported kindergarten is part of a state's educational system, offered free to all residents of the school district. Kindergarten used to be held for half a day—morning or afternoon—but many school districts are now instituting full-day kindergartens, mostly to meet the needs of working parents.

Parents whose primary purpose is giving their child an educational experience might look for a nursery school (listed in the Yellow Pages of the telephone directory under "Nursery Schools and Kindergartens"); those who need care for their children while they work or go to school look for a day-care center (listed under "Day Nurseries and Child Care"). Sometimes a parent's feelings dictate the choice. As one young mother, on the board of a new day-care center in a Long Island suburb, confessed, "I guess I ought to put my own little girl in the center, but I can't get over feeling that day care is for poor people." And a father stated emphatically, "They ought to come up with a better name. To me, day care sounds like you're putting your kid away somewhere."

If you look at both Yellow Page listings, however, you're likely to find the same facilities listed in both categories. These days many nursery schools and day-care centers have virtually identical programs and facilities. To meet the needs of the growing numbers of working parents, nursery schools have lengthened their school day and are now offering more

TYPES OF NURSERY SCHOOLS AND DAY-CARE CENTERS

Nonprofit Community Agencies

These charge fees to parents, sometimes on sliding scales based on parents' incomes, and are also funded by the sponsoring organizations. These include unions, colleges and universities, hospitals, churches and synagogues, and other social welfare organizations. Sometimes preference is given to families that are affiliated with the agency.

Publicly Funded Centers

These are often cosponsored by a community agency and receive federal, state, or city funding in addition to whatever the local agency provides. Attendance is sometimes limited to low-income families. Parents pay from nothing to a set maximum; if their income goes over a certain amount, their child must leave the center.

Individuals or Companies Operating for a Profit

Some of these centers are large, franchised operations of national chains, and some are small businesses run by individuals responding to a community need that meshes with their interests and abilities. All are totally supported by parents' fees. Some private centers have government approval to accept parents who receive child-care subsidies.

Employers

A very small number of private companies and public agencies operate centers, at or near their site of operations, for the children of employees. Fees are often charged on sliding scales based on parental incomes. Parents may be able to coordinate their lunch hours to eat with their children. As attorney Janet McCabe says, "It's wonderful to have workplace day care. It's great to see my baby at lunch!"

Public Schools

Some districts offer a prekindergarten program open to some or all children in the district. These operate for about three hours a day, usually in conjunction with regular morning or afternoon sessions. The program is usually free, but in a few cases a nominal fee is charged. A few school districts around the country are now providing kindergarten programs that run from 9:00 AM to 3:00 PM, and many offer supervised after-school programs.

Parent Cooperatives

Parents working part-time can sometimes participate in a cooperatively run nursery school or center, which requires all parents to devote a certain amount of actual classroom time, as well as time spent handling operations and raising funds.

services. And because of findings from research in child development, day-care centers are focusing more on children's educational and developmental needs. So when you look for group care for your child, don't worry about what a place calls itself. Instead, look at what it actually does and how well it does it. However, child-care experts advise parents not to worry too much about education in the day-care center. Says psychiatrist Dr. Nada Stotland of Chicago's Michael Reese Medical Center, "Your child shouldn't be bored there, but his or her skills will be developed in grammar school, not at the day-care center."

CHOOSING GROUP CARE

There are three basic types of group care, as defined by the Office of Child Development of the United States Department of Health and Human Services. You can use these types as standards for judging a day-care center or nursery school. What are the three types?

- *Comprehensive child-development program.* This kind of care embraces nearly all needs of growing children and their families—educational, nutritional, and health, including family counseling and instruction in child development for parents. This kind of care may be desirable for children from disadvantaged homes, but is unnecessary for middle-class children. Because it is very expensive, it is usually federally funded and offered free or at low cost to eligible families.

- *Custodial care.* This is at the other extreme, involving little more than baby-sitting, merely offering supervision over children's physical safety. Caregivers usually have little or no training; they provide the children in their care with hardly any books or educational toys, and the children usually spend most of the day watching television. This kind of care is the cheapest and probably the most common, but is hardly the kind of atmosphere most of us want for our children.

- *Developmental care.* In these programs children have many opportunities for social and educational development. Trained people work with them, a variety of good books and toys are available, the meals they're served are nutritionally sound, and medical care is offered. This is the most desirable kind of care for most children, and the kind described in the box "A Typical Day at Nursery School."

In a good developmental program, children have the chance to develop large-motor skills through riding bicycles, climbing ladders, playing with large balls, and so forth. They have the chance to develop their small-muscle coordination by stringing beads, building with small blocks, and playing with toys that they can nest or stack. They learn how to get along with other children and other adults—how to flourish socially outside the protected family environment. As they play with other children, they learn how to cooperate to reach common goals and also how to understand other people's

A TYPICAL DAY
AT NURSERY SCHOOL*

When Vicky arrives at school at 8:50 AM, she hangs up her jacket on the hook labeled with her name. She greets her teacher with a kiss and hoots at her cousin, Jason. She and Jason scamper over to the dress-up corner, where they don hard hats and play at being construction workers. When she tires of this, Vicky wanders over to the easel to paint and then goes into the washroom (shared by both sexes) and chats while washing off the paint. When she comes out, she finds a spot in the circle the children have formed around Tom, their new student teacher, who is about to lead some simple, catchy songs. Then it's time for juice and crackers. No one scolds Vicky when she spills juice on the floor. As the children munch and sip, conversation goes on at a brisk pace about baby brothers who spit up their dinner, Sunday visits to the zoo, overflowing toilets, new shoes, and all sorts of other important experiences. At rest time, Vicky sits quietly, putting together wooden puzzles. Later, she and Jason take turns being babies and pushing each other around in a sturdy wooden carriage. Thumb in mouth, Vicky listens to her teacher read a story, the last indoor event of the morning. The class dashes out to the playground, where, with whoops and hollers, yowls and squabbles, they climb on the jungle gym, go up and down on the seesaw, pedal furiously on tricycles, crawl in corners, or stand around deciding what to do. Just before noon, Vicky's father picks her up, and another day of school is over.

*From *A Child's World: Infancy Through Adolescence,* 2d ed., by Diane E. Papalia and Sally Wendkos Olds. New York: McGraw–Hill, 1979. Reprinted by permission.

rspectives and feelings. And when squabbles arise, they learn how to handle anger and hurt feelings. They experience success with new activities because activities in a well-designed center are at a level within the reach of most children and teachers go out of their way to help children learn new skills.

How can you tell which program is best for your child? Some suggestions are given in the box "How to Evaluate a Day-Care Center or Nursery School."

HOW TO EVALUATE A DAY-CARE CENTER OR NURSERY SCHOOL

- Visit while center is in session and stay anywhere from two hours to the entire school day.
- Look to see how children and parents arrive and leave, how they are greeted and said good-bye to by the staff.
- Note the way the staff handles incidents that come up throughout the day—crying, fighting, sleepy, or upset children; transitions from one activity to another; mealtimes; rest times; and so on.
- Listen for a busy hum of voices, the sound of cheerful activity, the absence of constant crying, quarreling, or scolding—or unnatural silence.
- Look for displays of children's artwork that show their own creativity rather than conformity to the teacher's patterns.
- Speak to other parents whose child(ren) attend the center, to find out how happy they and their children are with the center.
- Sniff for good, clean, inviting smells—and the absence of mildew, decay, poor plumbing.
- Ask the director to describe a typical day.
- Check the points raised on the next few sections with regard to policies, people, physical setup, the other children, and yourself.

Policies to Look For

- Encouragement for parents' visits at any time.
- A high enough adult–child ratio to ensure personal attention for all the children. (The National Day Care Study recommends one adult to seven three-, four-, and five-year-olds. Pediatrician T. Berry Brazelton recommends one adult to four infants under the age of two.)
- Not too many children in a single group. (The National Day Care Study found that small children do best when single class consists of no more than eighteen children.)
- Goals for development on all levels: physical, emotional and intellectual—neither custodial (just keeping children fed and protected) nor overly academic (preparing them too rigorously for school).
- Healthy and well-balance meals and snacks.
- Provisions for helping children adjust to the center when they first enroll.
- Degree of parent involvement compatible with your own desires.
- Insurance coverage for accidents to children.
- You should arrive at an understanding about fees, your obligation when your child is absent, the length of your financial commitment (by the week, the month, or the entire semester). If you need financial assistance, ask whether scholarship help is available. Does the center accept payment from the welfare department? Will it offer you help in applying for financial aid?
- Sensitivity to racial, ethnic, and gender-role concerns. (Books and toys should emphasize diversity and not perpetuate stereotypes relating to sex roles, race, religion, or age.)
- Provisions for a sick child. (Can she come to school? Are there backup provisions for care if she cannot? How is he welcomed back when he returns? Do you have to pay during his absence?)

The Ideal Caregivers

- Are interested in small children and sensitive to their feelings.
- Enjoy close physical contact with children, touching them a lot, hugging them, and taking them on their laps.
- Can set limits in a way that is both firm and kind.
- Plan and conduct interesting activities and stimulating conversations with children.
- Cooperate with other adults.
- Are able to deal with shy, aggressive, upset, and tired children simply and comfortably.
- Dress in easy-to-launder clothes that will let them participate in activities with children.
- Treat parents with respect for their intelligence, their child-rearing abilities, and their interest in their children.
- Have had some training in child development in high school, college, or special workshops. (The National Day Care Study found that neither the number of years of formal education nor previous experience working at a day-care center influences the quality of care but that specific knowledge of child development does.)

The Ideal Physical Environment

- There should be enough space, indoors and outdoors, for the number of children, so that the area does not seem crowded.
- Each child should have a special place to keep his or her own things.
- Children should have a place where they can go to play quietly, rest, or just be alone.
- If there is a television set, its use should be limited.
- Also see the box "Keeping Day Care Safe and Healthy," p. 177.

Toys and Equipment Should Include

- For large-muscle development: large balls, riding toys, climbing apparatus, balance beams, large blocks.
- For small-muscle development: beads to string, wooden puzzles, toys to nest or stack, small blocks.
- For dramatic play: dress-up clothes, dolls, tools, child-size furniture.
- For the arts: materials to paint, draw, cut, paste, and sculpt; musical instruments.
- For quiet moments: books; records; soft, cuddly stuffed animals.

The Children at a Good Center

- Are involved and interested in what they are doing.
- Are happy to come to school and content to go home.
- Are friendly to visitors, but do not cluster around one in a desperate plea for attention.
- Get along fairly well with each other, without constantly fighting.
- Are cheerful most of the time, instead of crying, whining, throwing temper tantrums, or clinging to adults.
- Can play by themselves or in small groups, without always being closely supervised by an adult.
- Are encouraged to do as much as possible for themselves and are helped to accomplish activities that are too difficult.
- Can wait their turn when necessary but do not spend a great deal of time waiting in line for toilets, toys, or equipment.

Your Personal Feelings

- Trust your gut reaction. Do you get a good feeling when you are there or an indefinable sensation that all is not as it should be?

- Do you feel welcome as a visitor? Do you feel that the center welcomes ideas and suggestions from parents?
- Are you encouraged to participate in decisions about policy, finances, or programs? (Such encouragement usually exists only in community-run programs, rarely in private centers.)
  Do center personnel seem to care about your whole family, as well as the child who attends the center?
- Are there any social or educational programs run for parents and your other children?
- Could you turn to the center as a backup to the nuclear family and an additional resource in times of crisis?
- Do you feel inadequate whenever you speak to center personnel? (Is this because of their attitude or yours?)

IF YOUR CHILD IS UNDER THREE YEARS OLD

Sixteen-month-old Bobby Collyer began attending the Infant Care and Resource Center in Ithaca, New York, when he was three-and-one-half months old. "So many people talked against it to me," said his mother Sandy Collyer, a bookkeeper for a small business, "but when I tell them what it's like, they realize why he's doing so well there.

"I thoroughly love the center. The people there have basically the same ideas I have of helping kids learn, but letting them do their own thing too. Bobby's very active and alert, and he's learning to do things for himself, which is important with my working and being a single parent."

When I visited the infant center, I could see why Sandy was so enthusiastic. Housed in two airy, bright rooms of a Cornell University building, the center was home to up to sixteen babies at a time, from the age of eight weeks to two years. At least four adults were always present to lavish individual attention and care on all children.

A nine-month-old sitting on the floor in a blue jumpsuit charmed me totally as he smiled and waved to me, as well as to teachers and children. An eight-week-old took in the group's activities from her comfortable perch, nestled in the folds of a yellow bean-bag chair. An undergraduate student intern sat on the floor rolling a big ball to a thirteen-month-old, who chortled every time he rolled it back. Both children and staff were obviously happy to be right where they were, doing just what they were doing.

Today this center is even more extraordinary. The Ithaca Community Childcare Center is now located in its own building, specifically designed for children eight weeks to ten years of age. Cornell University provided the three-acre site for the center, helped to get financing for the new building, and provides additional funding. In return, about three-fourths of the center's openings are reserved for the children of students or employees. It cares for twenty-four infants up to age one year and twenty-seven toddlers, as well as preschoolers and after-schoolers. The three infant rooms are clustered together in their own homelike wing, with a large parent lounge, a roof skylight shining over a little kitchen, and a covered outdoor patio.

There are, however, very few infant-care centers of the caliber of this one. Infant care is extremely expensive because of the high adult–child ratio required. Unless a center has considerable funding, few parents can afford to pay the full cost of operation, which can run up to about $200 a week. One Boston-area couple, who are paying (based on the parents' combined incomes) $182 a week for care of their fifteen-month-old, told me how much they're looking forward to the lower fees when their little boy is able to "graduate" from the Infant Care room to the Toddler room. And this child is in a nonprofit center especially set up for state employees! Many families, of course, cannot come close to affording this kind of fee, and few communities can or will underwrite the expense. So given the current state of child care, most child-development professionals advise—and most parents want—home-based care for their babies and toddlers.

You, however, may be among the few parents who have access to an infant-care center in your community. How can you tell whether it's good enough for your child? Besides checking out the points that are important for any center, you need to be aware of the following special concerns relating to very young children*:

- Are babies held and cuddled while they're fed, instead of drinking from propped bottles?
- Are cribs, highchairs, baby swings, and other equipment in good repair? Are they stabilized so they can't tip over? Do strollers and infant seats have safety harnesses?
- Are there gates in front of unsupervised stairways and doorways?
- Are there separate sleeping areas for infants who nap at different times?
- Does each child have his own crib or cot?
- Do crawling babies seem to be getting in people's way?
- Are the toddlers ignored because so much attention is focused on the infants or preschoolers?
- Are there special areas for diapering babies and disposing of dirty diapers—and are they well away from areas where food is prepared or served?

HELPING YOUR CHILD TO ADJUST TO THE CENTER

Throughout life, first impressions often leave lasting records. This is why it pays to invest extra time and thought in helping your child adjust to her first few days at the center. Some guidelines have already been given in Chapters 5 through 7. The following are a few additional suggestions:

- For about a month before enrolling your child in the center, get him used to being without you for increasing periods of time.

*These questions are based on the pamphlet "How to Select Child Care for an Infant or Toddler," available from the Child Care Resource Center, Inc.; 187 Hampshire Street; Cambridge, MA 02139.

- About a week before she is due to begin, take her for a short visit to the center. Let her spend about an hour there, meeting teachers and children, seeing the physical layout, and playing with the toys and equipment just enough to whet her appetite for more. Let her know that she will be coming back here soon and will be able to spend more time with the toys and the children.
- Go over with him the details of what his day will be like— from getting up in the morning and getting dressed, through going to the center and what he'll do there, to who will pick him up at the end of the day and what he'll do from then on (dinner, a bath, a story and bed, or whatever).

KEEPING DAY CARE SAFE AND HEALTHY

On your visit to the center, look for the following practices.

Safety

- Are there enough caregivers to supervise all children at all times?
- Does the building meet all safety codes? This is usually assured if the center is licensed.
- Are there enough exits, clearly marked?
- Are dangerous substances kept out of children's reach?
- Are toys and equipment in good repair, with no sharp edges, frayed electrical wires, and the like?
- Are potentially dangerous tools used only under supervision?
- Are all electrical outlets covered?
- Is there an exit plan in case of fire, as well as smoke detectors and fire extinguishers?
- Is tap water temperature kept below 110°F?
- Is heating equipment enclosed in fire-resistant material?

- Is there a fully stocked, easily accessible first-aid kit?
- Are instructions posted on treating an injured, poisoned, or choking child?
- Is at least one staff member trained in first aid, CPR, and the Heimlich maneuver?
- Are stairways well-lit, free from clutter, and equipped with child-height handrails?
- Are all climbable surfaces that are thirty inches high protected by barriers like guardrails?
- Do all windows above ground level have devices so they cannot be opened more than six inches?
- Are the floors free of objects that children could trip on?
- Are eating utensils safe (no styrofoam cups, plastic forks, or other items that can be easily broken and choked on)?

Health

- If there are any sick children present, are they cared for in a special, separate place?
- Is the area sanitary?
- Are floors and furniture clean?
- Is leftover food cleaned up and disposed of promptly?
- Are toilets in good repair?
- Are washing facilities adequate?
- Are children in clean underpants or diapers?
- Are children diapered and diapers disposed of away from areas where food is prepared or eaten?
- Do caregivers wash their hands after changing diapers and blowing their noses and before handling food?
- Do children wash their hands after using the toilet and blowing their noses and before handling food or brushing their teeth?
- Is the area well ventilated?
- Is there enough space so that the children are not crowded together?

- Read stories to your child that deal with the anxious feelings children have in response to big changes in their lives. Some good ones are *Are You My Mother?* by P. D. Eastman; *First Day of School* by Helen Oxenbury; *The Runaway Bunny* by Margaret W. Brown; and *Betsy's First Day at Nursery School* by Gunilla Wolde.
- If you can possibly take the time off from work, plan to stay with your child for at least part of the first few days—anywhere from ten minutes to the entire day—if she seems uneasy. Try to blend into the background, though, and don't play with her or even talk much to her. When you do leave, don't sneak off; tell her you'll be back to pick her up later, and say goodbye cheerfully but firmly, even if your child starts to cry. Chances are that the tears will stop by the time you reach the corner.
- Enroll him about a month before you begin your job, if you're making the switch from being at home to going to work.
- Be sure the clothes she'll wear to school are easy enough for her to handle for toileting. If she does need help, tell her how to ask, and alert the teacher.
- Sew or write his name inside sweaters, jackets, sneakers, or any other articles of clothing he's likely to take off at school. (For your child's safety, avoid putting his or her name on the outside of any item that can be seen by strangers.)
- Dress her in clothes that can get dirty—and that can even get lost without upsetting you. (Save the fancy outfits from Grandma for at-home times.)
- Encourage him to talk about his day at the center—what he likes about it, what he doesn't like, the people he likes and dislikes, his high points and low points.
- Play "center" from time to time, when she can take the role of the teacher and you can play the child. This may be a way to draw out her feelings about the center.

Your child will probably come home with more colds, sniffles, and sore throats after he starts going to the center. A number of studies have found higher rates of minor illness

PREVENTING SEXUAL ABUSE
IN DAY CARE

Over the past several years, a number of shocking stories have surfaced, reporting incidents of sexual abuse of little children by staff people at day-care homes and centers. Fortunately, such incidents are rare. But even one is too many. You can take steps to see that your child does not become a victim of such maltreatment. You need to strike a delicate balance, however, between teaching your child certain basic elements of self-protection and imposing such a burden for self-care that you alarm and stress the child. A three-year-old should not feel responsible for protecting herself; she needs to be able to depend on adults to put her in a safe environment. You can do the following:

- *Allow your children to take control of their own bodies from a very early age.* Let your children know that they never have to kiss or hug anyone—even Grandma—if they don't feel like it. You can explain to Grandma that you're sure Johnny will want to kiss her another time—and maybe suggest that Johnny blow her a kiss or shake her hand. Meanwhile, your child's sense of physical integrity is safeguarded.
- *Teach your child to say "no."* Children need to know that their bodies belong to them and that they can say "no" to anyone who might try to touch them in a way that doesn't feel comfortable—even if it's someone they love and trust.
- *Learn to recognize signs of sexual abuse.* Watch your child for such symptoms as loss of appetite or other extreme change of behavior; frequent nightmares, disturbed sleep, and fear of the dark; any new fears of objects, people, or places; bed-wetting, thumb-sucking, or unusual crying; torn or stained underclothes; vaginal or rectal bleeding; vaginal discharge or infection; painful, itching, reddened, or swollen genitals; unusual interest in or knowledge of sexual

matters; expressions of affection that seem preco-
cious or sensual; and fear or dislike of being left
with a particular caregiver or at the day-care home
or center.

If you notice any of these signs, call your pediatrician immediately. You might also speak to other
parents to see whether their children are reporting
any of the same signs. If so, take your child out of
the situation—and report the center to the police.

- *Encourage your child to talk to you.* Let your children
know that they can tell you anything about anybody,
and you will not betray their confidence or get angry with them. Also let them know that they are not
to blame for anything that anybody else does.

- *Research the day-care center.* If you have carefully
checked the credentials of the center and gotten
references from other parents, the probability is
that you have found a safe place. Two especially important provisions are your ability to drop in on the
center at any time without advance notice and the
presence of enough caregivers so that any individual staffer will not be able to step out of line unob-
served. However, even the most careful parents can
be hoodwinked, so always keep your eyes and ears
open to what your children are saying—or not
saying.

- *Reassure your child that most adults like and are good to
children.* You won't be doing your child any favors if,
in your fervor to protect him, you make him suspicious of all adults until they prove themselves trust-
worthy. If, on the contrary, you project the attitude
that most people are nice, your child is likely to
grow up a happier, more open person.

among children cared for in centers rather than at home or in
family day-care homes.

The good news is that most of these illnesses have not been
severe enough to warrant keeping children out of group care.
And some doctors have speculated about the possibility that

children who contract minor illnesses early in life may develop resistance to infections later on.

The bad news, though, is that some more serious illnesses are also spread in group care. So it is essential that children be up-to-date on their immunizations before they go to child care and that the center staff observe basic health practices as outlined in the boxes "Keeping Day Care Safe and Healthy" and "Preventing Sexual Abuse in Day Care."

MAKING CENTER CARE WORK

Your rights and responsibilities as a parent by no means end with the selection of the appropriate center. Child care is a two-way street. Keeping up your share of the responsibility assists caregivers in knowing and responding to the needs of your child and aids in the smooth functioning of the total program.

- *Be prompt* in paying all fees. Many facilities depend solely on the fees to remain in operation.
- *Follow through* on supplying caregiver or staff with current medical information on your child and with any other information that may affect the child's behavior from time to time (like the birth of a new sibling, a death in the family, or parental separation).
- *Participate* in conferences, formal or informal, arranged by staff or caregiver. Ask questions about your child and the program and ask for a conference if none is scheduled.
- *Be responsible* if you have volunteered for something special, like supplying a snack, making phone calls for a center activity, or driving on a field trip. If you have not yet volunteered, do try your best to make time for some contribution.
- *Be prompt* in picking up and delivering your child; she may come to expect you at a certain time each day. Smooth functioning of the program, as well as of the lives of the caregivers, depend on your promptness.
- *Be considerate* of the health of your own child and others

in the facility. If your child has a communicable disease or is so uncomfortable that he will be miserable all day, make other arrangements for his care (see Chapter 9 for emergency backups).*

Good center care can help the entire family, not just the one who happens to be enrolled. As noted pediatrician Dr. T. Berry Brazelton told me, "Day care can be an opportunity to back up the nuclear family and to provide extended family resources—a peer group and more caring people for the child and a peer group and source of emotional support for the parents.

"We all think about the child," Dr. Brazelton added. "We don't always think about the parent."

Most working parents are so pressed for time that they tend to think of the day-care center as a lifesaver for permitting them to go to work but as a resource they can forget the rest of the time. It may, however, make sense to squeeze some time out of your crowded days and weeks to participate to whatever degree you can in center activities.

If your child's day-care center plans social events for parents or for the entire family, make every effort to attend. Besides pleasing your child, who will enjoy letting you into her world, you may make friends among the other parents, many of whom are bound to have a great deal in common with you. If the center offers educational programs or workshops in child development, making the time for them can enrich your life as well as those of your children. If the center asks for help with fund-raising projects, remember that your child's future care may well depend on your participation. If you can possibly spare the time for these activities, you will probably find that you get as much as you give and that your child's day-care placement may well be a factor in strengthening your whole family's life.

*These suggestions, offered by the Day Care and Child Development Council of Tompkins County, Ithaca, New York, are reprinted here by permission of the council.

9

OTHER CHILD-CARE ARRANGEMENTS

Full-time child care—in your home, in someone else's home, or in a center—is not, of course, the only way to go. Furthermore, even if you have such full-time care, you'll sometimes want or need backups to take care of family crises or special needs that your regular arrangement cannot cover. In this chapter, you'll read about some of the other arrangements that work for many working parents.

PARENTS SHARE CHILD CARE

In about 15 percent of families that contain one or more children and a working mother, the father takes care of the children while the mother works. A real sign of progress in encouraging men to assume a larger share of their children's care will be seen when they—and other people—stop seeing what these men are doing as "baby-sitting."

"One of my biggest peeves," says Washington, D.C., filmmaker and consultant Jonathan Deull, "is hearing a father who takes care of his own child being referred to as a 'baby-sitter.' " Jon has shared at least equally with his wife, Sheryl Sturges, in the care of twenty-month-old David ever since the toddler's birth. When Jon is with David and is greeted with, "Oh, you're baby-sitting!", his stock answer is, "If David's mother were with him, would you say *she* was baby-sitting?"

Flexible and Part-Time Jobs

Jonathan and Sheryl realize how lucky they are because both have been able to arrange their work lives on part-time sched-ules, and they are able to employ a helper as backup when both are at work.

When one or both parents have flexible or part-time jobs, it is easier for them to dovetail their schedules to get their work done, care for their children, and still have some time for each other. One attorney who cut back on his work schedule while his children were small, in the belief that his whole family would be happier with a little less money and a little more of his attention, told me, "I wanted to have children just as much as my wife did, and I feel they're just as much mine as they are hers. So it only makes sense for me to put as much into the way they're raised."

Shift Work

For many other working couples, husband and wife pass each other like ships in the night for much of the week, as one goes to work and the other comes home to take care of the chil-dren. About one in three spouses (among full-time dual-earn-er couples who have small children) works an evening, night, or rotating shift, while the other spouse works days. Parents are more likely to show this pattern than childless couples. This route is hard on each of them and hard on the marriage because it usually means curtailed sleep for at least one of the parents and also cuts drastically into the time husband and wife have to spend with one another. It does, however, offer the child her own parents' care for most of her waking hours.

And its biggest appeal for hard-pressed families is its money-saving aspect. While some outside care is often required to piece together an hour or two between the parents' work schedules, this can often be obtained by family, friends, or neighbors as a favor.

This kind of pattern offers what sociologist Harriet B. Presser of the University of Maryland has called "a special type of single-parenting family," in which the child sees less of both parents together. These children may benefit in having each parent all to themselves for part of the day; another plus is that the children learn to pitch in and do their share of household chores. A drawback for the children, however, is that they seldom see their parents interacting on a day-to-day basis.

The greatest strain seems to be on the parents, who seem to experience more conflict both with each other and with their jobs, mostly around scheduling problems. These couples talk about being tired much of the time, never having dinner together, having trouble finding time for lovemaking—or even just talking. "Working nights is easier on the family, but harder on you," one wife said. But one husband expressed a positive side of this arrangement: "We never fight any more. And we hardly ever watch TV. Our time together is too special to waste, so we try to make the most of what we have."

The hardest task these parents face is keeping their own relationship going. Some do most of their talking by phone. Others leave funny or loving notes for each other on a daily basis, just to stay in touch. One husband found a unique way to remind his wife that even though he wasn't seeing much of her these days, he did love her. He recorded his voice on a tape recorder that he set, using an automatic timer, to go off about ten minutes after his wife arrived home.

Other Arrangements

Some couples set up long-range plans. Peggy, for example, stayed home with her two children for their first five years, going to college at night while Charles stayed with the children. For the next five years, Charles stayed home, working as a free-lance marketing consultant and pursuing the master's degree in sociology, which he had never had the time to obtain before. By that time, both children were in school all day; Peggy and Charles found a teenager to stay with them after school, and both parents took full-time jobs. Peggy made rapid advances in her advertising career, and Charles shifted career goals completely, moving from the business world to the life of an instructor at a community college.

Conceived in pragmatism, this kind of arrangement often produces an attitudinal rebirth, as fathers learn that the "maternal instinct" is not an inborn female characteristic but a skill that grows out of really knowing and being able to respond to one's child. Many families who have cast aside traditional viewpoints of father-as-breadwinner and mother-as-nurturer have found that sharing the delights and challenges of child care and the pleasures and pains of supporting the family brings about a happier balance within the home.

TAKING A CHILD TO WORK WITH YOU

When I walked into North Shore Surgical Supplies in Great Neck, New York, I received two greetings: "May I help you?" from a young woman—and "goo-goo" from her eleven-month-old baby in the playpen at the back of the store. On one of my visits to the CIAO Day Care Center in Brooklyn, director Terry Antonelli proudly showed me her three-month-old daughter, Amy, sleeping happily in a carriage next to Terry's desk. During a shopping trip in Hoosick Falls, New York, I was diverted during my baked-goods purchases by a pair of appealing infant twins, the daughters of the woman behind the counter, who in turn was the daughter of the owner.

Taking children to work is a long-time tradition. From time immemorial small children have accompanied their parents as they labored in the fields, have hung around small retail shops, and have gone along with physicians making house calls and salespersons calling on customers.

In recent years, children have been showing up again and in more and more places with their parents. A high school teacher whose baby-sitter hasn't shown up takes his infant with him in a pouch on his back. An editor at a women's magazine takes her child to the office for the first year and a half of the child's life. A television costume designer takes her infant with her as she shops, sews, and does fittings at the studio.

Day-care director Terry Antonelli summed up the feelings of many of these parents when she told me, "I like having Amy with me. It poses problems, but I wouldn't want to be away from her all day. I realize that I couldn't do this with many jobs, so I'm grateful for this opportunity."

And florist Richard Charlton, whose nine-year-old daughter Jessica spent the first three years of her life in the store with her parents and since then has been with them on Saturdays and holidays, says, "I think I've been the luckiest one. Most dads don't get a chance to see their children so often."

PARENT COOPERATIVE

In one Long Island suburb, a group of four women, who all work four days a week, worked out their own arrangement. On her nonworking day, each mother takes her own child plus the children of the other three women for the entire day in her own home. On the fifth day, a paid baby-sitter, whose fees are split among the four women, comes to the home with the biggest family room and backyard to care for all the children.

Parents who work part-time can often find other part-timers who are willing to swap child care on nonworking days. (Of course, these nonworking days often leave the parents more exhausted than the days they go to work!) Usually in this kind of arrangement, no money changes hands. Arrangements do have to be made with regard to meals, naps, and other aspects of care. When only a couple of children are involved, for example, the parent in charge generally makes lunch for them; when there are several, it is usually simpler for each parent to pack each child's lunch from home.

OUT-OF-SCHOOL CARE

After-School Centers

"When I was teaching fourth grade, a lot of my pupils would stay late after school to talk to me while I fixed up my class-room," Marilyn Deiner of North Merrick, New York told me. "These were mostly kids whose parents worked, who really didn't have anything to do after school." Those children who stayed after school stayed in Marilyn's mind even after she stopped teaching to raise three children of her own.

"Children whose parents work are often isolated," she said. "Out of concern for their safety, their parents often tell them to go home and stay home and not invite anyone over. They may need to talk to somebody, but they don't have other kids or a sympathetic adult around. Too often, they just sit in front of a television set and snack all afternoon. This is bad for their bodies and bad for their minds."

Acting on her feeling that children of working parents need something special to do after school, Marilyn Deiner organized the North Bellmore After-School Center. The center, a private, nonprofit corporation, drew on a network of community resources to enable it to offer a combined program of recreation and supervised study. The school district gave the center a rent-free site in one of its elementary schools; the National Council of Jewish Women contributed the money for a 160-book paperback library; the Long Island Savings Bank contributed funds for buttons to be given to "superreaders" in the center's reading club; the PTA underwrote a community survey; and local newspapers and radio stations publicized the new service.

Today the center has been expanded to five locations serving children from eleven schools; it provides transportation; and it has established a morning session from 7:30 to 8:30 AM, which includes breakfast, and all-day programs (with field trips) during some vacations, as determined by regular surveys on community needs. Children can come from one to five days a week or on a drop-in or temporary basis, according to their family situations and special needs. The after-school program includes indoor and outdoor play, arts and crafts, such self-care skills as sewing and cooking, exercises that include aerobics and junior body building, a reading club, and a study hour from 5:00 to 6:00 PM when the children do their homework under supervision.

This center, a pioneer when it was established in 1981, offered a model for the more than seventy programs that have followed it in the immediate area and is similar to many around the country. Such after-school programs are sponsored by local school districts, day-care centers, Ys, parent cooperatives, nonprofit educational associations, and religious organizations. Some employers have begun to participate too; they consider it good business to keep productivity high—and the hours between 3:00 and 5:00 PM, when parent–employees are often called to the phone by their children, can represent millions of dollars of lost time. Fees vary; some are set on a sliding scale based on family income; some run about $5 a day, with discounts for additional children; and scholarships are often available. Fees charged by private operators (more often found in big cities) can be considerably higher.

In general these programs try to create an atmosphere more like home than like school, in the philosophy that by 3:00 PM children have had enough school for one day. The best programs—according to the School Age Child Care Project (see below)—offer a safe physical environment, foster optimal development, employ enough well-trained staff members, are efficient, interact to some degree with parents, balance structured activities with free time, key activities to the interests of the children, use the community as much as possible, and communicate clear expectations and limits to the children while allowing for spontaneity.

The programs are not a cure-all, however. Their major problem for parents is that centers usually do not operate when schools are closed, and so other arrangements have to be made for days when children are on vacation but parents are not. Also, although centers usually invite all children from kindergartners to fifth graders to take part, children beyond third grade rarely attend, considering them too "babyish" and preferring to be home, even if that means being alone.

Other problems include difficulties in getting and keeping employees and transporting children from their regular schools to the center. And only a few offer part-time or drop-in care for parents with part-time or irregular hours.

Still, even with these lapses from perfection, such centers meet a major need in filling after-school hours with productive, supervised activities. By the time parents and children get together at home, they are readier for some of that precious "quality time" than they would be if a child has been bored and lonely all day and if the parent feels pressured to help with homework, along with everything else waiting to be done.

If you want to start a program in your own community or want to encourage your local school or community institution to do so, contact the School Age Child Care (SACC) Project for help (see the appendix "Helpful Organizations"). Since 1979 SACC has been conducting research, designing educational programs and conferences, publishing literature, and providing consultation and technical assistance in starting up centers. The project has also helped with innovative programs like "hot lines" that children can telephone for help, reassurance, or just company; special "self-care" courses and books; and workplace seminars for parents.

Other Arrangements

Center care is not, of course, the only answer for before-school or after-school care. Many parents have found good solutions by hiring individuals. And when a child is old enough to have a measure of independence, has friends to play with and things to do, the adult's presence in the home may be more important than the actual time he spends with the children. In cases like this, the after-school stand-in often does the breakfast dishes and the laundry and starts dinner. Or, your child may go to another person's home to do homework, have a snack, or just check in before going out to play or do some other activity, like music lesson or soccer practice. Stand-ins may come from the following categories:

- A college or high school student.

- An older person in the neighborhood.
- A family day-care provider.
- The at-home parent of your child's classmate or friend.
- An out-of-town or foreign college or graduate student who gets room and board and a nominal sum in exchange for being on hand when you are not.

These after-school caregivers can be found in a number of ways:

- Your local high school or a nearby college may have a student placement program.
- A note on your school's bulletin board or in the PTA newsletter will sometimes locate another parent who will, for a fee, take your child to school in the morning or bring your child home after school along with his or her own child.
- Many of the same resources listed in Chapter 6 may help you find an after-school helper.

Your Local Library: Not a Day-Care Center

Some librarians these days feel that they've succeeded too well in putting out the welcome mat for children. Yes, they want to encourage even the youngest children to come in to read or be read to and to use the library's facilities. But no, they emphatically state that they are neither equipped nor interested in serving as baby-sitters.

The bright, cheerful children's rooms of public libraries seem like safe, cozy spots to drop a child off in the afternoon to bridge the gap between the end of the child's schoolday and the end of the parent's workday or for a few hours on a Saturday when parents want to do errands or chores. But because so many parents have been leaving small children alone, sometimes up until closing time (which can be as late as 9 PM), many libraries have been setting tough policies regarding unsupervised children. Some ban unattended children under a certain age—seven or ten, for example; some warn parents they could face criminal charges of child abandonment; and some call in the police to take unsupervised children to social welfare agencies.

Aside from the children's being disruptive to other library patrons, libraries are not safe havens for them. Anyone can wander in, as one little boy found out; after having been left alone in the library for several hours, he became frightened when he walked into the washroom and found a naked man bathing there. And because the librarians do not keep tabs on which children are with adults and which are not, unattended children are left unprotected from any stranger who might want to take them away. While the library is not, of course, the ideal child-care facility, it will probably continue to be used as one as long as the demand for child care is so great and the supply is so meager.

CHILDREN IN CHARGE OF THEMSELVES

While many children need structure after school and need to be supervised by adults, others seem to do well on their own. Margaret Martin, for example, a bilingual coordinator for a New York City junior high school, stopped using baby-sitters when her twin sons were ten years old. "They could twist their way around anyone," Maggie says. "Left alone, they feel—and act—responsible."

The image of the latchkey child, lonely and forlorn, a key hanging around her neck on a dirty string, is pathetic. Often, of course, it is sadly accurate, describing a child who is left alone for long hours at a stretch, whose basic physical and emotional needs are not taken care of, who is thrust into situations he cannot handle. In other cases, however, the child who stays alone for two or three hours after school radiates a cheerful sense of confidence and independence.

Current estimates are that somewhere between 2 and 15 million school-age children—15 percent of six- to nine-year-olds and 45 percent of nine- to eleven-year-olds—regularly care for themselves at home without adult supervision. (The 2 million figure is the one reported to the United States Census Bureau, but the true number is much higher. Many parents don't want to admit that their children are alone after school, partly out of guilt and partly because leaving a young child

IS YOUR CHILD READY TO STAY ALONE?

Before you can say "yes" to this question, you need to ask yourself questions like the following. Can your child:

- Control his body well enough to keep from injuring himself?
- Keep track of keys and handle doors so she won't lock herself in or out?
- Safely operate the stove or other household equipment?
- Understand and remember spoken and written instructions?
- Be trusted to follow important rules?
- Stay alone without being too afraid or lonely?
- Be flexible and resourceful enough to handle the unexpected?
- Read and write well enough to take telephone messages?
- Use a pay phone in an emergency?
- Know what to say and do about visitors and callers?
- Know how to get help in an emergency?

If you can honestly answer "yes" to these questions, you and your child can give self-care a try. To make it as good an experience as possible, see the specific suggestions in Chapter 10.

alone is a criminal offense in some states.) Although most self-care takes place after school, some children spend some time alone in the morning or evening too. Most are alone for no more than two hours a day. Not surprisingly, the more hours a mother works and the older a child is, the greater is the family's use of self-care.

We have very little solid information about how this experience affects children. According to most of the few studies that have been done, there aren't any differences between supervised and self-care children on such important measures as self-esteem and school and social adjustment. According to others, children who care for themselves are more fearful and have more problems at school. One recent study blasted one myth—that most of these children are from poor, single-parents in high-risk, inner-city settings. In fact, most of them are from well-educated, middle- to upper-class families in suburban or rural areas. For these families then, self-care seems to be a choice rather than a necessity.

To decide whether this is the choice for your child, you need to take a close, hard look at your own family situation— and at what your options are. Most child-care experts believe that if you *can* provide adult supervision for your school-age child, your child will be better off. But suppose this is a true hardship? How then do you decide whether your child can be alone for a few hours of every day?

You need to look not so much at your child's age (although nine years does seem to be a minimum age when a child can safely be on her own) but at the child's maturity. For some criteria, see the box "Is Your Child Ready to Stay Alone?" Then, if this is the route you choose, you can help your child feel secure and mature by structuring the "alone time" in a way that encourages safe, comfortable self-direction. (For specific suggestions, see Chapter 10.) The sense of being trusted—of being treated like a responsible person—is a heady feeling. In fact, in some homes, the direst threat that parents can make to their children is, "If you don't behave, we'll get a baby-sitter!"

THE "LIMITED-RESPONSIBILITY" BABY-SITTER

As the mother of three grown children, I've often bewailed the fact that when they were most eager to work around the house, they were the least efficient. When they became accomplished enough to make real inroads in the work load, the competence was there but the enthusiasm had waned. The same is often true of baby-sitters. Young boys and girls—aged about nine to fourteen—often love babies and small children and would almost pay *you* to let them stay with your youngsters. Yet you (rightly) may be reluctant to leave your children with sitters who are still children themselves.

But these eager caregivers can play an important role in your and your children's lives. A mature preadolescent can give gentle and exuberant care that your children will love and you will appreciate, provided you structure opportunities for supervised baby-sitting when you or another adult is close at hand.

Health writer and lecturer Dian Dincin Buchman used to have a "Sunday morning baby-sitter," a very young girl who had a key to the Buchman apartment, who would let herself in at 7:30 Sunday morning, when the only person awake in the apartment was baby Caitlin. The baby-sitter would give Caitlin breakfast, dress her, and amuse her all morning, letting Dian and Bucky catch up on much-needed sleep and enjoy a leisurely breakfast together. The baby and her special Sunday friend adored each other, and the arrangement went on for years. A Sunday-morning sitter can be a low-cost blessing to parents who share child care by working different shifts. Having someone come in when both are home gives them a little bit of time together.

These young sitters can save your sanity at other times too. They can come in during the "witching hour," that hour or two before dinner or bedtime, to bathe and feed your baby while you are busy with your older children. Or they can play games and help a first grader with homework while you play with the baby. Or they can meet your children at school and walk them home, to the baby-sitter or day-care center, or to such after-school activities as scout meetings or music lessons.

SWAP WITH A NONPARENT

For backup emergency help or for an occasional weekend or evening stint of baby-sitting, a person with no children of his or her own may be willing to stay with your children in exchange for service you can render. You might be able to do errands for an older person, drive a teenager who is too young to have a driver's license to the shopping mall, cook a little bit extra every night and provide meals for a single person, do the laundry for an apartment dweller without washing and drying machines, or perform some other appreciated service.

HELP! IT'S AN EMERGENCY!

No matter what regular arrangement you make for child care, you need to protect yourself and your children by having backup plans for those times when your primary plans collapse. Be prepared ahead of time. Don't wait until you realize that school will be closed the following week for spring vacation, or your sitter calls to tell you she's sick, or Johnny throws up as you're going out the door.

Start now to draw up a list of emergency backup people (see suggestions below). Get to know three or four of them before you *need* them. Either call them to baby-sit for a few hours on a weekend once or twice or just invite them over to your home to meet you and your child. In a pinch, you can call a reliable agency.

One young mother in West Germany organized a community emergency service. Tina Breitinger, a twenty-nine-year-old divorced mother of two sons, ages six and seven, started the "Granny Emergency Service" to find older men or women to provide child care in an emergency. From appeals in a popular magazine addressed to parents and on local radio stations, Ms. Breitinger heard from hundreds of parents interested in such a service and from men and women, ages fifty-five to seventy-five, about twenty of whom have registered to help out when a child or parent is sick or in other family crises.

Here are some other approaches you could take:

- Place an ad in your local paper, along the lines of "Occasional baby-sitting, from 7:00 AM–6:00 PM, for children of working parents. Boy, seven, and girl, eight, usually in school, sometimes need care on school holidays and when minor illness keeps them home. Call 883–7511, evenings."

FOR EMERGENCY CAREGIVER

- Introduce sitter to child (if they haven't already met, which they should have).
- Show her around the house.
- Give her the basic house information and phone numbers (see box on page 142).
- Give her numbers where you, your spouse, or a close relative or friend can be reached during the day.
- Call home once or twice just to seek how everything is going. (She may hesitate to call you.)
- Tell her your child's basic routine—when he eats, when he sleeps, what he likes to do. Give her suggestions for meals, snacks, and activities.
- Tell her when you or your spouse will be home.

If Your Child Is Sick

- Leave a signed medical permission slip with the babysitter, with her name written in (see box on page 225).
- Tell her how sick your child is, what special care she needs, and what medicines she should be taking.
- *Write down* how much, and at what times, medicine should be given.
- Alert her to symptoms she should watch out for.
- Ask her to jot down the following, so she can give you a report on your return: What your child eats and when; how much he sleeps and when; any unusual urine or bowel patterns; temperature and what time taken; medicine taken; any other symptoms; progress throughout the day.

- Place a similar notice on church, school, and supermarket bulletin boards.
- Ask everyone you know whether they know nonemployed parents of school-age children, retired or unemployed

people, high school or college students, or others who might have occasional time available. Sometimes two people can dovetail their schedules, sharing the job.

- Check your closest child-care information and referral service to see whether it keeps such a list.
- Contact nearby hospitals, colleges, high schools, and nursing schools, to see whether they keep a list.
- Call on friends, relatives, and neighbors and think of some wonderful way to reciprocate if they won't accept any money.
- Relax your standards a little. Someone who'll be with your child for a week or two shouldn't have to meet the same criteria as a full-time person.

Once you have found someone, you can help her to take good care of your child by following the suggestions given in the box "For Emergency Caregiver."

Other Emergency Quick-Fixes

FOR HEALTHY CHILDREN.　When school is closed or your regular child-care arrangement is unavailable, you can do one of the following:

- *Take your child to work with you.* Arm her with a sheaf of colored pencils and paper, books, games, and puzzles. Or, give her a task to do, like collating or stapling papers or addressing envelopes. Take her out to lunch. She'll see what you do all day; she'll get a special treat; you'll have some bonus time together; and you'll save money on babysitting.
- *If you work at home, hire a baby-sitter for at least part of the day.* This way you can spend some time with your child—and still get some work done. The sitter can spend a morning or an afternoon with a sick child, playing games and fetching and carrying. The sitter can take the child out for at least part of every day. This is a good time for your child to get to the zoo, the movies, the park, or the Christmas-decorated store windows.

- If your schedule is flexible or if you have vacation days coming, you may be able to take some time off from work to enjoy with your children. This is a good time to do some shopping together or to work together on special projects, like pasting photos in albums. Years from now, you won't remember that you took a week longer to complete a project at work, but those hours with your children are likely to build lasting memories for both of you.

FOR SICK CHILDREN.   Some of the above solutions will also work if your child is not too sick. For guidance on keeping a child home from school or day care, see the box "How Sick Is Too Sick to Go to School?" During bouts of childhood illness, though, the following are usually a better choice:

- *Leave your child at home alone if he is a mature nine-year-old or older.* Be sure he follows your safety instructions. Phone home two or three times during the day. Let him enjoy some usually forbidden treats—like watching television "soaps" or eating ice cream for lunch. Ask a neighbor to look in during the day and ask a friend or relative to phone. Be sure to leave a phone number where you or someone he knows well can be reached.
- *Stay home with her.* Parents usually use their own sick leave for this, unless their employers have unusually liberal family policies. You can also use personal or vacation days. Sometimes spouses alternate days or half-days so that neither one's schedule falls too far behind; others decide who stays home based on which one can best afford taking the time. Some parents bring work home on these days.
- *If the child is not too sick, your regular baby-sitter or day-care center may be able to make special provisions for him.* Centers will often take a child with a slight cold or cough, but not if he is vomiting or has fever. A family day-care mother will often take a child with a mild cold but will not accept one with fever, diarrhea, or vomiting.
- *Take her to a "get-well" center or "sick bay."* These centers, with names like Chicken Soup and Grandma's House, are specially set up to take care of children with a mild illness. More than fifty of these centers exist around the country

HOW SICK IS TOO SICK TO GO TO SCHOOL?

The American Academy of Pediatrics (AAP) advises that "there are very few illnesses for which children need to be excluded from day care." A child who feels slightly sick may be distracted from his discomfort by school activities, may feel good about his ability to overcome an obstacle, and may not endanger the health of the other children.

Yet many centers exclude all sick children, even those who are mildly ill. In cases like this, pediatrician Dr. George Sterne, chairman of the AAP Committee on Early Childhood, Adoption, and Dependent Care, recommends that children stay in familiar surroundings with familiar people—a separate area in the classroom, day-care center, or family day-care home.

Sometimes, however, the child's symptoms may signal a more serious illness, when the child should indeed stay home. Symptoms that warrant keeping a child home include:

- A fever of more than 100° F orally or 101° F rectally
- Vomiting or diarrhea
- A rash you can't identify
- Stomachache, earache, headache, or other pain
- Impetigo or any other highly contagious disease
- Feelings of weakness or dizziness

If any of the above symptoms last more than a day, you should call your physician.

Furthermore, if the child *says* she is too sick to go to school, you should pay attention. Says pediatrician Dr. Mary Howell, "Children who know that they will be allowed to stay home when they ask for that opportunity usually do not abuse the request." Sometimes the problem may be more emotional than physical. You don't want to make a habit of keeping a child home, but if he rarely asks to do so, it may well be worth keeping an upset child home.

(in clinics, hospitals, or separate areas in day-care centers), and more keep opening all the time. The centers are themselves the center of controversy. Child-care experts disagree about whether they should be licensed, whether they help spread childhood illnesses, and whether they are good for children's mental health. Some are partly funded by community or municipal funds, offering care at a range from no charge to $10 a day; those operated privately, for profit, generally run from $25 to 35 a day. To find one in your community, contact your local child-care council or information-and-referral service.

TAKING A CHILD WITH YOU TO NONWORK ACTIVITIES

Most work environments in this modern world are not compatible with the needs of small children, requiring other provisions for care. More and more parents, however, are taking their children along on many nonwork outings that used to be off limits for babies and toddlers. The ability to do this is especially important for working parents. Aside from the financial savings involved, taking a child with you provides more of that precious commodity, parent–child time. It's usually easiest when you have only one child.

Evenings Out with Friends

If you begin when your baby is young, she will become used to sleeping in strange places. All you need is a quiet room, away from the socializing. She can graduate from the center of a big bed (for an infant who can't turn over yet), to a car bed or carriage, to a portable crib, to a regular bed or a sleeping bag on the floor. To take her home, you can just wrap her in a blanket, put her in your car, and let her wake up in the morning in her own bed.

Movies

A baby held on your lap or made comfortable in a car bed will often snooze happily at a drive-in theater. Some infants will even sleep through a movie in a regular theater—if they're sleepy enough and used to falling asleep in your arms, especially after being nursed or bottle-fed. A toddler who has learned to whisper can often sit through a movie, enjoying it and not interfering with anyone else's enjoyment.

Church

Many churches have baby-sitters to care for small children in a separate room while the parents are at services. Very young babies (like some of the older parishioners) will often snooze right through the service in their parents' laps.

Restaurants

Most casual restaurants (and even some elegant ones) provide high chairs, booster seats, and children's menus. You'll probably want to find an establishment where the noise level is high enough so that your own small fry's high-decibel conversation won't make heads turn and waiters shudder. And you'll want fast service rather than leisurely dining. You can usually find this in small ethnic restaurants (Chinese restaurants seem particularly welcoming to families), in the kind of rock-music spots that you may have loved when you were single, and, of course, in the ever-present fast-food franchises. No matter how fast the service is, though, it's a good idea to take along some finger food for your baby or toddler while you're waiting to be served. Eating out can be fun for everybody and will mean one night when no one has to worry about cooking dinner or doing dishes.

Where Else?

The possibilities go on and on. All it needs is a "why not?" attitude and taking some special steps to make your child more comfortable, so that you and the people around you can be more comfortable too. This may mean, for example, calling your eye doctor ahead of time to be sure your baby can remain on your lap while your eyes are examined; calling the museum to make sure they permit baby strollers; remembering to carry some healthful, easy-to-eat, not too messy snacks like raisins, pretzels, bagels, or apple slices (food is a great pacifier); and equipping yourself with a back or chest carrier, an infant seat, or whatever other special contrivances are available for your youngster's comfort and your convenience.

10

YOUR CHILD'S WORLD

Your child's world encompasses many settings. At home, in the day-care center, or at the baby-sitter's house, in school, and in the community at large, children grow and develop. This development takes place in all spheres of their lives—the physical, the intellectual, and the emotional. As a parent, of course, you want to foster that development as much as you can. You want your children to be physically healthy and safe, you want them to stretch their minds, and you want them to be well-adjusted, well-functioning emotional beings. Let's take a look at the special concerns that working parents have in all these realms.

WHEN YOUR CHILD IS HOME ALONE

Many children come home after school, take out their own keys to open their front doors, and stay alone in their own homes until a parent comes home from work. While some of them feel anxious about being alone, they can be helped to overcome these anxieties. On the other hand, many other children feel independent and adult at the idea that they are responsible for themselves.

Which children do best on their own? Two factors in their lives seem important. One is an increasing degree of control that they have had over the years over how they spend their time, so that they now have a strong sense of how they should be spending those two or three hours without adult supervision. The other important element is the presence of the parent—even if it's on the other end of the telephone. According to Laurence Steinberg, a psychologist at Temple University who has conducted research on children who are alone after school, those whose parents keep track of where they are respond to that parental interest. They are better able to resist peer pressures and to stay out of trouble.

Eleven-year-old Benji Wilder is in this second group. When he comes home after school, the first thing he does is call his father at work. After that, he feeds his cat, folds any clothes that are in the laundry basket, sets the table, and he may even take a few steps toward starting dinner. If the weather is good, he knows he can go out to play ball until 6:00, when his father is due home. If not, he may go to a friend's house to play, providing he calls his father to tell him where he'll be. He can't invite any friends over when he's home alone. Some days he does his homework after school so it won't be waiting for him after dinner, and he can read or watch television instead.

"One think I learned early on," says Benji's father, "is that I got nowhere trying to make rules that I had no way of enforcing. Like, at first, I told Benji he wasn't allowed to watch television after school. And then I realized I had no way of knowing whether he was watching TV or not. So I dropped that rule. I told him, 'Look, kid, you could be doing a lot of stuff that's more interesting and better for you than sitting glued to that tube. But I can' make that decision for you. You have to do it yourself.'

"The only thing I could do was set up some jobs that he had to do—and I could tell as soon as I came home whether he did them or not. And I'd know whether he got his homework done. So I stopped asking him about the TV. Most times, if his friends are around, he'd rather be out playing with them anyway. And if not, well, let him have his hour or so with the set. I know I watch plenty of junk myself when I come home at night."

Parents whose children have reached the age when a baby-sitter is no longer absolutely essential have worked out a number of guidelines that help maximize their children's self-confidence and minimize anxiety (for both child and parent).

California attorney Barbara Flicker, for example, never put her eldest son in charge of his younger brother and sister. "Instead of making one kid the boss, I always thought it was better to make all the children be responsible for themselves," she says. "This way, the younger ones learned what was expected of them and were forced to take responsibility for their own behavior. And it kept Billy from having to be the 'bad guy.' I think that's one reason why they all get along so well now."

A strong argument for this practice of making every child responsible for his own behavior is the pattern noticed by Billie Rosoff, director of the voluntary sterilization program at Preterm Clinic in Brookline, Massachusetts. Rosoff found that practically all women who had decided to be sterilized before giving birth to any children had had the primary responsibility for bringing up a younger brother or sister. "I'd like to put up a billboard," she says: " 'To All Parents: Don't Let Your Older Children Take Responsibility for the Other Children.' "

Some parents pay all their children for "baby-sitting" with themselves. When they behave well, they all receive a sum of money (that, totaled, might equal what the parents would have to pay a baby-sitter); when they fight or act up, no one gets paid.

For suggestions that have helped other children who take care of themselves for part of the day, see the box "Helping the Child Alone at Home."

Being Prepared for the Unexpected

"Do you know where my mother is?" the young voice on the phone asked me. "She was supposed to be back in time to drive me to my tennis lesson, but nobody's home and it's time for me to go." Because I work at home, I was able to drive my next-door neighbor, seven-year-old Eric, to his lesson.

HELPING THE CHILD ALONE AT HOME

You can do a lot to make the self-care experience as safe and as comfortable for your child as possible, by taking steps like the following.

Safety

- Tell your child what to do in an emergency: how she can reach you—or if that's impossible, which friends or neighbors to call; how to call fire fighters or police; what other resources to call on.
- Teach your child not to tell telephone callers whom he doesn't know that he is alone and not to open the door to anyone but family and close friends.
- Be firm in setting safety rules: for example, no use of gas or electric stove or other electrical appliances (except for radio, television, or record player) until the child is mature enough.
- Tell your child to keep her house key out of sight, so other people will not realize that she is alone after school.
- Check out escape routes from fire for every room in your house (including an escape ladder, if necessary) and show them to your child. Tell him that if there is a fire, he should not try to put it out himself but should round up any siblings and leave the house as fast as possible. He should then call the fire department from a neighbor's house, and he should not go back into the house for any reason.
- Teach your child how to call for an ambulance—and when (if the child or anyone else in the home has a burn, heavy bleeding, a possible broken bone, or has swallowed what may be poison).

General Well-being

- Stay in touch by telephone. Set up a regular time for check-in calls, either for you to call your child or for her to call you.

- Teach your child what to do in a minor emergency—
  how to replace a fuse or switch on a circuit;
  how to shut off the main water valve; where flash-
  lights are kept (there should be several, with working batteries that you check on from time to time).
- Put each child in charge of himself. Don't make the
  eldest the "boss."
- Pay each child to behave well. If you get reports of
  fighting, no one gets paid.
- Set up a schedule of chores like feeding pets,
  folding laundry, setting the table, and doing
  homework.
- Be sure the child has enough change for a phone
  call and a bus or taxi ride home.
- Don't bother making rules that you can't enforce
  (like "No TV in the afternoon").
- Leave healthy snacks in easy reach (like carrot and
  celery sticks, cheese, fruit, peanut butter, juice,
  and milk).
- Set up a central message center for notes. These can
  be businesslike messages to tell each other about
  special things that need to be done or to give
  information about each other's whereabouts. Don't
  forget cheerful greetings and jokes. And be sure
  not to make every note an order to do something!
- Buy a good book. One addressed to nine- to
  fourteen-year-olds who take care of themselves for
  part of the day is *Alone After School: A Self-Care Guide
  for Latchkey Children and Their Parents* by Helen
  Swan and Victoria Houston (see the appendix
  "Recommended Reading"). It offers children and
  young adolescents useful guidance for mastering
  difficult situations.
- Reassure your child by letting her know that even
  though this solution has some problems, it seems to
  be the best thing to do now, and even though the
  child may sometimes feel worried and anxious,
  you're sure that she can handle whatever may come
  up. And anytime she wants to talk about any
  concerns, you're ready to listen.

Because we know each other well, he felt comfortable calling me, as my children, when they were young, felt comfortable calling on his mother.

Your children should know what to do and whom to consult when life does not go according to plan. What do they do, for example, on the day when you're an hour late because you were caught in the traffic jam behind an overturned tractor trailer? Not only are you still far from home at the time your first grader is due home, but you can't even get to a telephone to alert anyone. Will Beth know what to do?

Even kindergartners should know what to do if they come home after school to find the house locked and no one at home. Should they go to a neighbor's home? If so, whose? Should they go to the corner grocery store whose proprietor knows the family?

Should they phone you, your spouse, or Uncle Pete? Children should be taught as soon as possible how to use a pay phone, and they should always carry enough change for a couple of telephone calls, along with a slip of paper with the most important numbers (both parents and two or three neighbors or relatives). They can carry the change and the numbers in a schoolbag, a pocket (pinned shut to prevent loss), or in one of those shoe-purses designed for joggers but attachable to any lace-up shoe.

While working out plans for the unexpected, it's important to find out from your children what *they* would like to do and whom *they* would feel comfortable calling on for help.

YOUR CHILD'S SAFETY

"Will my child be safe?" This is the first question most parents ask themselves when they hire a baby-sitter, when they check out a day-care center, and when they nervously begin letting their children stay home alone. What can you do to ensure your children's safety? First of all, you should observe all the safety precautions spelled out in Chapter 6, with reference to hiring and giving instructions to your household helpers. Other precautions are included in the box "Helping the Child Alone at Home."

Then there are a number of other steps you can take to make your home a safer place for yourself as well as your children. Sociologists and journalists are not the only people in our society who have noted the rise of two-job families. Unfortunately, burglars also have kept up with this change, and they capitalize on it all the time. Police departments in both urban and suburban areas have been receiving more reports of burglaries that take place between 10 AM and 4 PM—after adults have gone to work and children to school and before they return. If you live in a community where most families are away during the day, you are particularly vulnerable during these hours. Even if you have a baby-sitter at home with your children, you don't want them to be alarmed or endangered by someone trying to get into the house or by someone whom they surprise on their return. So you should see that certain practices are followed by whoever is at home day or night. For suggestions see the box "Keeping Your Home and Your Child Safe from Burglars."

YOUR CHILD'S SOCIAL LIFE

Some children are unhappy because they cannot spend as much time with their friends as they would like to. Most parents realize that two or three children are two or three times more likely to get into mischief than is one alone. So working parents of children who are in charge of themselves after school often do not permit their children to entertain their friends in an unsupervised home. Children who go to an after-school center or to a family day-care home also grumble sometimes because they are not free to play with the friends they like best.

"I used to be overcome with paroxysms of guilt," one mother told me, "every time Jamie would start complaining about how he never got to play with his friends. But then one day I suddenly realized that I never see my friends during the week

KEEPING YOUR HOME AND YOUR CHILD SAFE FROM BURGLARS

- Lock all your doors.
- Install more than one type of lock on your outside doors (a spring latch in addition to a deadbolt, for example).
- Lock all your windows with jimmy-proof locks.
- Leave a radio playing when no one is home.
- Do not hide keys outside the house. Leave an extra key with a trusted neighbor or with the building superintendent.
- Ask your neighbors to report anything unusual to the police (strange people or cars loitering in the area, any activity that doesn't seem quite right). Most police departments encourage citizens to call them on any suspicion, rather than hold back.
- Put short chains on all outside doors, so that you can open them far enough to take in a letter or to sign for a package, without allowing access into the house.
- Put peep holes in solid outside doors, so that you can see who is outside.
- Check references carefully for anyone you hire to work in your home. Some people who don't burglarize will help out their friends.

If You Live in a House

- Keep your garage locked, especially if it is attached to your house.
- Don't leave any ladders around where people could use them to find a vulnerable spot.
- Install floodlights at the back of your house and keep them on at night.

If You Live in an Apartment

- Know your building well. Be aware of places where criminals might enter, hide, or escape (front and

rear doors, elevators, stairways, passageways,
garages, fire escapes, and laundry and other utility
rooms).

- Press your landlord to install security measures.
- Don't go alone at odd hours to the laundry room.
- Report burned out lights in hallways and stairways.
- Report suspicious people or activities to the
management.
- Avoid getting into the elevator with anyone who
looks at all suspicious.
- Get to know a few of your neighbors, so you can
look out for each other.
- Be sure your baby-sitter and your children know
how to get the superintendent quickly.
- Do not buzz anyone into the building unless you are
expecting a caller or unless you recognize the name
and voice.

Tell Your Baby-sitter and Children

- Don't tell strangers that you are not home during
the day.
- Don't tell anyone who calls on the telephone that
the "lady" or "gentleman" of the house isn't home,
or that a child is alone. Your child can tell a caller
that you cannot come to the phone now, but that
you'll call back. And, if your job permits, he can
then call you at work. Or he can be instructed to
answer the phone only on a prearranged signal.
(One ring, followed a minute or so later by regular
ringing of the telephone.)
- Do not let anyone in they don't know. Have delivery people leave packages outside.
- Let service people in only if they have an appointment. Check their credentials.

either. This just had to be a fact of life for our family. Work
and school and family during the week, and the outside social
whirl—such as it is—on weekends. As soon as I laid it out

straight for him, he seemed to accept the fairness of the situation a little better. What's probably more important is that *I* accepted it."

Other working parents are able to help their children find time to socialize with their friends by letting one child at a time invite a buddy home for dinner and a sleep-over. The host parent can often pick up the visitor on the way home from work. As with so many other problems, willingness combined with ingenuity can often provide a solution.

YOUR CHILD'S EMOTIONAL HEALTH

Study after study shows that the children of working parents are, by and large, just as well adjusted as children who have the full-time care of at least one parent. Still, working parents need finely tuned antennae. The *quality* of parenting may indeed be more important than its *quantity*, but the two *are* related. It's hard to create quality time when you rush home, tired and frazzled at the end of the day, tear around making dinner, then catch up on chores. It can be done, but it requires thought and planning and, sometimes, superhuman levels of patience and humor.

Chapter 14 presents more about some of the ways by which you can build quality time into your family life. Meanwhile, you need to be aware of certain specific situations that are likely to arise in a home with children and employed parents.

At Day's End

Whether you are at home or at work, it's likely that the late-afternoon or early-evening hours—when both your child and you are tired and hungry—are likely to be the lowest points of your day. This nadir may be especially intense for the child of working parents—and the worse it is for the child, the worse it is for the parents.

"It's a terrible strain for a small child to behave well all day," pediatrician T. Berry Brazelton pointed out to me. "Just think of the effort it takes for little Johnny to hold himself together for hours at a stretch. He feels angry sometimes during the day; he feels afraid; he feels anxious. So what does he do? He saves it up till he goes home to his parents.

"All too often, the parent who's the butt of the temper tantrum that finally erupts says, 'Uh-oh, he's falling apart,' and feels guilty and inadequate. But when parents see that Johnny needs to let some of those strong feelings out, and that he's doing it when he feels safe, at home with people who he knows love him, they can look at themselves in a different light. They can sense how important it is, what they do at night with their child."

When parents recognize the vast importance they hold in the lives of their children, it becomes easier for them to save up something of themselves for the end of the day, so that they can give more to their children. The less burdened parents are by an unhealthy load of guilt, the easier it is for them to reach out to their children.

Reading Signals

Just as new parents learn to distinguish a baby's cries—the cry that means "I'm hungry," from the one that means "I'm sleepy," or "Something hurts me"—they learn how to read other signals too. They learn when a bout of crankiness signals fatigue, when a child's disposition changes so drastically that it indicates that she is under too much stress, and when a child's fussiness seems to indicate that something is awry enough that it bears further investigation.

It's often hard, of course, to read a child's signals. So parents need to be inordinately sensitive, so that they can learn to recognize when their children are troubled. At that point, they can either help them themselves or bring in professional help if it seems warranted.

"Children have troubles for all sorts of reasons," says pediatrician Mary Howell, warning parents not to blame everything that goes wrong in a child's life on the fact of his parents' being at work. "Problems," she goes on, "are part and parcel of living, and the problems of children cannot always be traced to one specific cause, much less be blamed on anything that their parents have done."

What, then, are some of the distress signals that point to real trouble? One thing to look out for is change, and some of the ways that change may show up are listed in the box "Signs of Trouble in a Child's Emotional Life."

SIGNS OF TROUBLE IN A CHILD'S EMOTIONAL LIFE

- Does your child cry much more often than she used to?
- Do the kinds of slight setbacks that he used to take in stride now upset him?
- Is there a sudden increase in temper tantrums?
- Is she more silent?
- Is he more irritable?
- Is she doing things she'd already grown out of, like wetting the bed or sucking her thumb?
- Is he letting his homework go for the first time ever?
- Does she suddenly keep "forgetting" to let you know where she is after school?
- Is he evasive when you ask him who his friends are?
- Are you starting to get bad reports on schoolwork or classroom behavior?
- Is she waking up with bad dreams or having other sleep problems?
- Has his appetite suddenly left him?

What to Do

What can you do when you receive an SOS from your child? First, of course, you want to discover the underlying causes of the unhappiness so you can make her feel better. Depending on the age of the child, you may want first to speak to the youngster himself or else to his caregiver or teacher.

You may in this way uncover some fairly clear-cut problem—another child who's making your child's life miserable, difficulty with schoolwork or in making a sports team, or a teacher or caregiver your child doesn't like. If you come up with something you can put your finger on, you may be able to devise some sort of quick, practical solution to the problem.

Chances are, though, that you won't be able to spot the source of the problem so easily. You'll end up feeling only that your child is suffering for some unknown reason. You may still be able to improve the situation. We don't always need to know the precise cause of unhappiness to do something about it. No matter what is troubling Janie, she may feel better if you spend more time with her alone, if you think of some treat that makes her feel special, or if you give her a few extra privileges to raise her status within the family.

Sometimes just offering an interested and sympathetic ear can work wonders, even when you cannot change anything in your child's life. Suppose your son is feeling neglected because he is the only child on the block whose parents work nights and sleep in the daytime? Or suppose your daughter feels "freaky" because she's the only one in her class whose parents have a "commuter" marriage (in which your spouse and you work in different cities and get together only on weekends)? In either of these cases, you may not be able to change the basic circumstances of your family life. But you can give your child a chance to talk about his or her feelings. You can help your son understand why you work the way you do and why your neighbors criticize you for it—if they do. You can let your daughter know that you appreciate how much she misses her other parent. When children hurt, we can often relieve some of their pain just by being there and reassuring them of our love, of our involvement, and of our confidence in them.

Sometimes, though, no matter what you do to help your child, you don't see any improvement in the way she or he feels. If you have been seeing signs of distress over a period of several weeks—a long time in the life of a child—you may want to seek outside help. If you have a relative or a friend whose judgment and discretion you trust, you may want to talk the problem over with him or her. Or you might go to your family doctor, a family-service agency, or a child-guidance clinic. Sometimes an objective pair of eyes and ears that don't know your family are best able to help you understand and meet your children's needs as well as your own.

When Children Resent Their Parents' Work

"Why can't you be home when I get home from school, like Mark's mother is?" David often asks his mother. "She always gives us milk and cookies—and she makes the cookies herself!" By the age of nine, David has learned just where his mother is vulnerable. As a child of his time and his society, it would never occur to him to ask his father the same question. Because his father is, however, sensitive both to David's feelings of being neglected and to his wife's feelings of being unfairly singled out as the parent who *should* be home, David's father took it on himself to explain to David the importance his mother's work holds for her, for the family, and for the people she helps as a hospital social worker.

David's mother also picked up some nuances in his complaints that are common among children whose parents have the kinds of jobs that involve helping other people—teachers, social workers, doctors, nurses. An often unspoken worry is, "You love the people at work more than you love me. If you didn't, you'd be home doing things for me instead of for them." While this worry can be—and should be —dealt with directly, the more effective way to allay it is to demonstrate as often as possible how much the children do mean to the parents. When children know that in the crunch they and their needs come first, they won't feel they're playing second fiddle to their parents' job. We'll talk more about the ways parents can make their children feel loved, wanted, and taken care of in Chapter 14.

Sometimes the protests are an occasional thing, surfacing only after vacations and holidays, when the family has spent a good amount of time together and the child wants to prolong this togetherness. Sometimes the protests are more frequent.

Whatever their frequency, their outcome is often guilt on the part of the mother, especially when she knows she likes going to work more than she would enjoy being home full-time with her children.

"I have a good excuse," one pharmaceutical saleswoman told me. "We need the money I earn. But I don't know what I would tell my child if I didn't. He just can't understand why I don't want to stay home with him all the time. And at four-and-a-half, he can't understand why I love my work so much."

Parents do need to be sensitive, of course, to children's needs for reassurance of parental love. But they don't need to apologize for the fact that they, as adults, enjoy the work they do. They can explain their interest in their work as an "adult thing." Work is something that people prepare for through many years of education, of thought, and of special training. Work is the principal vehicle through which many of us experience the fulfillment of exercising our abilities, making our contributions to society, and getting the gratification that comes from other people's recognition of our competence. Work is something that most grown-ups do, and something that your child, too, can look forward to doing for most of her adult life.

One big plus of presenting your attitude toward your work in this positive way is the role model you are offering your child. How much brighter the future will seem if he can look forward to work as a positive enhancement of life rather than a necessary evil!

One way to convey this sense of enthusiasm for your work is to bring your child into your working world when it's appropriate. You might want to introduce your preschooler to your work site for only an hour at a time, possibly on one of your days off when you can come in for a short visit, or else on a working day when someone else (your spouse, your caregiver, or a friend or relative) can bring your child in for a short stay. Depending on the nature of your work and the atmosphere there, all-day visits may be possible for an older child, who may be pressed into service to answer a phone, run errands or collate papers. Sometimes an especially meaningful parent–child experience can develop from taking an older schoolchild with you on a short business trip. Your child can be encouraged to go to a museum, a park, and/or a movie for part of the day, while the two of you are together the rest of the time.

Norma Deull, director of the theatrical division of Clark Transfer Company in Trenton, New Jersey, remembers the fun she had when at the age of four she began going to work every Sunday with her father, himself an executive with the same firm. "I played on the platform and I rode up and down on the dumbwaiter while he was busy in his office or doing other jobs around the terminal. Then when I was ten, I took the train by myself from Philadelphia to Washington, where my father was working for a few days. He would put me on a sight-seeing bus every day while he was at work, and then we would have our evenings together. It was great fun for me, and I got the sense that his work was fun for him too. It wasn't like work—it was more like play. And that's the attitude I've always had about what work should be.

"It's funny," Norma muses. "I just realized that in the job I have now I'm doing a lot of the same things my father did; and I realize, looking back, that from the time I was a little kid, I wanted a job like my father's."

Sometimes children need to learn that the kinds of frustrations they complain about are simply among the realities of life. Just as children learn that the toy store is not open on Sunday, they have to accept the fact that father can't take them to the ball game on Monday, and mother can't rush with them to the shoe store on Wednesday.

One mother met her child's resentment head-on. After about the twentieth time ten-year-old Lisa had asked petulantly, "Oh, why do you have to work, anyway?", her mother stopped what she was doing, curbed her feelings of defensiveness, and sat down with Lisa. She let Lisa know that she understood her annoyance, but she pointed out to the child—without anger—how unhappy, bored, and restless she would be staying home.

"What a responsibility it would be for you," Lisa's mother told her, "to feel that my happiness and sense of who I am depended on how good you were and how much time you wanted to spend with me. Instead, I'm helping you to grow up and be independent." As mother and daughter talked over their concerns and their feelings, each seemed to understand the other a little bit better. Life was not all roses thereafter, but it was far less thorny than it had been.

YOUR CHILD'S PHYSICAL HEALTH

When European explorers first set foot on many islands, unknown until then to the world beyond their shores, they brought with them the seeds of many illnesses new to the native population. The same thing happens, in reverse, when your children leave the home for other places, especially those full of other children. Your children will come up against bacteria and viruses to which they have not yet built up resistance. And so it's not uncommon to find them coming home from the family day-care home, the day-care center, or the kindergarten with one runny nose or sore throat after another.

Although some of these minor illnesses are inevitable and may even benefit your child in the long run by building up resistance to germs at an early age, you can do your part to keep your children as healthy as possible.

The latest medical research shows that the best way to prevent the spread of infections involves something very simple—washing hands. So you can do a lot to help your children stay healthy by teaching them, from a very early age, to wash their hands after playing outside, after using the toilet, and after blowing their noses—and before handling food or brushing their teeth. You should also, of course, wash your own hands in the same situations, as well as after you have come into contact with a lot of people (shaking hands, riding public transportation, and so forth).

Probably the best thing you can do for your entire family is to provide the kind of home environment that will help everyone be as strong and as germ-resistant as possible. Nothing exotic about this: just eating the right kinds of food, getting enough sleep, dressing appropriately for the weather, staying away as much as possible from people with known contagious or infectious diseases, and being up to date on all immunizations.

Ensuring the Best Emergency
Medical Treatment for Your Child

When my daughter Jennifer was ten years old, she fell off the playground jungle gym. Because both my husband and I were unreachable at the time, the school nurse called my next-door neighbor, who took Jenny to the hospital, where they X-rayed her immediately and diagnosed fractures of her wrist and elbow. Not until my husband and I reached the hospital some three hours later, however, could the necessary operation be performed to set Jenny's arm.

Some years later, my youngest daughter Dorri suffered a concussion in a serious automobile accident, 1500 miles from home. Emergency crews immediately helicoptered her to the nearest major hospital where she was put into intensive care; her split lip was sutured to minimize scarring, and her abrasions were cleaned and covered with protective salve before we were even called.

Both these cases typify usual emergency medical practice. When an injury is not life-threatening or almost sure not to leave lasting scars or deformities, hospital authorities usually prefer to wait for the parents or someone who has the parents' written permission to authorize medical care. In instances of extreme emergency (which different hospitals define in different ways), physicians *will* act. Many cases, however, fall somewhere in between. A deep cut that is not treated immediately may leave a large scar, and a broken bone that has to wait to be set may not heal perfectly, leaving an impairment in functioning. So, to be on the safe side, the caregiver in charge of your child should always have in her possession a statement authorizing medical treatment. You may prefer to name a relative, friend, or neighbor who is likely to be accessible as the person to authorize treatment in case you cannot be reached. In either case, it is best to have such a letter of authorization notarized, but an unnotarized letter is better than none at all. The form in the box "Authorization for Emergency Medical Care" should cover any eventualities.

AUTHORIZATION FOR EMERGENCY MEDICAL CARE

Child's Name _____

Mother's Name _____

Telephone no. where she can be reached during the day: _____

Father's Name _____

Telephone no. where he can be reached during the day: _____

Doctor's Name _____ Telephone: _____

In the event that there is an immediate medical emergency or a situation in which medical care must be administered to my child and we cannot be reached, I/we give authority to _____ to call the doctor listed above. In the case he or she cannot be reached, the pediatrician on duty at the hospital may provide or obtain medical care for my child, which may include arrangements for the administration of anesthesia, to provide the necessary treatment for my child. If feasible, I would like my child to be taken to _____ Hospital. If she or he is at such a distance from this hospital that an intolerable delay would be created, the above-named person has the authority to designate another hospital.

Date _____ Signed: _____

(Mother)

Signed: _____

(Father)

Signature of Notary Public

To be sure that your child will be adequately covered, it's a good idea to make about a dozen copies of this form, so that you will always have extra blanks. This way, when you have a new or a substitute caregiver, you can quickly write in the name of your child, the name of your caregiver, and your own signature.

Your Child's Doctor

Your partner in your efforts to keep your children healthy is your pediatrician or family physician. You need someone who can administer routine examinations, who can diagnose serious illness, and who can spot a problem that you're not aware of, even if that problem is emotional in origin rather than physical.

What happens then if your partner acts more like your opponent? If your children's doctor is convinced that the children of working parents get poorer care than do children who have a parent at home full-time? If she feels that baby-sitters or day-care centers are bad for children?

A pediatrician once said to me, "I can always tell the working parents. They're the ones who call me frantically in the middle of the night because they're feeling so guilty about leaving their kids that they overreact to the slightest thing. I'd like to tell them not to overreact—and not to go out to work." A doctor with this attitude is bound to show it and bound to add to your already full knapsack of guilt, anxiety, and other pressures. You don't need that.

If your pediatrician's bias is as evident as his stethoscope, in such remarks as, "Well, if your business trip is more important than your child's health" or "If it were *my* child, *I* wouldn't leave him with a baby-sitter," you have two basic options. You can shop around for a physician who is not only good at medicine but also good at relating to your life. Or, you can embark on a campaign to educate your doctor, an approach that will, in the long run, benefit other families as well as your own. Without becoming defensive, you can emphasize your willingness to see that your child gets the best care possible; support this by working into the conversation the way you accomplish

this aim. You can also take several concrete steps in this
direction:

- Ask your child's caregiver to accompany you on at least
  one occasion to the pediatrician's office. This way, she will
  learn the route as well as the routine, will meet the physician and the office staff, and will feel more comfortable
  should she have to go to the doctor's office when you are
  not along. Your caregiver will, of course, have your doctor's phone number.
- Be sure that your doctor has your caregiver's phone number. She should also have your phone number at work and
  should be encouraged to call you there with any questions
  or reports or to speak with you mornings or evenings.
- Ask how you can facilitate the doctor's treatment of your
  child. Are there special telephone hours when the doctor
  prefers to be called? If these hours conflict with your work
  or commuting schedule, ask for a convenient alternative
  time for nonemergency phone calls.
- Familiarize your caregiver with the hospital where your
  doctor is affiliated. Show her where it is; point out the
  emergency room entrance.
- Be sure to fill out a medical form (see box). Leave one with
  your caregiver and give another completed copy to your
  child's doctor. That way, emergency medical care for your
  child will not have to await your arrival.

YOUR CHILD AT SCHOOL

Rachel, age six, didn't feel well at school. Right after the 9:00
AM bell rang, she began feeling a little weak and dizzy. Not
seriously ill—just draggy enough so that she wanted to go
home. The school nurse thought she should go home. But Rachel had to stay in the school infirmary all day because the
nurse couldn't locate Alice Swersey, Rachel's mother, who
was attending a conference of music therapists and was unavailable by phone. Rachel was feeling so miserable that she
couldn't summon the energy to tell the nurse to call her father
instead. Burt Swersey's business office—where he had been

all day—was in his home, a fact that had been duly recorded on Rachel's medical card, a fact her teacher knew, a fact that Rachel's mother had taken pains to point out at the beginning of the semester.

The Swerseys were living in a Westchester County community that has become synonymous with the good suburban life. Even though in this school district, as in many others around the country, a growing number of women are going to work, school personnel still cling to outmoded thinking patterns. Although men and women often break out of gender-stereotyped roles unselfconsciously when it benefits the family, institutions often act as if these roles were unchangeable. Families have to do what the Swerseys did after this fiasco. Burt and Alice made an appointment with Rachel's principal, emphasizing Burt's important role in Rachel's life—and also emphasizing his availability to her in an emergency, an availability that was much greater than his wife's because Alice's job was a half-hour drive away.

In this case, the school had blinders on, ignoring the presence of a second parent. For single-parent families, when the school is in effect the second parent, the attitudes of personnel are often even more insensitive. A survey conducted by the National Committee for Citizens in Education found that more than half of the parents responding had had to take time off from their jobs to attend conferences with their children's teachers. Nearly half had heard teachers talking about "broken homes" and using other disparaging language to describe single-parent families. Schools were sending messages home to "Mr. and Mrs. Smith" even when there was only one parent in the home. After Mr. Jones cooked a dish of lasagna for a class potluck dinner, his son's teacher wrote a note that said, "Thank you, Mrs. Jones." Children were being invited to functions that involved bringing a specific parent ("Breakfast with Dad" or "Mother–Daughter Sports Night"), when that parent was not living in the home. Schoolbooks were still showing the ideal family as the one in which there were two parents—a breadwinning father and a full-time-homemaker mother.

"I keep saying they should call it the 'Nonworking Parents and Teachers Association," one working mother told me soon after she moved to an affluent suburb precisely because of the good reputation of its schools. "All the fund-raising events are scheduled during the day, so of course I can't take Peter to the after-school movie or attend the Wednesday-morning boutique tour. I'll take time off from work to go to something that Peter is personally involved in, like a class play, but not for a bake sale. So the parents on the committees call me, and I tell them that I can't go—and they say in a very disapproving tone of voice, 'Oh, yes, that's right, you *work.*'

"Then I say, 'Richard can't go, either.' And there's this blank silence. 'That's my husband,' I add. 'Peter's father.' And they're stunned that I should even bring him up because nobody *expects* a child's father to be at any of these events. It's all up to the mother. And it's all terribly guilt-producing.

"I keep telling them, 'I'll be glad to do anything—bake cookies, lick envelopes, do anything useful—as long as I can do it in the evenings or on weekends.' But they keep scheduling these things during the day. So I don't get to any of them."

That conversation took place eight years ago—and a lot of changes have occurred in the meantime. Today, this school—like so many others around the country—has changed its scheduling, so that most events involving parents take place in the evenings or weekends, making it possible for working parents to attend. Aside from enabling working mothers to retain their close ties with their children's schools, this change also acknowledges the interest that fathers have in their direction. So the entire family benefits.

Still, of course, there are conflicts. Field trips and class plays still take place during the school day, and, as one money market trader told me, "My eight-year-old daughter is very vocal in reminding me that other mothers help in school and go with the class on trips. I feel guilty that I can't be there for her as much as she would like me to, but I tell her that she has to let me know which events are *really* important to her. When she does, I do everything that I can to be there. So it's a constant compromise. But then, that's what my whole life is."

Many teachers and other school personnel are, of course, extremely sympathetic to the needs of working parents and their children. (And not only because so many people in education are working parents themselves.) Often, if you assume that an interest and a concern exist, you can enlist your child's teacher as a friend of your family.

"I always call each of the children's teachers early in the year," says Bernice Cohlan, manager of a unisex haircutting salon. "I make an early-morning appointment of just fifteen or twenty minutes, when I can tell her my work schedule, give her my phone number at the shop, and tell her that I would appreciate her calling me at any time if there's any problem at all. This way, we get to meet each other, she gets to see that even though I'm a single parent without much time I am *very* interested in my children. While I won't be bugging her, I do want to stay informed."

The approach has worked well for Bernice, as well as for seven-year-old Gary and for nine-year-old Bonnie, who have had consistently good experiences with their teachers. Bernice has received calls from time to time—once when Bonnie seemed obsessed with bullying a smaller child in her class, once when Gary was refusing to participate in any group games, and on a couple of other occasions. "I wasn't always sure just what to do after these calls," Bernice says, "but at least I knew that some extra TLC was called for, and between the teachers and me, the problems usually cleared up fairly soon."

YOUR CHILD IN THE COMMUNITY

As children grow older, the pathways of their lives stretch farther and farther beyond home and school. They want to participate in more activities, and most parents want them to participate. But even though extra programs for children would seem to help out the family in which both parents are working, they often pose logistic roadblocks.

The problem may begin with signing up a child for an activity. Says Cleveland attorney Marie Grossman, "Our whole society has to move toward more flexible hours for people who have children. For example, when I wanted to sign my boys up for art classes, I had to take a morning off from work because the first sign-up day was scheduled on a Friday morning, and the enrollment had to be done in person. When I wanted to go with my sons to a mother–child swim class, that was totally out of the question because all the classes were held during the day. It wasn't until a lot of us working parents protested that the Y changed it to Friday night. Everything like that helps, but it just gets so exhausting having to battle this mentality all the time."

Change comes, however, only as a result of battling this mentality. Community leaders need to recognize how even the simplest changes in procedures (accepting enrollment by mail or phone, for example) can make life go so much more smoothly for working parents and their children. They need to weigh the value of making more substantial changes (like moving daytime sports practices to early evenings or weekends, so that working parents can participate as coaches and assistants). They need to recognize how an openness to change and the willingness to break out of old ways of doing things can benefit the entire community.

Another bugaboo for working parents is transportation, a special problem for people who live in suburban or rural areas, where there is no good mass-transit system.

"Without some way for my children to get around, they become prisoners in their own homes," says rural Wisconsinite Dan Littlefield. "They can't play ball after school, they can't go to visit their friends, they can't even be Boy Scouts."

Some parents solve this problem radically, by moving. When the Flicker family moved from the suburblike community of Whitestone, Queens, into the heart of Manhattan, both parents were nearer their jobs, the older boys were nearer their school, and all three children had easy access to the New York City bus–and–subway system. Like many other city youngsters, Julie Flicker learned to get around by herself at a very early age—learning the routes while at the same time learning how to be "street-smart" and "subway-smart" to avoid trouble.

Other families find more modest solutions. They join car pools in which some parents drive during the week and others make special trips on weekends. They hire older neighborhood residents or high school or college students whom they know to be careful drivers, to shepherd their youngsters around. Or, they use local taxi companies, taking advantage of charge accounts so their children and caregivers can get where they want to go without having to have cash in hand. (The Delux Taxi Service in Port Washington, New York, asks the parent opening an account to give the company the names of all persons who will be authorized to ride and to sign, eliminating the possibility that overly generous children will start giving their friends rides all over town!)

One of your child's greatest needs is to feel at home in the community. Working parents often feel isolated from their neighbors because they are gone from the home all day long and are swamped with family and household tasks evenings and weekends. It's important, however, to make the effort to build bridges within the community. Without feeling as if you have to join the kaffeeklatsch crowd (which in many communities has dwindled or disappeared outright), you *can* make friendly overtures.

One good way to meet your neighbors is to say "yes"—once—to one of the fund drives that ask you to solicit. Another is to take the children and call on the neighbors on a weekend afternoon. This way your children will get to know the teenagers next door, the elderly couple across the street, the big family in the house on the corner. And you and your children will become more than shadowy figures glimpsed on the street. Should you, your children, or your caregiver ever need anything, they will have someone familiar to turn to. Most people like to help others in times of need, but that basic first connection has to be made so that you may feel you are asking for help from a caring neighbor rather than a stranger.

In our mobile society, many of the traditional community roots no longer exist for children in the way they once did. With your interest and your effort, however, you can plant such roots for your family.

11

YOUR WORLD

―――――

As a working parent, you probably spend so much time thinking about and doing things for your children, your work, and your spouse (if you have one) that you may sometimes feel as if some essential part of yourself, ignored and uncared for, is slipping out of sight—or even out of existence. According to many psychologists, these years when children are young and work is demanding are the most stressful in the entire life span. Your circuits are overloaded, your energy is stretched to the limits, and you end up asking, "What about *me?*"

This chapter is about you, about the kinds of issues that working parents have told me—and other researchers—are major ones in their lives. Not all the concerns in this chapter, of course, will apply to you. But if you come away with the realization that you're not the only one who has these feelings, you may be able to deal with them more effectively.

―――――

YOUR GUILT

"All the time." "About everything." "Guilt is a constant in my life." If there is one refrain that I keep hearing over and over again as I speak with working parents, it is the persistent presence of guilt. Few of us are untouched by it. And many of us torture ourselves with it, retaining perfect memories for every crisis in our children's lives—especially when we think we failed them. My friend Elaine often thinks back to a day some fifteen years ago.

At about the same time Elaine was stepping into a subway train on her way home from work, a car was screeching around the corner of the quiet street where her children and their housekeeper were walking the family dog. The dog bolted, the car swerved—but not quickly enough—and in an instant the beloved pet was lying dead by the curb. The children were beside themselves with grief. The housekeeper did her best to comfort them, but, feeling inadequate to the task of taking in the dog's body and comforting the children, she anxiously awaited their mother's arrival.

Meanwhile, the train that Elaine was riding was sitting motionless in a tunnel, stalled for forty-five minutes by a fire on the track ahead. The housekeeper wanted to get home to her own family, so when the time came for her bus to leave, she told the oldest of Elaine's sons, then about ten, "You be in charge now. I have to go."

By the time Elaine got home, half an hour after the housekeeper had gone, she found all three of the children—the three-year-old, the eight-year-old, and the ten-year-old—crying hysterically over the body of the dead dog, feeling totally alone and abandoned.

"That was absolutely the worst moment I ever had as a working mother," Elaine recalls, her own anguish and that of her children still fresh in her mind. "I had had a rotten day myself at the office, I was furious at the housekeeper for having left the children at a time like this, and I felt overwhelmed by guilt that all of this happened."

Yet as bad as that evening was, as painful for everyone involved, it left no lasting scars that anyone can see. All three of Elaine's children are now well-adjusted adults, leading busy, productive lives. Elaine and her husband are both successful in their absorbing careers, no longer torn by the demands of caring for small children. The housekeeper, too, came out of the experience only slightly bruised. At first remorseful at leaving the children and then angry at being fired, she decided that this kind of work was not for her and got a job in a factory, which she could leave the second the whistle blew.

We all have our own stories, but I think we can all learn from this one. It was an experience no one would ever have chosen children to go through. But from all the evidence, these three were not irreparably harmed. And this is what parents need to remember when we begin to feel sick with guilt about how we think we are failing our children.

Even if we parents were never to leave our children's sides, we could not protect them from painful moments. Nor would we want to. For it is precisely through such traumas that a great deal of growth takes place. As parents, we have to keep a balanced view of what we can and cannot do. We need to do our very best, but not torture ourselves with the things that we think we should be doing but are not.

In interviewing parents for this edition of this book, it was dismaying to see that guilt is as much of a specter as ever in working parents' lives. One new wrinkle in the guilty-parent syndrome, however, is that it's no longer confined to working mothers. Now fathers are taking their parenting so seriously that they're feeling guilty too. Even though women still seem more susceptible to the disease, men also show its symptoms.

What Do Working Parents Feel Guilty About?

"About keeping my son in day care from 7:30 AM to 5:30 PM five days a week—even though my wife assures me he's better off with his peers than with us."

"About making Andy the same kind of sandwich every day (peanut butter and jelly, what else?)."

"About not answering my friends' letters."

"About not being a better person."

"I lose my patience much too quickly and start snapping and yelling—and then I see the hurt on my daughter's face."

"Because I'm not with my child for more hours of the

day—and because the time I spend with her is too often filled with chores."

"I feel guilty when I'm with my son and not concentrating on my writing—and guilty when I'm writing because I'm not spending the time with my son."

"It rips at my heart to leave my daughter each morning knowing I'm going to miss one more smile, not be able to comfort her when she cries, hug her when I want to."

"For spending time grocery shopping when my children are home, instead of devoting my full attention to them."

"For not having their friends over on the weekends because I want to catch up on all the things I didn't do all week long."

"For going to work when my kids are sick."

"For staying home from work when my daughter just has a cold."

"For being preoccupied with my problems at the office and not hearing my little boy when he asks me a question."

"For being upset about not being at the fifth-grade play and making mistakes in typing the budget figures for my company."

"Sometimes I feel guilty for not feeling guilty!"

Everyone feels conflicts occasionally, but working parents—and especially working mothers—seem to suffer more than most. You're less likely to feel guilty if you need the money and you don't like your job. But if your financial need is not so pressing and you really love your work, guilt is more likely to attack. Furthermore, your symptoms may be aggravated by the comments of neighbors or relatives or by the pleas of your own children, who very quickly learn how to use your guilt to their own advantage.

Once guilt takes hold, it can infect your whole life and that of your family. It can force you to make too few demands on your children. It can make you be too indulgent, saying "yes" even before Susie gets her question out of her mouth. This isn't good for the children, and it certainly isn't good for you.

Guilt can drive you to be a "superparent," to feel that you have to do everything that you would do if you weren't holding a job. You have to lead that scout troop, bake those cookies, make those elaborate Halloween costumes, and do all the other things that many a stay-at-home parent wouldn't dream of doing.

Getting Rid of Guilt

Guilt does not have to go with the territory. Working parents need to remember that they are people themselves, with legitimate needs, and that when these needs are met, they function better as parents, as workers, as spouses, as friends—as people.

There are two basic approaches for giving guilt the gate. First, *if you think your guilt is justified, change the situation that gives rise to it.* When we talk about guilt, we are usually describing that extremely painful feeling we experience when we have not lived up to our own standards of behavior. Sometimes this ancient emotion is not all bad. As psychiatrist Willard Gaylin wrote in his wise book *Feelings,* "Guilt is a guardian of our goodness." The only people who never feel guilty, says Dr. Gaylin, are psychopaths, or antisocial people, who are capable of committing the vilest crimes without feeling any remorse.

So take a good look at what you're feeling guilty about. Do you feel conscience-stricken over the poor care your children are getting? If it's really poor, you owe it to them—and to yourself—to do whatever you have to do to change your child-care arrangement. Are you remorseful because you are preoccupied when your children talk to you? Then force yourself to clear your mind of work problems and to give some undivided attention to your children. Even fifteen minutes of total attention is better than an hour of time when your body is present but your mind is miles away. Do you feel you're short-changing your employer because you spend so much time at work mediating your children's arguments? Tell them they are to phone you *only* in case of emergency—and if they don't, refuse to deal with the kind of bickering they can handle themselves.

But then, after you have analyzed what you are doing and

SOME SUCCESSFUL CHANTS
FOR CASTING OUT GUILT

- I remind myself what I was like before I went to work.
- My presence at home doesn't solve all problems either.
- I would be a wretched mother if I were home all the time.
- If I weren't working, my children wouldn't be able to have music and dance lessons or summer camp.
- You can't have everything, and the independence my children show reassures me that I have not failed them in an undermining way.
- My children would hate having the suffocating mother I would be if I focused all my energies on them.
- I do the very best I can at home and at work.
- My family likes the vacations that are possible only because of my income.
- We've gotten used to eating.
- What I'm doing is for their sake too.
- I created an indispensable image out of my own need to feel special and worthwhile. Now I know I *am,* so I can let go.
- When I'm happy, so is my family.
- My kids don't seem to be suffering. In fact, they're doing just fine.
- The kids of the nonemployed mothers I know don't seem to be in any better shape than mine.
- I accept the inevitability of some conflict between work and family, but my family realizes that when push comes to shove, they come first.
- My children get all the mothering they need. Any more would be too much.
- When I'm constantly with the children, I become too irritable.
- It's the only life I have. If I couldn't enjoy it and feel that I was making the most of it, my kids would bear the brunt of my frustration.

- Save the mother and you save the child.
- Work is my therapy. It's cheaper than paying a shrink, and it works just as well for me.
- My work is socially useful. I'm helping to make the world a better place.
- I am not superwoman. I cannot do everything.
- If I weren't working, I would probably be an obsessive, overprotective mother; if I didn't have children, I would probably be a workaholic. Having to combine mothering and working has enabled me to keep my perspective in both areas.
- When I feel I've abandoned my daughter, I force myself to see how she is thriving and to remember that abandonment is my own issue.
- I'm the breadwinner now, and I'm doing the best I can to make a good life for my children.
- Remember that mothers who stay home feel guilty these days too. One told me, "I feel guilty that I'm not earning anything. I don't 'have to' work and yet I still want to get away sometimes. I work on accepting the feelings and realizing that you can't have it all—at least not all at the same time."

feel that in fact you are doing the best you can, relax. Forgive yourself for not being able to do everything. Accept your strengths and your weaknesses, your needs, your limitations. Be as accepting of yourself as you are of others. And at this point, switch to the second technique for getting rid of guilt.

Second, *tell yourself that the children of working parents do not need labels saying "My parents' working is injurious to my health."* There is no research that proves that the simple fact of either or both parents' working hurts children. If you need some magic words to exorcise your guilt, look at the incantations in the box "Some Successful Chants for Casting Out Guilt." They have worked for other parents who have used them to get rid of the demons of unnecessary guilt. And this is the key word—*unnecessary*. You are not Superman or Wonder Woman. You are not perfect. You cannot be all things to all people. You are one human being who is doing the best you can. That's all you can do.

YOUR STRESS

No one's life is free of stress. Nor, probably, should anyone's be. Some stress is energizing: It poses challenges, stimulates us to achieve, and makes life interesting. Too much stress, however, takes its toll in physical or emotional illness or an overwhelmed feeling that interferes with our ability to do our best at home or at work.

If you're like most working parents, you are probably under more stress than you'd like. You could, no doubt, do with fewer challenges and a little less stimulation. You wouldn't mind leading a life that was just the tiniest bit less interesting if it could also be that much more restful. You might even welcome a little boredom from time to time. Yet even though you know that your life-style is more stressful than that in which only one parent works outside the home, you'd probably choose to do practically the same thing if you were starting all over again.

Still, you always have too much to do and too little time to do it in. This is what sociologists call *overload*. And what one father described to me as "the feeling that I'm that guy in Poe's story *The Pit and the Pendulum*. It's just like everything's closing in on me, and I'll never catch up with all that I have to do." The more important your family life is to you and the more you care about your job, the more you're likely to feel this overload. Because you want to do everything.

Trying to do everything is, of course, a big part of the problem. This everything may be a woman's feeling that she is the primary parent, the primary housekeeper, the primary person in charge of the million and one details of daily life—as well as a person with commitments and obligations around her work. Or, it may be a man's feeling that he wants to succeed in his career, but he also wants to be a major presence in his children's lives—and that often these two goals are in direct conflict with each other.

One way that married working parents are alleviating their stress is by redefining their roles. This means sharing not only the work of child care and household chores but—just as, or even more, important—sharing the responsibility for knowing what has to be done. (Some suggestions for making these changes are given in Chapters 12 and 15.) Of course, while this relieves the woman of some of her traditional burden, it adds to the stress level of a man who may be handling household, parenting, and relationship tasks for the first time.

As Los Angeles rabbi Harvey J. Fields wrote in the "About Men" column of the *New York Times Magazine,* "I liked the way we were. . . . Now it's all in flux, and I am scared. . . . I see myself being stripped of my masculine, dominant, father, success image. . . . The curtain has fallen on old assumptions, and it's painful and bewildering."

As with any change, this kind of reshuffling of traditional attitudes is stressful. Still, men are benefiting in one way from these changed roles. The presence of women in the work force seems to have given men permission to admit and deal with their own family-related stress. As researchers at the Wellesley College Center for Research on Women have written, "It is becoming more acceptable for men to acknowledge stress associated with their roles within the family, in part because of increased awareness of the importance of men's roles as fathers."

How else can working parents ease their high-stress lives? Some ways are listed in the box "Strategies for Easing the Transition Between Work and Home." And some guiding

---

STRATEGIES FOR EASING THE TRANSITION BETWEEN WORK AND HOME

- Tell everyone you have to watch the TV news and will be available in a half-hour. You can all view together as you unwind, or you can go off into a room by yourself, even if you want only to stare mindlessly at a flickering screen.
- Close your bedroom door for fifteen minutes while you lie down with the mail, the newspaper, a magazine, music on the radio, or just total silence and total rest.
- Take a fifteen-minute herbal bath or a bracing shower.

- Exercise for fifteen to thirty minutes: run, walk, bicycle, or jump rope, either alone or with any other family members who want to join you.
- Change from work clothes into comfortable shoes and jeans, a caftan, or whatever else spells relaxation. If you're not going out later, you might even get into pajamas and robe. In some families, everyone does this early—and then they do their day's laundry before they go to bed.
- Nurse the baby. (While available only to breast-feeding mothers, this option is one of the most satisfying and relaxing ways to make the switch from working person to family person.)
- Lie down on a couch or bed for fifteen minutes to half an hour, issuing an open invitation to all family members to come tell you their news while you're stretched out. As little bodies crawl all over you, this lying-down break may calm them down as well.
- Get off the bus two stops earlier than you have to and walk the rest of the way home. The exercise is good for you, and the fresh air acts as a decompression chamber. If you're driving, detour by the park for a ten-minute stroll to accomplish the same effect.
- Put a favorite record on the stereo and listen to music while you look at the mail.
- Have informal appetizers right away, so you can relax and serve dinner a little later. Good, easy, fast first foods are cheese and crackers, raw vegetables, and a cottage cheese or yogurt dip, salad and soup.
- Meditate, daydream, or fantasize for fifteen to thirty minutes.
- Find a quiet spot where you can be alone for a few minutes before or after work, have a cup of coffee or tea, and indulge yourself in some light reading. And don't feel guilty about these stolen moments!
- As soon as you get home, put your baby or small child in a warm bath—and maybe climb in yourself. It's a relaxing way to bridge your two worlds.

principles are listed below. These have worked for some of the working parents I've spoken to. And they've worked for some two-career couples interviewed by Professor Denise A. Skinner of the University of Wisconsin's Department of Human Development, Family Relations, and Community Educational Services. Some of them might work for you.

- *Realize that stress is an inevitable part of your way of life.* You can alleviate it to some degree, but you'll never make it go away altogether, so don't waste your energy trying to do the impossible.
- *Do, however, change what you can.* According to research, stress is the flip side of guilt—at least regarding women. Although mothers who like their jobs and are not in great financial need are more likely to feel guilty around family issues, women who hold low-paying jobs with few opportunities to make their own decisions are more vulnerable to stress-related illness than are women in higher-level jobs. Also, say researchers at the Wellesley College Center for Research on Women, situations that increase working women's stress levels include having very young children, having a large number of children, being a single parent, and having primary responsibility for family work. What, then, can you do about all of this? *If* you can upgrade your job and *if* you can spread the responsibility for family work around (neither of which can, of course, be done with a snap of the fingers!), you may reduce your stress level.
- *Learn to tell the difference between the things you can change and the things you can't.* Then correct the former and accept the reality of the latter.
- *Don't do it all.* Just do some. And be sure it's the most important or the most satisfying some. Set priorities for the projects you'd like to accomplish, rating them in order of importance. Only do those at the bottom of the list if they give you great personal satisfaction and can be classified as pleasurable, leisure-time activity.
- *Ruthlessly squash any perfectionist tendencies.* Remember time-management expert Alan Lakein's rule that "anything worth doing is worth doing badly." If you have to do everything perfectly to satisfy yourself, (a) you'll never be

satisfied, and (b) a lot of things will never get done. If you can accept a less-than-perfect job, you'll relieve yourself of a large burden, and you'll increase your productivity.

- *Compartmentalize your work and family roles.* Don't bring work worries home, and don't take family worries to work. Abide by the motto, "Be here now." If, instead of immersing yourself in whatever activity you're doing at the time, you constantly allow your mind to wander to the other sphere of your life, you won't be fully productive in either place—and you won't enjoy either side. If you do find yourself thinking about a problem in your "other life," jot down a note to yourself—and then forget about it until you can pay full attention to it when it's time to shift gears again.

- *Learn to say "No"*—to your children, your friends, your spouse, your boss, your neighbors, and representatives from community agencies. Just because someone asks you to do something doesn't mean you have to do it. You do have to learn to set your priorities, how to decide what you can and what you cannot do.

- *Ask for help.* Don't be shy. Take your help anywhere you can find it—from spouse, parents, children, neighbors, friends, employer. Very often you'll find that once you tell people what you need, they'll come through for you. But people usually don't know what you want unless you tell them.

- *Learn how to handle the little hassles of everyday life.* Seemingly trivial events often have more effect on physical and mental health than do many more dramatic events. Years ago, my mother spent two precious hours baking and decorating a cake for a friend, then accidentally knocked the cake over. Her father came upon her in tears, took her in his arms, and said, "Don't ever cry about anything that can be replaced." She made another cake, and I've heard those words in my mind many times in my life, when I've had a wallet stolen, lost a favorite earring, and dented the fender on a new car.

- *Always carry something to read or do* for those times when you get stuck in traffic, in line, on a stalled train, or at the bus stop. If you're caught without anything, go over a specific problem in your mind (what you'll ask Johnny's teacher at this evening's conference, who in your office should receive the report you're writing, or what the family will do over the weekend).

- *Look for the silver lining.* Our upset feelings come not from an event itself but from the way we perceive it. So focus on positive perception. Instead of fretting because your missed bus will make you late for work, concentrate on the added bonus of time that you'll have to finish the morning paper. Finding something positive in the most frustrating experience can be a challenging and interesting exercise in itself!

- *Reorganize who does what.* Just because the mother has always phoned the baby-sitter, bought the birthday cards, and planned the family meals doesn't mean she always has to do it. The father or the children or a hired person can take over not only the jobs themselves but also the responsibility for remembering when they need to be done. (More about this in Chapters 12 and 15.)

- *Plan your life.* Set up daily "To Do" lists, weekly schedules, monthly goals, and other plans for using your time as productively as possible. For specific suggestions, see the next section, "Your Time."

- *Baby your body.* Get enough sleep and rest. Eat healthy, well-balanced meals. Listen to such physical signals as an upset stomach or an aching head—and slow down in response.

- *Do some kind of regular exercise* for at least half an hour, three times a week. Do something you like, and if possible, do it with a friend. You'll enjoy the socializing for which you have so little time, and you'll be more highly motivated to keep up with the exercise. If you don't want to take too much time, get out a jump rope and jump in front of the TV set for a ten-minute stretch.

- *Give yourself one treat,* just for you, every day. This day will never come again, so be sure it includes at least one of the joys that make life worth living, whether it's reading one chapter of a novel, watching one silly TV show, eating one favorite food, taking one bike ride, or relishing one conversation with a good friend. You deserve your own special treat, and you have every right to take it. In fact, occasionally, beg, borrow, or steal the help you need so you can take a complete day for yourself—to go to a movie, go window-shopping, or catch up with a good friend.

- *Choose fight or flight.* When something important bothers you, either express your anger or anxiety about it to an appropriate person or put it out of your mind temporarily by some escapism (a long walk, a good movie, a flight of fantasy). Don't brood over it without taking any action.
- *Live in the present.* Don't dwell on past mistakes or grievances and don't dream about what you're going to do "someday." Concentrate on what needs to be done today—and do it.
- *Learn to recognize symptoms of overstress.* If you find that you're habitually late, constantly forgetting things, not doing your work as well as usual, losing your temper a lot, or getting sick a lot, take a good hard look at your life and see whether you can reduce any of its demands on you.
- *Think positively.* Give yourself credit for all that you do instead of running yourself down for what you don't get done. And recognize that some of your stress comes from some of the best things in your life—your relationships with people you love and the challenges of work that you care about.

YOUR TIME

"I wish I had more time for myself."

If any one sentence could sum up the feeling of most working parents, this would be it. How do they find the time to do their jobs, care for their children, run their homes, see family and friends, get to the dentist, read a novel, run a mile, write a poem, or just sit and daydream? Too often, the things they *want* to do never get done, shut out by the things they *have* to do. Yet the time is there. Says San Francisco time-management consultant Donna Goldfein, author of *Everywoman's Guide to Time Management,* "Everyone deserves some guilt-free time each day that is rightfully theirs to spend as they choose. And everyone—no matter how busy he or she is—can find it. It's all in the planning."

Of course, as engineer and mother Cynthia Fabian Mascone points out, "Regardless of how well you organize your time, there are still only twenty-four hours in a day." Still, planning can help. To find out how, I went with Donna Goldfein to the home of JoAnna Brandi, a twenty-eight-year-old divorced mother.

At the time of our visit, JoAnna was living with her five-year-old daughter Jeanine on the first floor of a fifty-year-old two-family house in Great Neck, New York. The five rooms of their home overflow with an eclectic, chaotic abundance of luxuriant plants, interestingly framed photographs and quotations, old bottles, charming antiques, and creative crafts projects in various stages of completion.

What is a typical day like for JoAnna? Her alarm rings at 7:45 AM. She showers and dresses and makes coffee for herself and oatmeal for Jeanine, in between helping Jeanine choose and get into her clothes for the day, brushing and braiding the little girl's long dark hair, and making both their lunches. At 9:00 JoAnna goes across the street with Jeanine to wait for the kindergarten bus and then comes back inside.

In the next forty-five minutes, JoAnna drinks her coffee and talks on the telephone as she does the dishes from breakfast and last night's dinner. She spends less than fifteen minutes putting on makeup and running a comb through her own casually cut dark hair. Then she leaves her house to walk the two blocks to her twenty-hour-a-week clerical and administrative job at the local parks department.

At 3:30 PM JoAnna comes home for her car so she can pick up Jeanine from the after-school center and then drive to the home of a woman who has advertised quilts for sale. JoAnna has good taste and good luck in finding treasures on back roads, in thrift shops, and even out on the street in trash heaps, but today decides that the quilts are not worth stretching her limited budget.

JoAnna usually doesn't plan meals ahead of time. ("Plenty of nights I don't know what I'm going to make till just before I make it," she says.) So on the way home, when she realizes how close they are to Jeanine's favorite hamburger stop, she takes her there for dinner. Afterward they stop in at a supermarket to buy several items she forgot when she went marketing the day before. ("I never make a list," she says. "Most of the time I don't know I'm out of something till I look for it and can't find it.") She also picks up a few boxes for rubbish; one of her projects is clearing out her cluttered back porch.

JoAnna hates marketing, even though she finds herself standing in line at the store three or more times a week. She arrives home tired and cross. While Jeanine gets ready for bed, JoAnna hunts for space on her crowded pantry shelves to put away the groceries. She also puts a load of towels in the washing machine, and at the bottom of the hamper finds Jeanine's shoe, which has been missing for three days.

After paying some bills and talking on the phone to a good friend for about an hour, it's 11:00 PM. JoAnna goes to the pantry to get her typewriter and lugs it over to the kitchen table, hoping that the sight of it out in the open will be a constant reminder of all the schoolwork she has to do. She is doing independent study to complete the eighteen credits she needs for her bachelor's degree. She has to finish a portfolio demonstrating college-level conceptual knowledge of business management. Although JoAnna had planned to type at least one page of her long bibliography tonight, she is so tired that she changes her mind, decides to let the typewriter remind her tomorrow, and goes to bed.

What does JoAnna see as her biggest problem?

"I waste a lot of time," she acknowledges, "and so I don't have time for myself. I get very angry with myself after I've spent too much time on the phone when I could have been doing other things. I'm having a hard time forcing myself to sit down and finish my portfolio, which is due in six weeks. And I need physical organization. I have no place to put things so everything is all over the house, and the outside really affects the inside for me. When my house is orderly, my mind functions better."

What does time consultant Donna Goldfein see as JoAnna's problems, and what does she suggest doing about them? "JoAnna's biggest problem is the reverse side of her charm," says Goldfein, "It's the childlike exuberance that leads her to tackle one project after another with a burst of enthusiasm, yet prevents her from seeing anything through to completion." Goldfein had seen the sheaf of poems JoAnna wants to revise and put in book form, the half-covered chair sitting in the living room, and the worry and guilt over the incomplete portfolio.

Donna Goldfein made these specific suggestions for JoAnna, which could apply to other working parents too:

- *Set up a "Think Center."* Every home should have a spot where a parent can sit down, do both short-range and long-range planning, and manage the executive tasks of running a household. (JoAnna can move a charming and capacious antique desk from her bedroom, where it is never used because it is too close to Jeanine's room, into the den. Here she can set up her typewriter, spread out her school papers, and work whenever she can, without having to clear everything away between times.)

- *Make a daily "To Do" list.* Every evening take ten minutes to think about the next day. Take a clean sheet of paper each time. List job hours, appointments, and other "musts." Mark one block of time—at least an hour a day—"me" for your own personal time. Group together tasks of one kind such as phone calls, errands, and household chores. Transfer any tasks left undone from the previous day to the new list.

- *Choose one major project at a time and attack it in digestible pieces.* If it can't be completed in one day, it keeps going on the daily list until it is done. Only then is a new project substituted. (JoAnna's most pressing project is her portfolio. If she wakes up an hour earlier—as she is used to doing—and does her dishes, dressing, and makeup while Jeanine is still home, she will have forty-five minutes every morning to devote to her portfolio.)

- *Control the telephone instead of letting it control you.* Invest in a telephone answering machine and use it to screen your messages. If the phone rings at an inconvenient time or if the call is not urgent, let the machine be your secretary and return the call at *your* convenience.

Place a note on your phone with the one word *time*. This will remind you to ask yourself whether this conversation is important or enjoyable enough to warrant spending your precious time on it.

Get a long telephone cord, so you can cook, do dishes, or get other chores done while you chat.

Use postcards instead of phone calls for extending or replying to invitations, imparting information, and just keeping in touch.

- *Select clothes the night before.* If you can do this for yourself and your child, you can eliminate morning indecision and save a few steps in the most hectic time of your day.
- *Use space well to save time.* Reorganize your storage spots. Items that you use often deserve to be up front and close to hand. Keep often-used utensils on counters, less often-used items down lower, up higher, behind closed cabinet doors. Group similar items together and label them by categories, like "canned soups," "plant-care needs," and "craft supplies." Store them logically. For example, alphabetize your spices the way supermarkets do.

  If you have limited closet and drawer space, make maximum use of your walls. Use shelves for clothes you can fold and hooks to hang jewelry and belts. Put your children's things on shelves and hooks that are low enough for them to reach themselves.
- *Market efficiently.* Plan seven days worth of menus at a time and list the items you need to buy. (JoAnna does *some* pre-planning: because one of Jeanine's favorite dishes is spinach pie, JoAnna usually keeps frozen spinach, ricotta cheese, and eggs in the refrigerator and makes two pies at a time, freezing one for later use.) When you start to run low on any item, mark it on a running list. Save time by buying case lots of paper goods and canned foods if you have the room to store them.

JoAnna doesn't have to suppress her vitality and spontaneity to run her life more effectively. Incorporating a few simple suggestions like the ones above will, however, enable her to simplify her life; carry out her responsibilities as mother, student, and worker; and still maintain the warmth of her personality and her home. She will probably always set herself more goals than she can realistically finish, but she can do *more* of what she wants to do, and she can feel better about the way she is running her life.

YOUR FRIENDS

"The one thing I miss most about being back at work is not seeing my friends," my friend, caterer Fran Zaslow, proprietor of Incredible Edibles, told me. "The only women I talk to at all regularly are the women I work with. Once you're not at home during the day, nobody calls you. They say, 'Fran? Oh, she's working.' And you might as well be on a desert island.

"So I do miss my friends. I keep telling myself I'll call them and take the first step, but so far I never seem to have a minute to do it. But that part of my life is important to me, so when things settle down a little, I'll make the time."

For most working parents, things don't seem to settle down until their children grow up. So the difficulty of finding or making the time to see friends persists. Again, as for the other issues dealt with in this chapter, this problem looms larger in women's lives than in men's; research supports the common opinion that intimate friendships are generally more important for women.

Both women and men do need their friends, however. Single parents need them the most. While family is wonderful—and some of us are fortunate to count our siblings or other relatives among our closest friends—there is nothing like that soulmate whom you've chosen because you understand each other so well, because you know you can talk about virtually anything together, and because you feel so good being with each other.

It is worth making the effort to keep up your old friendships and to make new ones. Here are some suggestions from other working parents:

- Write a quick postcard from time to time, just to let a friend know you're thinking of him or her.
- Visit by phone while you're cooking, doing dishes, or folding laundry.

- Order a theater or concert subscription series with special friends to ensure your seeing them at least a few times over the year.
- Get together with another family for an activity the children will enjoy, such as the zoo, an amusement park, or a picnic. If you drive in separate cars, you'll have special family time during the trip there; once there, the adults can talk while the children are enjoying the special attraction.
- Keep a supply of gifts (wrapped by the store) on hand suitable to take to a hostess or a sick friend, so you don't have to make a special trip to the store each time.
- Pay your children to address your Christmas card envelopes.
- Write a holiday letter bringing friends up to date on your family's news and activities, the kind of news that you'd tell everyone on your list. Photocopy the letter and add handwritten notes at the bottom to personalize each letter. Or, if you have access to a computer, personalize it. In the group letter, discipline yourself not to put in a lot of information about people many of your friends don't know or activities they don't care about. The letters of this kind that I like best tell *only* about the activities of the immediate family and are written in a way that conveys the writer's personality.

Entertaining Made Easy

"*What* entertaining?" or "Hah!" working parents say when asked what they do about entertaining their friends. Still, having people come to your house is a wonderful way to keep the bonds of friendship strong. And, with a little planning, it need not be expensive nor terribly time consuming. *Every*body is busy these days, so the elegant gourmet meal that takes days to prepare is out of the question. But there are plenty of ways to help you spend time with your friends that are fast and easy and fun. Here are some ideas:

- Invite people in for make-your-own sundaes after dinner. Your guests love it, and you don't have to do a thing except buy the fixings, set them out, and clean up the spilled chocolate syrup afterward.
- Invite people for Sunday brunch. The menu can be fast and easy, and you have Saturday to prepare and Sunday afternoon to clean up.
- On a cold winter's night, a big pot of chili or a hearty soup, a good bread, a salad, and dessert and coffee make an easy, soul-satisfying meal.
- Outdoor parties featuring the all-American menu of hot dogs and beans, hamburgers, corn on the cob, and watermelon are always popular. Cooking is minimal, and you don't even need silverware.
- Potluck get-togethers for which everyone brings part of the meal and then takes home their dirty pots or serving bowls are ideal these days when *everyone* is busy.
- A group of friends can take turns sharing take-out food at each other's homes. Whether it's Chinese food, hamburgers, fried chicken, pizza, heroes, or other favorites, you can all split the cost of the main meal, while the host provides beverages, paper plates, dessert, and coffee.
- If you do want to go all-out and give a more formal dinner party, give two, two days in a row. The idea sounds overwhelming, but it has a number of pluses: You can shop for both parties at once, polish your silver once for both occasions, and wash the dishes and glassware from the first party and put them right back on the table. You can use the same centerpiece, the same menu, and if your friends are obligingly neat, the same tablecloth.
- Another variation on this theme involves giving two parties back to back on the same day. Sounds crazy, but it works! We once invited half our friends for a Sunday afternoon party to run from 1:00 to 4:00, and the other half to come from 4:00 to 7:00 the same day. We invited the early risers, the people who lived nearby, and the football fans for the early shift. Since it was "SuperBowl Day," enough people left promptly at 4:00 to watch the game at home, so that we didn't have more overlap than our house could handle.

- Pay your children to help serve and clean up. They'll enjoy participating, relish earning money, and free you to be with your friends.

YOUR MONEY

Ed had always made the family's financial decisions: how much they could afford to spend on a house, a vacation, a car. Content to play the role of a little girl, Nell would even ask him what to do with her paycheck—whether she should cash it or bank it. Now, however, Nell has decided that it's time to grow up, and she wants to make decisions herself. Ed is worried. If Nell can make her own decisions about money, maybe she can make up her own mind about other things too. Maybe she'll even become independent enough to leave him.

Fights about money often aren't about money at all. As this example shows, money is often only the outer wrapping of something that runs far deeper. Something that has to do with power, competition, self-esteem, anger, guilt, and love.

Study after study shows money to be the major single area of conflict in marriage, with more than half of all couples fighting about it. In general, the less money people have, the more they argue about it, but even the affluent are not immune from fiscal squabbles. According to psychologist and psychoanalyst Dr. Joseph Newirth, "Money often becomes the barometer for a marriage. How people handle money, an intrinsic part of everyday life, can show how they handle other aspects of their relationship, as well." Not surprisingly, money is the pivot on which the bitterest arguments between divorcing couples usually resolve.

Sometimes, of course, fights about money are really about *money*. In these days of rising expectations and of prices that are rising faster, many families find the good life always just beyond their reach. The more frustrated they become as they try to juggle expenses and income, the more their money worries take over their lives.

Fortunately, there are ways for money-troubled single parents or two-paycheck couples to improve the way they handle money. Some suggestions are listed in the box "Suggestions for Working Parents Who Fight Over Money, Cry Over Money, or Just Wonder Where It All Goes."

SUGGESTIONS FOR WORKING PARENTS WHO FIGHT OVER MONEY, CRY OVER MONEY, OR JUST WONDER WHERE IT ALL GOES

- Conduct a weekly review of what you spent or charged over the past week and what expenses you'll have during the coming week. Couples should do this together.
- If your review shows an excess of purchases or services charged over the previous week, lock up your credit cards till the next week, at least.
- Set a dollar limit on what one partner can spend without having to consult the other.
- Immediately record in your checkbook all checks, withdrawals and deposits, even if you wait a few days to do the arithmetic.
- If you don't carry your checkbook with you, carry two blank checks. The minute you write them out, note on a slip of paper the number of the check, the amount written, and the payee. Put this note in your wallet and transfer the information to your checkbook as soon as you get home.
- Use a pocket calculator to balance your checkbook and keep other financial records.
- Use a bank that has branches near both home and work—or keep accounts at two banks.
- Be sure each partner knows where all your important financial papers are. Be sure they're in a safe place.
- Decide who'll pay the bills and keep the checkbook on the basis of who has the better head for figures and who will be responsible about paying the bills on time.

- Carry "mad money" with you in a separate pocket or handbag compartment. In case your wallet gets lost or stolen, or you suddenly have an unexpected expense, it's handy to know you have a ten-dollar bill and a one-dollar bill tucked away. Replace it as soon as possible after spending.
- Try to forecast financial implications of events in your life at least one or two steps in advance. Ask yourself, for example: "How will we change our life-style during the months after the new baby comes while we have only one income?" "What should I do when that raise comes through?" "How will we meet the children's college tuition charges?" "How will we keep up two households after we separate, on the same amount of money we've been earning for one?"
- Be sure your benefits don't duplicate each other's. If payroll deductions are being taken from your salary for, say, medical insurance, and your spouse's policy covers most of the same provisions, it may pay to drop one policy.
- Learn the basic skills of money management. Read a good book, take a course at the Y or consult your local consumer credit counseling center (for the name of the nearest one write to The National Foundation for Consumer Credit; 8701 Georgia Ave., #507; Silver Spring, MD 20910).
- Keep accurate financial records. Save canceled checks and receipts and make notations in a diary. This is especially important for any items that you claim tax deductions or credits on (like child care, medical expenses, charitable contributions) and for contributions made by the spouse who earns the smaller amount to prove that she or he made substantial contributions toward jointly owned property (like your house).
- Talk, talk, talk. "The biggest problem we see in families that have gotten over their heads in debt is a lack of communication," says credit counselor Gerard A. Lareau. "We see couples who have been

> married five or ten years and who have never
> discussed money realistically." One reason for this
> silence is the belief held by many women that it's
> unfeminine to know about money or even to talk
> about it. But because money represents indepen-
> dence and power, it has to be understood and dealt
> with. Being informed about financial affairs is *not*
> unsuitable for a woman; it is essential for *every* adult.

How Two-Paycheck Couples Handle Money

In these days of open discussion about sex, politics, religion—
virtually every aspect of life—only one conversational taboo
remains. Money. Rarely do we know what our best friends or
our closest relatives earn, and to ask them would generally be
considered the height of bad manners and the depth of snoop-
iness. We are more likely to know how often a man and woman go to bed together than how they handle their finances!

One nice thing about being a writer is that you can ask im-
pertinent questions when they're pertinent to your research.
So after treading on this delicate financial ground, I did come
up with some findings on the ways working parents manage
their money. First, practically none of the parents I ques-
tioned keep their earnings separate as "his" and "hers." Most
dump whatever comes into a common account, to be with-
drawn to pay the most pressing common bills. Within this
overall philosophy, however, different couples handle the me-
chanics in different ways.

Ann and Aaron Adams, for example (these names are
changed to protect privacy in this most intimate of topics),
pool both their salaries in one joint account. Each week they
deposit enough to cover that week's immediate expenses, as
well as one-fourth of the monthly bills (rent, utilities, car payment, and so on). After allocating a modest amount to their
savings account, they put the remaining cash in a locked drawer to which each has the key, so that they can both draw on it
for personal needs during the week. Neither Ann nor Aaron
likes managing the money, so Ann pays the bills and balances

the checkbook for three months, and then Aaron takes over for the next three, and so forth.

Betty and Bob Black, both of whom are self-employed, both write a great many checks. It makes more sense for them to keep two separate accounts. Each one keeps his or her own account, and each pays part of the joint bills. Because Bob earns much more than Betty does (a typical situation in a society in which women earn only 70¢ for every dollar earned by men), he pays the higher bills (like mortgage, utilities, and child-care payments), while Betty pays for such items as insurance and clothing.

Celia and Charles Carter also have two different accounts in two different banks, but both of theirs are joint accounts. While Celia and Charles also assume different responsibilities, the joint nature of their accounts gives them more flexibility. When Charles, for example, has a big bill coming up but a smaller balance in "his" account than the account Celia usually handles, they trade checkbooks for a few days.

Debbie and Dick Davis like having three accounts—one joint account for the major household bills and two individual accounts, one for Debbie and one for Dick. "We talk about the big things we buy and even a lot of the little things," says Debbie, "but I like being able to buy a present for Dick without his having to know what I spent for it, or just buying something I want for myself that I know he would think was a silly purchase. I'm not extravagant, but I think I'm entitled to be silly sometimes."

This "his, hers, and theirs" approach can often solve both men's and women's number-one complaints. What bothers men? Let's listen to Frank, a thirty-five-year-old insurance salesman: "It just doesn't seem fair. All these years, both of us always considered my income our money. Now that Marjorie's gone back to work, she opened her own bank account, and I never see her check. So it comes down to what's mine is ours and what's hers is hers."

And women? "You don't understand," Marjorie said to Frank. "Your money was always yours. When I needed a new coat, I said something to you about it before I bought one, but I never knew what clothes you were going to buy till you came home with them. We always took the vacations you wanted

HOW TO ESTABLISH YOUR INDIVIDUAL CREDIT RATING

- Open both a savings account and a checking account in your own name. Your name is *not* "Mrs. John Smith"; it is "Mary Smith." Make regular deposits to both accounts. The deposits need not be large; they must be regular.
- Open a charge account in your name only—with a retail store, a gas company, or a bank card such as MasterCard or Visa.
- Pay the bills for these accounts from your own checking account.
- If you are turned down for credit, write to the company to request the reason in writing. If you feel you were wrongly rejected, protest, giving reasons both to the company itself and also the central credit bureau in your locality. (To find out the name and address of this bureau, look in the Yellow Pages of your telephone directory under "Credit Reporting" or "Credit Rating.")

because I always felt, 'He worked hard for that money. He deserves the vacation he wants.' I never felt I could spend much money on my mother's birthday present because I didn't feel right about buying a really good present with money you had earned.

"But I never really understood how much we both thought of the money as yours until you invested two thousand dollars without even asking me about it—and lost it. So now this is my money, and I just have a different feeling about it because I earned it. And I love the feeling."

Another advantage to a woman's having an account in her name alone is its contribution to her establishing her own credit rating, apart from her husband's. Many a divorcee or widow has been shocked to find that even though she contributed to amassing joint property with money she earned and also kept the books throughout her marriage, once she is no longer a wife, she cannot open a charge account or get a loan. While such practices are changing, they are still widespread enough so that working women should protect themselves by doing what they have to do to assure their own credit ratings.

12

YOUR MARRIAGE

"Ginny and I are great working partners and problem solvers," Chuck, a retailing executive in Tulsa, told me. "But is that all there is to marriage? I had always thought my wife would be a lot more interested in hearing about my problems and my feelings. Sure, I can understand intellectually that Ginny doesn't have either the time or energy to 'make nice' to me, but still I feel I'm missing something. And so is she—because I don't have the time or energy to give her the strokes she needs, either."

And Massachusetts lawyer Jeanne Smith bemoaned the fact that "we never seem to find any time to talk except for 'task assignments.' " Her complaint—"Our lives are too frantic, and my relationship with my husband is always short-changed"—is one that I have heard from many working parents. The kind of overload so many people are under, day in and day out, strains the most loving relationships.

Some problems, of course, cut far deeper. One woman told me, "I would like to share my work successes with my husband, but since he is jealous and insecure about my being a successful businesswoman, I turn to my close girlfriends instead. All I get from him are complaints about shortfalls in the household. I used to overcompensate, especially around cooking. I would try to play superwoman and prepare these wonderful dinners in advance. But the more I did, the more he demanded; so then I went to the other extreme and did practically nothing at home. But he didn't do anything, either, and our kids were the big losers. So I've gone back to doing more—at least a little bit more—and my efforts seem more appreciated now by everybody."

Two-job families don't seem to have any *more* problems than those with just one breadwinner, according to researchers who have studied marital happiness, but they do have special ones. Especially when there are children because their arrival also makes new demands on a couple's relationship.

The most common marriage pattern today—that in which both husband and wife hold jobs outside the home and share duties within it—represents a major change from traditional family patterns in the United States. It holds both benefits and drawbacks over the family patterns that most of us grew up with.

A major benefit, of course, is the increased income. One out of every eight wives earns half or more of the family's total income, while one out of three contributes between one-third and one-half. Most new home buyers these days are two-wage-earner families. If it weren't for the second income, the house—and many other niceties—would be out of the question. But the benefits in this life-style go beyond the merely material.

Husbands and wives in two-income families are likely to be on more equal footing. Employed wives tend to have higher self-esteem compared to at-home wives—and higher self-esteem generally makes people happier and more appealing. And fathers in these families tend to be closer to their children. Furthermore, each partner has more opportunities for developing his or her potential in many areas.

But the stresses are here too, as every working parent knows. You have extra demands on your time and energy, conflicts between demands of work and family, the danger of competitive rivalry between husband and wife, and anxiety and guilt over meeting your children's needs.

Sociologists say that many of the problems of working couples stem from the fact that you are part of three role systems—the work system of the wife, the work system of the husband, and the joint family system. Each role makes its own demands, and you constantly have to decide which role should take priority—the family, your work, or your spouse's work. Family roles are most demanding when children are small, and work roles ask the most when you're first getting established in your career or when you take on new responsibilities. It's hard to juggle all these demands, especially since—if you're typical—you grew up in a family that lived quite differently.

A TIME OF TRANSITION

"The parents of today were brought up with a different kind of socialization," marriage and sex therapist Dr. Shirley Zussman told me when I met with her and her late husband, gynecologist Dr. Leon Zussman, in the Manhattan office where they conducted their joint-counseling practice. Both Zussmans agreed that this period in history—of changing standards, roles, and behaviors—is difficult for both men and women.

"Who were the role models for today's parents?" Dr. Shirley asked. "The father was the one who went out to work and was tended to and, to a degree, waited on when he got home. The mother might have worked, but her emphasis was not on her job but on her family. She was there to soothe her husband's brow and to kiss her children's hurts away.

"The typical young husband we see who is in a two-job marriage does give this new way of doing things his all-out effort, but underneath he feels gypped and deprived. He likes the fact that his wife goes out and earns money; he's proud of her, and he feels he *should* be doing more to lighten her burden. But he really doesn't want to. His conflict is that he wishes things were different.

"At the same time, the wife, with all her demands and wishes and expectations of help—justified because she's doing a full day's work too—feels guilty about asking for it and even about accepting it when it is freely offered. So in a sense, neither partner is winning."

"It all sounds pretty hopeless," I said. "Not at all," Dr. Leon assured me. "Not if a couple are willing to struggle to overcome these old, ingrained patterns. It's okay to struggle because after the struggle comes the reward of a better relationship and a better life."

Transitions seem especially hard for those couples—rarer these days—who married with the expectation that the woman would stay home with the children while the man supported the family. Maybe the wife did this for a few years and was perfectly happy to stay home and spend her days with small children. But now the children are older, money is tighter, and the wife feels she has to go back to work. The husband, however, may have grown used to things as they are—knowing that his children are well cared for by a loving mother and that his meals are beautifully cooked by a loving wife. Even if he knows the family needs the money his wife's job will bring in, it is often hard for him to give up his role as sole provider.

Many a husband feels that his whole being is threatened when his wife wants to change these things. If she goes out to work, she'll be independent financially and won't need him so much. She'll be meeting other men, who will find her attractive and may be a threat to him. He already comes home tired from work. How will he manage to find the energy to help with the housework and to comfort her with her business worries, as she always has with his?

Even when the husband was the one who suggested that his wife continue or begin working, some of these fears may still lurk beneath the surface of his awareness. And even when both husband and wife feel comfortable themselves about their life-style, their marriage is still likely to encounter problems revolving around two time-frames—the day-to-day time that neither one has enough of and the time of transition in which they live and in which the marriage exists.

The big squeeze in two-job marriages comes from what seems to be finite supplies of time and energy. Between meeting the demands of the job, the children, the household chores, and the logistics of coordinating the details for everything, most working parents have little left for each other. They're too tired to make love, too preoccupied to make conversation, too overwhelmed to make time just for fun.

Working parents who want their marriages to work, too, need to focus their energies toward each other on two fronts: first, on making the time for each other so that their relationship doesn't get buried under the morass of phone calls to the baby-sitter, trips to the day-care center, punch-in cards at the time clock, reports handed in to the supervisor, conferences with the third-grade teacher, and all the other details that can swamp them.

Second, they need to restructure their family lives so that one spouse (usually the wife) doesn't end up working a full-time job for which she gets paid and then comes home to the other full-time job of managing home and children. Let's look separately at these two separate pathways toward a better marriage.

MAKING TIME FOR EACH OTHER

When both husband and wife have full-time jobs, there never seems to be enough time for everything. They don't have a wife in the old sense—a person who can devote full-time energies to filling the refrigerator, cooking meals that are as delicious as they are nutritious as they are economical, mopping the floors, balancing the checkbook, taking care of children's emotional needs along with their physical care, and all the other tasks that are part of maintaining a family.

Each partner becomes harried and feels harassed, and the pressure mounts. Either or both are apt to feel overworked and underappreciated, and from this injury to the psyche, hostility toward the spouse often spurts out, like blood from a cut artery. Even in the absence of hostility, lack of time can drain life from a marriage, as intimacy between husband and wife becomes the lowest priority in the couple's hierarchy.

One way to find time is to reallocate your priorities, to take stock of the way you are spending your time now, and to think about whether you are spending it the way you really *want* to spend it. Take advantage of the time-saving suggestions offered in this boook—and anywhere else you can find them.

Time you don't have to spend on cleaning can be spent on caring.

No matter how much time you are able to save, however, through using your hours efficiently, the fact remains that you do have an enormous amount of work to do. You could be busy every moment of every day and night, focusing your energies on your job, your children, your household, your in-laws, and your religious affiliation—and find that you and your spouse haven't really spoken to or listened to each other in an intimate way for weeks.

It's something like building a savings account. Financial counselors consistently recommend deciding up front what you plan to save from each week's paycheck. If you spend your money on all the other expenses that come up and plan to save what's left over, you usually find that your bank account goes unfed. It's the same with time. If you count on devoting to your marriage the time that's left over after both of you have attended to everything else, you'll find that the clock ticked away when you weren't looking—and your relationship has been going unfed.

The trick to finding quality time together is to plan for it. You can make a date to spend private uninterrupted time with each other, just as you would make a date to go out with friends.

When Drs. Shirley and Leon Zussman first suggested this to me in our conversation, I was gratified because my husband and I had already been doing this. "You're playing tennis tonight, I'm teaching tomorrow night. Let's make a date for Wednesday night—no outside plans, just the two of us." Yet somehow I had been embarrassed by it. It seemed so unromantic to plan ahead for intimacy, so unspontaneous. And yet, as the Zussmans point out, "We live in a society that thwarts our spontaneity. Therefore, we have to create opportunities when we *can* spontaneously express our feelings and our sexuality."

Interestingly, spontaneity seems to be considered a requirement only of licit, married sex. During my research for my book *The Eternal Garden: Seasons of Our Sexuality,* which explored sexual development throughout life, I spoke to a number of people who were involved in extramarital affairs. They told me of preparations worthy of a military campaign. Such lovers often hold innumerable telephone conversations to find time when both partners can get away from their respective spouses, to locate a place to meet, and to formulate a network of explanations for the stolen time. And yet the excitement of such encounters generally seems to thrive in direct proportion to the complexity of the arrangements.

If people would have "affairs" with their spouses—set aside time, think about creating a romantic setting, and concentrate on pleasing their partners—these planned-for assignations between husband and wife who are married to each other might well be as exciting as the most illicit fling. One good current book suggesting ways to bring this kind of excitement into the marriage bed is by sex and marital therapist Dagmar O'Connor, *How to Make Love to the Same Person for the Rest of Your Life (and Still Love It!)* (see the appendix "Recommended Reading").

Not that every marital date has to end in sex, of course. Sometimes my husband and I have just needed a block of time in which we could talk, knowing that neither of us would have to rush off to a meeting, tend a child, or answer the telephone (bless our answering machine!). The important thing is that you set aside time for just yourselves—whether it involves getting a baby-sitter so you can get out to a neighborhood coffee shop to catch up with each other over a sandwich, or taking turns with another couple who'll take your children for a weekend so you can have two precious days together.

You could even set a kitchen timer or alarm clock for an hour or two and tell your children that you and your spouse want some privacy and they are not to interrupt you until the timer goes off. Then go to your bedroom and lock the door.

One couple I know have a regular Saturday afternoon date right in their own bedroom. They hire a neighborhood teenager to give their children an early supper, they leave instructions that they are not to be disturbed unless the house is on fire, they take a plate of snacks and a carafe of wine into their room, and then they lock the door. Usually they are so turned on by their elaborate preparations, the lush music they play, and the special nightgown she wears that they make love.

MAKING A PLACE
AND TIME IN YOUR LIFE
FOR MAKING LOVE

- Put a lock on your bedroom door. Nothing dampens ardor so effectively as the knowledge that a pajama-clad cherub could wander in at any time.

- Create an attractive setting in your bedroom. Is it neat and inviting, or is it the depository of all the clutter you're embarrassed to leave around the rest of the house? It would be better to have a neighborhood reputation as a sloppy housekeeper than for you and your spouse to have to slog through piles of laundry and old newspapers in order to reach the bed.

- If you're always to tired at night, set the alarm for an hour earlier than you usually get up. Funny how waking up at 5:00 A.M. is much more inviting when the object is lovemaking.

- If one of you is an "owl" who likes to stay up late and the other a "lark" who is energetic early in the day, take turns accommodating to each other's schedules. The "lark" can take an early evening nap to stay up later, for example.

- If your children have begun to go to sleep later than you do, don't wait. There's nothing wrong with telling the children that you and your spouse are going into your bedroom and that you don't want to be disturbed. This is the *best* kind of sex education—letting them know that the two of you are interested in each other. You can even ask them to answer the telephone and to tell callers you're busy and will phone back the next day. (Chances are, if they're staying up so late, they're the ones getting the calls, anyway.)

- Think "Why not?" when your partner expresses interest in making love, even if you're not in the mood. If you set aside the time for sex and concentrate on pleasing your partner, you'll often be pleasantly surprised to find that before you realize it, you *are* in the mood.

- Occasionally telephone each other during the day with a sexual invitation. A throaty voice promising splendid pleasure later on arouses a mouth-drying sense of anticipation even among long-married couples.

- Plan ahead. As the Zussmans wrote in their book *Getting Together*, "Look, you plan everything else in life. You plan your ski weekends, even though you don't know whether or not it's going to snow. You schedule going church services on Sunday, although you have no idea whether you will be open to religious inspiration on any given Sunday or not. As for getting in the mood, the key usually lies in arousing your expectations. The best way to put yourself in the mood is to make a date so that both of you have 'equal time' to fantasize in advance." Couples who have followed this advice have found that it can result in some of the most memorable times of their lives.

Other times, though, they just use their date to be close to each other in a nonsexual way. Either way, they emerge with a renewed feeling of closeness.

It says something about the values in our society that one of the biggest stumbling blocks to keeping a date with your own spouse is your hesitation about telling anyone else why you can't go to a movie or have coffee with them or attend a meeting. To the same people whom I'd have no hesitancy at all about saying, "I'm going out to dinner with so-and-so" or "I promised to go to a meeting of such-and-such committee," the words "I have a date with my husband" stick in my throat. So I usually just say, "I have another appointment." Now that I've owned up to this in print, though, maybe it will be easier to say it over the phone!

MAKING YOUR MARRIAGE
A FAIR PARTNERSHIP

Many couples began their marriages with the attitude expressed by Mary Ann Russo, age twenty-seven, of Tucson, Arizona, the mother of John, age four, and Melanie, age three. "I used to think that because I was a female person it was my responsibility to do everything in the house and that because my husband Michael was a male person he had no obligations at home besides his job. So I took it all on myself, even after the children were born, and I continued to work full-time at the bank."

Every morning Mary Ann woke at 6:00, did one or two loads of laundry, dressed the children, made a hot breakfast (although she was too busy to eat it herself), and took the children to the day-care center on her way to work. After working all day, she picked up the children, rushed home, cooked dinner, cleaned up the kitchen, and then attended to all the tasks that always seemed to be waiting for her. Many nights she didn't get to bed until 1:00 AM. She kept this pace up for about a year.

"Finally, when I was so run down that I couldn't get out of bed in the morning," recalls Mary Ann, "I told Michael, 'Hey, you know, I work, too. It's just as hard for me as it is for you. I can't handle everything at home by myself. You *have* to help.' He saw how pale and thin I was getting and that I was so nervous I would scream over any little thing. So he started doing more and more."

Now Michael does the dishes, vacuums, cleans the bathroom, and takes turns with Mary Ann at bathing and putting the children to bed. The long-overdue righting of the unequal balance of work in this marriage has helped Mary Ann and Michael in their relationship with each other. Michael has a wife who is more energetic, more fun, and friendlier toward him, and Mary Ann respects and values Michael's contributions to the family, partly because she now feels that he respects and values hers.

However, many marriages are still at the stage where Mary Ann and Michael's was before she spoke up. According to a 1988 report from the Women's Research and Education Institute, married women working full-time are spending twenty-five hours a week in household work, while their male counterparts are putting in thirteen, just about half. And a nationwide survey done by *The New York Times* in late 1987 found that 90 percent of married women who work full-time do almost all the food shopping and 86 percent do most or all of the cooking. One of the understatements of the year was uttered in response to these findings by Joseph Pleck, the Luce Professor of the Family at Wheaton College in Norton, Massachusetts, when he said, "The family as an institution changes rather slowly." Dr. Pleck's own research underscores this snail-like pace: in 1965 men said they did 20 percent of the household chores, while by 1981 they were doing 30 percent.

Still, a December 1988 report in *American Demographics* magazine by John P. Robinson, a sociologist at the University of Maryland, based on a 1985 survey of 5000 men and women, indicated that the housework gap between women and men has narrowed. The present two-to-one ratio contrasts with a three-to-one share of housework in 1975 and almost a six-to-one share in 1965. However, women used to do most of the gardening, pet care, and handling bills; now these jobs are about evenly divided between the sexes. Men still do most of the yard work and home repairs, and women do most of the laundry and cooking. (In my own informal survey of working parents, I was pleasantly surprised to see how many men have taken over the ironing—in those families that do any ironing at all.)

Although this trend is in the right direction, it is discouragingly slow. As one recent survey of married men, conducted by a New York advertising agency, concluded, "It's easier for men to accept the possibility of women as brain surgeons than to release their own wives from the drudgery of laundry and cleaning the bathroom." Even when couples share child care equally, as many young working couples do, the other household responsibilities tend to fall into the wife's hands more often than the husband's.

The Meatloaf Syndrome

And even when men do pitch in with more child care and household tasks, women are still almost always responsible for *thinking* about what needs to be done. It's the old "meatloaf" syndrome, a story that has made its rounds among a generation of working wives.

One night Mary has to work late, so she calls her husband Bill at work to tell him that there's meatloaf sitting in the refrigerator all ready to pop in the oven. Would he pop it in? Next week Mary has to work late again. She calls Bill and tells him she has all the fixings for the meatloaf in the refrigerator. The recipe's on page 381 of the blue cookbook, and would he just throw everything together and pop it in the oven? Another week passes. The phone rings at Bill's office. "Listen, darling, I just haven't had a chance to go marketing this week. On your way home, could you stop at the store and pick up stuff for a meatloaf? If you don't get it ready in time, it's okay if dinner's a little late tonight." And Bill learns he can whip up a pretty good meatloaf.

But not until Bill himself thinks about the fact that the family will need to eat dinner and makes plans for it will he and Mary really have an equitable relationship. The same thing goes for thinking about when Billy Junior needs new shoes— and who's going to take him and when. Or, about when little Marybeth has to go for her doctor's check-up. Or, when the laundry has to be done so nobody runs out of socks. Or, all the other concerns related to bringing up children and being part of a family.

Making Changes

What *is* the secret ingredient in marriages like that of publishing executive Dennis Dalrymple and editor Jamie Raab? Dennis does at least half of the child-care and household chores and maintains that "every male should do his share." He appreciates the care Jamie gives their one-year-old son despite her own work, which she often brings home. And she recognizes his involvement and makes an effort "to do my share."

What makes one man his wife's ally, while another sabotages his at every opportunity? Are some men "good guys" and others "bad guys"? The answer is not so simple. How a man feels about sharing the household duties depends on many things—his own upbringing, his current life goals and work situation, his sense of his own masculinity, whether he considers himself a success or a failure, how many children there are and how old they are, and what the basic marital relationship is like, among other factors.

How a wife deals with her husband's feelings also depends on many things—how much the family needs her income, how great her need is to get out of the house, how much reassurance her husband needs of his importance in her life. A husband's support shown through attitude and action is crucial. Balancing job and family demands is never easy, and it's much harder when a woman has to do the juggling all by herself.

These days, few men openly object to their wives' working. They recognize that the family needs the income. And that women work for all the additional reasons that men do. But, mired in unspoken (and often unrecognized) assumptions, a man often gives lip service to his wife's needs while still feeling that his work comes first and that her role is to help him.

As a lawyer married to a social worker confided, "My husband's job is emotionally depleting, and because he gets so worn down and is under so much pressure, he expects me to take care of petty errands and phone calls from my office. He's rarely willing to do any of that unless I remind him constantly, and reminding him is more work than the chore itself."

And a college professor described her husband as "verbally supportive": "He always wants to talk about my job and my problems with it, but he's not supportive when it comes to household tasks. Yesterday, on my day for preparing classes at home, I did six loads of laundry, shopped for groceries, and cleaned for house guests (his relatives)."

And most ironic of all, a real estate salesperson and mother of three small children said that her husband encourages her to work more, "but does not provide the emotional support at home that I feel I need." His profession? A psychiatrist.

So here are men who mean well, who want to do more, but who are not doing it. What can a wife do when she wants or needs to work outside the home, when she's overworked inside it, and her husband is either actively opposed or passively unhelpful? For the situation to change, one partner has to raise the issue. Since the partner who feels unfairly treated is usually the wife, she's generally the one who has to rock the boat. Many women have proved that it's possible to do this without capsizing the marriage. On the contrary, facing the issue squarely usually brings about smoother sailing.

Brenda B. Even, Ph.D., and Elizabeth B. Yost, Ph.D., both on the faculty of the College of Education at the University of Arizona in Tucson, have counseled hundreds of women, especially around life-change issues. In listening to the women, Drs. Even and Yost discovered a major difference between those who had their husbands' support and those who did not. They found almost invariably that the wives with supportive husbands had approached their husbands differently from the others.

Dr. Yost, assistant professor of counseling and guidance, and Dr. Even, assistant professor of secondary education, analyzed the different approaches the women had followed and the reactions of their husbands. The counselors then worked out a step-by-step plan to encourage a husband to be an ally rather than a saboteur. Many other professionals who work with couples in the throes of change confirm the basic principles in this plan, which calls for communication, love and encouragement.

Communication

The best time to talk about who does what, where, and when is early in the relationship—ideally before the first child is born or even before marriage. Couples who discuss their expectations about chores and child care ahead of time have an easier time handling them. But even after years of traditional divisions of labor, putting the issues on the table can result in more equal portions of work for both of you.

Whenever you want to raise thorny issues, the first consideration is picking a good time to talk, so you'll have enough time and enough privacy. You may even want to make an appointment ahead of time, so your husband won't be expecting to watch a ball game while you are expecting to let him in on your life plans or deep feelings. Some couples have their best heart-to-hearts at a quiet table in a neighborhood restaurant. There's a big advantage to dealing with important issues outside the house: being out in public makes it that much harder for a discussion that starts out sweet and reasonable to end up in tears, shouts, and name-calling.

The better prepared you are for this conversation, the more likely it is to go well. So before you sit down, have a fairly clear idea of what you want—and why you feel you're entitled to it. Then you will be ready to tell him why you want to make changes and how you want him to help.

Many men do not realize how much is involved in caring for children and in running a home. Never having had to make the many decisions and follow up the incredible number of details required for smooth functioning, they have no concept of the time and emotional energy that these activities demand. Often, a husband just needs to be told what is involved and how skewed the levels of responsibilities are between him and his wife for him to agree to do his fair share.

Furthermore, husbands and wives often have different perceptions about how much each one does. One woman answered my question about who does the housework and then added, "I'll bet my husband's responses would be very different from mine. He thinks he does more work than I think he does."

Sometimes this information is best conveyed by a dramatic demonstration of the disparity. Tanya, for example, took out legal pads, one for herself and one for her husband Larry and suggested that they both write down all the tasks each one performed relative to the children and the household, giving the approximate time each one took. When Larry realized that Tanya was writing away furiously long after he had stopped and that her time total was four times his, even though they both worked the same number of hours at their jobs, he said somewhat shamefacedly, "Not fair, is it?" A turning point in the marriage had been reached.

Many women think they are consulting with their husbands by moving in angrily with a series of demands, but, says Janice

LaRouche, coauthor of *Janice LaRouche's Strategies for Women at Work* and leader of career-planning and assertiveness workshops in New York City, "When the wife moves into a head-on confrontation, the husband gets up all his defenses, and they get nowhere."

Says Bernard F. Guerney, Ph.D., professor of human development at Pennsylvania State University and president of the Institute for the Development of Emotional and Life Skills, "I would advise a wife to express her true feelings to her husband, but to concentrate on the nonthreatening feelings first, so she's less likely to turn this into a power issue." The wife can talk as positively as possible about what she wants out of life, what some of her personal goals are, and what she would like her husband to do.

In line with the communication skills he outlines in his book *Relationship Enhancement*, Dr. Guerney advises the wife to present her situation briefly and then stop to get her husband's reaction. She goes then from being the presenter to being the listener when he concentrates on *his* feelings. Dr. Guerney advises an appeal to the husband's better nature first—his desire to help her and make her happy—before bringing up issues of fairness (as in phrases like "you owe this to me").

Amanda Robinson used this positive approach with good results. "For months before I went back to school, Greg and I talked constantly," she says. "First I told him how important it was to me to get my college degree. Later, when I had registered at school, I told him I would have classes two or three nights a week. Would he stay home with Brendan, who was then only eighteen-months old? We discussed the fact that we wouldn't be able to go out as much as in the past because money would be tighter until I could turn my degree into a job. And I appealed to him for more help with the housework. We really put in a lot of time hashing things out, and I know it paid off because now I couldn't ask for anyone more understanding and helpful."

Some women may resent having to plan a "strategy" to get their husbands' support. "Why should *I* be the one to bend over backward?" they may ask. "It's about time *he* took some responsibility for making changes. Besides, if I have to figure out every little thing—like when to talk to him and how to state what I want to say—isn't that manipulating him?"

Psychologist Elizabeth Yost says to such women: "There's a difference between manipulation and tact. Furthermore, you can't expect your husband to change overnight. Every marriage is a contract, and when you want to change the expectations both of you had when you married, you're breaking that contract."

The most important reason for a woman's making extra efforts is simply that otherwise she is not likely to get what she wants—her husband's support.

Says Janice LaRouche, "The woman who resents having to take responsibility for her husband's feelings has to remember that she's doing this not only for him, but for herself. She has to tell herself, 'It's my life and I want it to work and I'll take whatever steps I have to to make it work.' If you're going to carve out a career, you have to take the responsibility."

Love

A wise wife makes a special effort to show her husband that even though their life together may not conform to his initial expectations, she still loves and respects him. She is also sensitive to his special quirks or problems and she is content with one change at a time.

Linda Urbanczyk, for example, had to enroll at an out-of-town college and sleep away from home one night a week in order to get the courses she needed for a master's degree in counseling. Her husband Don, she suggested, could drop four-year-old Matthew off at nursery school on his way to work. A neighbor would pick Matthew up and take care of him until Don came home from work. Don would then take over. Don had always shared in Matthew's care because Linda had continued to work after his birth. While Don looked forward to spending more time alone with his son, every time he talked to Linda about her plans, he would ask anxiously, "But how will we eat?"

"I was tempted to tell him to just buy frozen food those nights, or to take Matthew out for pizza," says Linda, "but I knew Don had come from a food-oriented home. Furthermore, I recognized that he didn't need the food so much as he needed to know that I had cooked it for him."

TEN WAYS TO SAY "I LOVE YOU"

- Tuck a loving note in an unexpected place (brief-case, underwear drawer, engagement book).
- Phone during the day, even when there isn't a crisis, just to let your spouse know you're thinking of him.
- Mail a funny card to her place of work without wait-ing for a special occasion. (Write "Personal" on the front of the envelope if you don't want to be inti-mate with her secretary, too!)
- Make a gift of time. Give your spouse a two-hour block of time to do anything he wants you to—including chores you hate.
- Cook or buy a favorite food.
- Make a date to go out—and handle *all* the arrange-ments, including making the reservations, phoning and picking up the baby-sitter, and inviting friends your spouse is particularly fond of.
- Notice when his pajamas are torn or her bathrobe is held together with safety pins and surprise the other with an unbirthday present.
- Seduce her as ardently as if you were courting a new lover.
- Prepare and serve breakfast in bed.
- Bring home a book you know he wants to read and write a loving inscription in the flyleaf.

So Linda began planning meals to fit her schedule. Some weeks she made stew in double batches, freezing portions for Don and Matthew to reheat on their "bachelor" nights; at other times, she cooked a roast or put together a casserole the day before. "It meant more work for me," says Linda, "but it was worth it, especially since we would often have quick meals on the nights I was home. Once reassured that Linda would continue to think about his needs, Don became free enough to experiment in the kitchen himself and has since become the family's weekend chef.

Remembering to "be content with one change at a time," Linda realized that Don's taking full responsibility for Matthew on her days away was so important that she did not push him to take over any other household activities at that time.

Encouragement

Any way in which a spouse shows willingness to change—no matter how small the change is—can, and should be, recognized. When Dick, who never even knew where the baby-sitter's telephone number was written, assumed the responsibility of calling her for the first time, Claire wisely recognized his action for what it was—a first step in a totally new direction.

The wife who says, "What's the big deal? Am I supposed to do handsprings when he does one tiny thing? Look at all I've been doing for years!" is missing a valuable opportunity for encouraging her husband to do more. One of the major principles of behavioral psychology (as well as good common sense) rests on the proved fact that people thrive on recognition. The person whose small efforts are commended becomes motivated to make large efforts. If what the husband sees as a major concession is not appreciated by his wife, he tends to say, "Why bother?" Yet this encouragement is difficult for many women.

Paula Kaplan, a bookkeeper, told Elizabeth Yost, "Harry does the dishes every night, but he doesn't really want to and he grumbles so much that it ruins the whole thing." Dr. Yost pointed out that neither Paula nor Harry ever dreamed he'd be doing dishes on a daily basis and that she would do better to focus on the positive change in his *actions* instead of on the negative aspect of his *attitude*.

"How often do you say positive things to him?" asked Dr. Yost. Paula was silent for a while, then admitted that most of her comments to Harry these days come out as complaints. Dr. Yost suggested that Paula keep a "diary of encouragement," a written record of all the times she uttered a word of encouragement to Harry and that she systematically and gradually utter these words more frequently, especially in those areas where she wanted the most change.

"DIARY OF ENCOURAGEMENT"

Keep a diary for two weeks, in which you record all the positive things you say to your spouse, recognizing things he or she does now that contribute to the work of the household or that help you in your work. At the end of the two weeks, review your entries. Have you increased your recognition of his or her efforts? Can you?

At first Paula felt strained and artificial when she praised Harry or expressed appreciation, but soon she was saying things like this: "You don't know how wonderful it is for me to know that when I come down from putting the baby to bed, all the dishes will be done, and you and I can have a little time just to sit together and talk." Or, "You finish up the kitchen so fast, I can't get over it." By the time Paula noticed that Harry was complaining less about doing the dishes, she was finding it easier to express all the loving feelings she had for him.

Women too fall prey to old assumptions that we drank in with our mothers' milk and absorbed just as fully. When a wife complains that her husband isn't gentle enough with the baby or doesn't sweep the kitchen floor thoroughly enough, she may really be expressing her anxiety about losing a role that she identified with—that of ruler of the home front. Even though she's not happy with all the work that being a full-time wife and mother entails, she really doesn't want to give up any part of it because she derives so much of her identity and self-esteem from these aspects of her life. Very often she doesn't realize how deeply ingrained these feelings are until she is actually in a position where she can shed some of the responsibilities she also wants to keep. Caught in such a conflict, she may sabotage herself.

Margo Wolff, assistant to the sales manager in a plastics manufacturing firm, had often taken two- or three-day trips out of town before the birth of her baby. When Beth was three months old, Margo hired a baby-sitter, went back to work and was once more faced with the fact that she'd have to go out of town from time to time. When Beth was one year old, Margo was asked to attend a three-day conference. Her husband Tim agreed to take care of the baby mornings and evenings when the baby-sitter wasn't there, and Margo left. When she returned, she complained to counselor Brenda Even that she found Beth holding her arms out to her father more often than to her. Margo didn't like that. She expressed her unhappiness by criticizing the way Tim had dressed the baby, managed the meals, kept the house in her absence. Dr. Even helped Margo to understand why she felt as she did.

Says Margo now, "It didn't seem right for a baby not to prefer her mother; being Mother had become a part of my identity, as close to me as my name. Then I realized that I was also afraid of being unfeminine and a bad mother. Once I got straight about it—that I wanted two opposing things, to work *and* to be the kingpin in Beth's life—I saw how silly I was being. When I relaxed and let things take their course, I was grateful that Tim and Beth had such a wonderful relationship."

Many women hold to the "boss" role as they delegate work to their husbands. A woman will *say* she wants her husband to take on more managerial responsibilities, and yet when he does, she shoots him down for it. If she can back off from feeling that everything has to be done her way, she'll get more cooperation.

"The first time Ray did the marketing," Jane Scott told me, laughing, "I was so tickled that he had done it that I nearly went wild. You should have heard me squealing, 'Grapefruit! Lasagna! Fabulous! Look at all these great things I never think of buying! Will we eat!' I didn't criticize one thing he had bought, even though I knew some of the stuff would end up in the garbage. Now he does the marketing every week, and he's learned the kinds of things we need. And I still don't criticize him."

Jane's decision to hold her tongue is strategic. The husband who is criticized for the way he bathes the baby, scrambles the eggs, or sorts the laundry will not rush to do it again. Of course, there are those husbands who—deliberately or unconsciously—do a bad job just so they won't be asked to repeat the task. But whether a husband is genuinely doing his best or not, the wife who can pick up on positives and ignore the negatives is assuring herself of more help in the future.

It is one thing, though, to recognize that a husband's feelings are valid and to support and encourage his efforts to change and quite another to grovel before him, begging for favors. Shirley Sloan Fader, a working mother herself, collected the experiences of 500 job-holding wives for her book *From Kitchen to Career* and concluded that the wife's own feelings often shape the husband's reaction. Ms. Fader noted that as long as a woman felt her husband was helping *her,* there was trouble. For many of these 500 women, the breakthrough came when the wife realized that because supporting the family was now a joint husband–wife project, logically, home and children were also a joint responsibility.

One Chicago woman said, "As long as someone is doing you a favor, you have to wheedle and coax and be constantly grateful. It makes for emotional tension and eternal bickering. Once you realize that you've taken on a regular commitment to bring money into the family, then it's fair to insist that some of the home and child care should now be your husband's *regular responsibility.* My husband now does the weekly grocery shopping and the Monday, Wednesday, and Friday dinners, as well as some of the children's chauffeuring. He's not helping me, and he's not doing me a favor. They're *his* children, it's *his* home, and doing something regularly about caring for them is now *his* job."

Another way a wife can encourage her husband's participation is to recognize that every family is unique and that different men make their contributions in different ways. One may love his children but be too impatient to care for them for long stretches at a time, whereas he will be perfectly willing to take over the heavy cleaning. Another will do anything for the children and nothing in the house. And a third may feel that all the time and energy he puts into such traditionally masculine tasks as shoveling snow, tending the lawn, and making house and car repairs go unappreciated by his wife. A husband and wife can make trade-offs for the work each one does, to share it fairly.

Sometimes, doing chores together is the answer. Caryl and Carlo LaTorre, for example, often spend Sundays cooking in quantity. They both love to cook and enjoy the shared activity as well as the time together. The whole family appreciates the delicious meals they feast on all week long.

Chores, of course, are not the only issue in the two-job marriage, even though they are often a handy-dandy focus for other conflicts. It's easier to say "you never do the dishes" than "you don't care about me."

The basic point is that if love and understanding are at the wellspring of the marriage, good things flow into every branch of it. From this source comes the wish for each other to be happy and fulfilled. Out of this same font of good feeling comes your wish to be fair and your genuine desire not to burden one another with more than each of you can handle. You respect each other's strengths, offer help where the other is weak, show compassion on bad days, share the rejoicing on good ones. All these course together in the currents of a vital, life-sustaining relationship.

13

THE SINGLE
WORKING PARENT

———

"I know that however much difficulty I make for myself and others by my choice to support myself and my children and to live apart from my husband, it more than makes up for the slow death I had been living before," publishing assistant Carol Leonard told me. "The choices are hard and so is the struggle, but we're all healthier—even the plants!"

"Within weeks of trying to be both breadwinner and housewife—whirling at speeds several times what the machinery was built for—I began to notice pieces of myself breaking off, whizzing dangerously close to everyone within reach, especially my children," wrote single father Robert Miner in *Ms.* magazine.

Chances are that every single working parent has at different times in his or her life identified with both these feelings, both the joys and the pains of the kind of lives they lead.

The concerns of single parents are addressed throughout this book because your concerns include virtually all those faced by the married working parent. This chapter is here in recognition that you have other special concerns also. Whether you are single because you never married or because you have lost a spouse to death, divorce, or separation, your life is

285

more difficult in some ways than that of your married colleagues, just because of arithmetic. You don't need a calculator to tell you that when one person has to do all the work and the caring that is usually shared by two people, more time and more energy are called for.

For the most part, single parents do rise to the challenge. One recent study found that 75 percent of single-parent families are doing well, according to reports by both parents and children. Another has found that while the first two years after divorce are the hardest, most divorced adults and their children are able to forge satisfying new lives for themselves.

EFFECTS OF LIVING IN A SINGLE-PARENT FAMILY

Like most other things in life, the effects of single-parent life are not all one way. Let's look at both sides of this common situation.

Pluses of the Single-Parent Family

This life-style, with all its pressures, often holds benefits for both parents and children. One woman I know, for example, refers to her split-up as "a divorce made in Heaven," talking about how much happier and at peace both she and her children have been since her difficult marriage ended.

Many times the single parent finds it a relief to be able to make all the basic decisions about children, job, and general life-style without having to cope with a spouse who disagrees. "It's wonderful," one divorced teacher told me, "not to have somebody questioning my judgment all the time."

As sociologist E. E. LeMasters writes, "It is obvious to any clinician that the two-parent system has its own pathology: The two parents may be in serious conflict as to how their parental roles should be performed; one parent may be competent but have his (or her) efforts undermined by the incompetent partner; the children may be caught in a 'double bind' or crossfire between the two parents; both parents may be competent but simply unable to work together as an effective team in rearing their children; one parent may be more competent than the other but be inhibited by the team pattern inherent in the two-parent system.''

There are benefits after a divorce to the children, too. By and large, research has shown that even though the adjustment to the breakup of their parents' marriage is usually painful for children, they fare better in peaceful single-parent homes than in those with two adults always at each other's throats. And an inaccessible, rejecting, or hostile parent is worse for children than an absent one.

One survey of the way third-, sixth-, and eighth-grade children feel about themselves found no differences among children in intact families, in households in which a parent had remarried, or in single-parent homes. Those children with the poorest self-concepts, however, were the ones in homes wracked by fighting.

Children gain from divorce in other ways, too. As six-year-old Jamie said to her father, "I'm glad you're divorced. This way I get a lot of alone time with you and a lot of alone time with Mommy."

"In a way," Jamie's father said to me, "she gets the best of both worlds."

Social psychologist Robert S. Weiss points out other advantages that come to the children in a single-parent family, in his book *Going It Alone: The Family Life and Social Situation of the Single Parent* (see appendix "Recommended Reading"). In his studies and interviews, Dr. Weiss has found that the children in these families assume a different place in the life of the family than do those in families with two parents.

Because these youngsters have more responsibilities in seeing that the family runs smoothly, they tend to be treated more as equals than as subordinates. Even very young children become, in effect, "junior partners" in the running of the household. Their opinions are sought and listened to regarding times meals should be eaten, what food should be served, how chores should be parceled out, what major household purchases are needed, what vacation and weekend plans should be made, and how a move to a new apartment or house will affect the family.

As one mother told Dr. Weiss, "Now things are different. Instead of more or less being a family of mother and four children, we're all one family with all equal responsibility, and we all have a say, and we're all very important. And if it's going to work right, we all have to be able to cooperate with each other." Children who are treated this way tend to respond by acting more responsibly and by being more self-reliant.

Reading Victor and Mildred Goertzel's book *Cradles of Eminence* (see appendix "Recommended Reading") about the childhoods of 400 eminent Americans, I was struck by the high proportion of prominent people who had been raised by widows and widowers, by parents whose partners had deserted them and their children, and by mothers who never did marry the children's fathers. It's possible that, freed from the conflicting loyalties toward spouse and children, these people's parents reared them more intensely, devoting vast amounts of time and energy to the development of the children's talents and abilities.

Before you tell all your friends to leave their spouses for the good of the children, however, it's important to look at the other side of the picture.

Minuses of Single-Parent Life

Some of the problems in single-parent families are shared about equally by mothers and fathers, while others are felt more by one gender or the other. More than nine out of ten children of divorced parents stay with their mothers—although the proportion of father-headed one-parent families has soared by almost 300 percent since 1970. Those who live with their fathers tend to be school-age or older and are more often boys.

Both men and women share the problem of task overload and emotional overload. Too much to do, too little time to do it in, too much worry about what isn't getting done. Both share the anxiety of having to be both father and mother to their children; both feel the frequent pressures of having to be in two places at once; both feel the painful isolation and awesome responsibility of being the only parent in the home on a daily basis. Both feel the awkwardness of having to reorient their social lives around their new status, of finding out (often painfully) which of their married friends are no longer interested in seeing them, and of making new friends.

PROBLEMS FOR SINGLE FATHERS.   Men have more trouble coping with the minutiae of home life—the cooking, the cleaning, the laundry, the chores that oil the wheels of day-to-day living. Not surprisingly, research shows that the ones who do best after divorce were actively involved in child care and housework within the marriage.

The single greatest concern of single fathers, though, bores more deeply into the core of their feelings for their children. They tend to feel at sea when it comes to meeting their children's emotional needs. Because our society has not encouraged men to be in touch with and to express their own emotions, nor fostered their nurturing abilities, it is not surprising that this is *the* area in which most single fathers feel their inadequacies most strongly. Faced, however, with the need to be the nurturing parent, fathers do come through. Those fathers who cope best with these issues have sought extra counseling and education about children either before or after the divorce and have consciously worked toward forging a good relationship with their children.

Robert Miner, author of *Mother's Day*, a novel about a single father, wrote in *Ms.* magazine, "I began to find scattered about the house, like debris on a battlefield, bits of the emotional armor that I would never again be willing to wear. Because along with my rage and terror, I was now dealing with vast seas of warmth and love that I had never experienced before. Comforting an injured child, rocking away fierce monsters for a wide-eyed, midnight toddler, watching the baby wrinkle her nose at her first comprehended joke—such flawless intimacies made it clear to me that what I had taken before to mean 'family' would never again be satisfactory for me."

PROBLEMS FOR SINGLE MOTHERS.   The worst problem for most women is the economic one. The average income of the woman-headed family is less than half that of the two-parent family, a fact that helps explain the high proportion—eight out of ten—of single mothers who are in the labor force. This is one especially stark effect of the inequity in pay scales and job opportunities between men and women. While single fathers who keep up their child-support payments (unfortunately, a minority of those who are ordered to) also feel the pinch of contributing toward a second household, they are not affected so drastically as single mothers, who usually have to drop their living standards sharply after their marriages end.

Another area where women experience more difficulty than men is in dating. Men are often lonely too, of course, and unsure of starting over again in the dating arena. Still—even today, in these "liberated" times—men generally find it easier to meet and to go out with women. Divorced women are also less likely to remarry than are their ex-husbands.

The problems are, of course, there for children, too. Children hurt all over when their parents' marriages break up, feeling as much confusion as the separating couple—maybe more.

But the results of research by child-care professionals show that parents who are sensitive to their children's feelings can help them overcome their fear of being abandoned, resolve their feelings of guilt, and recover well enough to be able to form intimate relationships without repeating their parents' mistakes.

HOW PARENTS CAN HELP THEIR CHILDREN

The following guidelines, drawn from a number of family relations experts, should help parents handle the break.

- *Tell all the children about the divorce.* Though this seems obvious, social worker Judith S. Wallerstein and psychologist Joan B. Kelly, whose research findings are presented in their book *Surviving the Break-up: How Children Actually*

Cope with Divorce, find that some 80 percent of pre-schoolers are given no explanation because their parents think they are too young to understand. But according to child psychiatrist Richard A. Gardner, author of *The Parents Book About Divorce* and *The Boys and Girls Book About Divorce,* very young children frequently understand much more than parents realize. Children, he says, need to be told about an impending separation. Toddlers should be told often, in different words, until they understand what is happening.

- *If possible, both parents should tell all the children at the same time.* Too often the scene resembles that in the Gould household. "*You* want the divorce," Marian told her husband. "*You* tell the children." Jerry took their three children aside, one by one, and gave them his explanation. The children ran to their mother for confirmation and then anxiously compared notes—"What did they tell you that they didn't tell me?" The fissure between Marian and Jerry spread to isolate everyone in the family.

  Both parents should gather all the children and tell them together, a few weeks before the parting takes place, if possible. This way there is not only less chance of parents blaming each other, but also more trust between children and parents, more closeness among siblings, and more of a feeling that they will all continue to function as a family in certain ways. The children see that both parents are still deeply involved with their lives and will continue to be available to them.

- *Explain the situation in language the children understand.* What you tell them depends on how old the children are, how obvious your unhappiness has been, and what special circumstances may exist. One father said, "We used to love each other, but we've changed so much that we now make each other too unhappy to live together anymore." A mother pointed out, "You know how much we've been fighting; we've decided it would be better for everybody if we didn't live together, so we're going to get a divorce."

- *Tell the children only as much as they need to know.* It may be tempting to discuss openly what you see as causes for the divorce—an affair, alcoholism, compulsive gambling, sexual incompatibility—yet this talk may confuse and wound children far more than it helps them.

It is often misleading to tell children, "We're getting a divorce because Mommy has a boyfriend she loves more than me" or "because Daddy has a drinking problem," for such causes may be indicative of deeper and more complicated problems. Furthermore, explaining such details puts a heavy burden on children. Faced with an implication of parental wrongdoing or weakness, it's hard for them not to judge that parent. At a time when they need as much emotional support as possible, they may lose faith in at least one, and possibly both, of their parents.

• *Make the point very strongly that your children did not cause your divorce.* Whatever parents tell children and however carefully they couch their words, children process the information in their own way, transforming it into terms that make sense to them. Young children see the whole world as revolving around themselves and often assume that something they did or thought drove their parents to divorce. The guilt that ensues can torture a child.

When a social worker asked seven-year-old Amy why her parents had divorced, she said, "Because of me. Our apartment was too crowded. If it hadn't been for me, my Mommy and Daddy would have liked living in our apartment and wouldn't have fought so much."

• *Emphasize the finality of your decision.* The fantasy of parental reunion is almost universal. Many children try to sabotage any new love relationships in hope of keeping the path open for their parents to reunite. As long as they dream of this eventuality, they are unable to progress in accepting reality. Once children give up feeling that they caused the divorce (and therefore have the power to bring their parents together again), they can think more constructively about ways to lessen the pain of the rupture. Parents who remain on good terms sometimes unwittingly fuel children's fantasies of parental reunion. After one eight-year-old said, "If you still kiss each other hello and goodbye, that means you love each other and should get married again," her mother quickly answered, "We *like* each other—but we're *not* going to get married again."

- *Explain, carefully and in detail, how the children will be cared for.* More universal than guilt and self-blame is the overwhelming fear of abandonment. Although children may not speak up about that fear, they do need reassurance that they will continue to be cared for. After custody arrangements have been worked out, parents should explain them in detail. Meredith will live with her mother during the week and her father on weekends, for example, or Jason will be with his father for the school year and his mother during the summer.

  When parents are fighting for custody, they can say something like, "We both want you to live with us, so we're asking a judge who knows a lot about children to help us decide what will be best for you. Whatever happens, you'll be well taken care of and you'll still see both of us."

- *Reassure your children that both of you will continue to love them.* Dr. Matti Gershenfeld, a psychologist at Temple University in Philadelphia, urges parents to emphasize one message: "There is no such thing as divorce between parent and child." She stresses the importance of telling children over and over of both parents' continuing love for them. "No matter what happens," a parent might say, "I'll always be your mother [or father]. No matter what you do or what changes occur in our lives, you'll always be my child. I'll never stop loving you."

- *Encourage children to express their feelings of fear, sadness, and anger.* The breakup of any marriage leaves much for children to mourn—the loss of one parent, the loss of a familiar situation, the loss of membership in a complete family. Intrinsic in the mourning process is the rage that surfaces in many ways and is usually felt most by the custodial parent.

  When nine-year-old Tony had a tonsillectomy and his father failed to visit him, he didn't say anything. But he hit and screamed at his mother when she came to the hospital. When children can express their feelings openly, they can begin to understand and deal with them. Parents can help by admitting their own sadness, anger, and confusion. They can also seek out a discussion group for children of divorce. Such groups are often sponsored by schools, mental health clinics, and other community agencies. Those who participate realize that other children have many of the same problems. Discussions help them to deal with various situations and cope with disturbing feelings about themselves and their parents.

- *Set limits on your children's behavior.* Understanding the roots of anger does not mean letting children act it out. On the contrary, the single parent needs to maintain firm, friendly discipline. Children need to know that someone stronger loves them enough to stop them from losing control. When a child gets out of hand, a parent may benefit from learning behavior-modification techniques that help deal with specific irritating behavior such as rudeness or disobedience.

- *Enlist the help of other adults.* Teachers, scout leaders, volunteers from Big Brothers or Big Sisters (see appendix "Helpful Organizations"), relatives, or friends can often demonstrate a caring concern that helps a child through a crisis. When Brian told his teacher in June about his parents' coming separation, she made sure he would be with his best friend in the room of an especially sensitive teacher the next fall.

- *No matter how angry you are with your spouse, declare a truce around your children.* One of the most important determinants of how children come through a divorce is the parents' relationship with each other after they decide to part. When six-year-old Ginny drew a picture of her mother, her father, and herself all holding hands, her mother said gently, "This is a beautiful picture, Ginny, but we're not a family anymore." Yet in many ways they are a family—because of Ginny. Her parents are still her parents and both have her welfare at heart. The more they can retain this sense of connection, the better off Ginny will be.

After studying the parenting of forty-one divorced people, Constance R. Ahrons, professor of sociology at the University of Southern California and coauthor of *Divorced Families,* found that those couples who were most successful at coparenting had flexible visiting arrangements. They rarely discussed other aspects of their lives with each other and tried to avoid talking about issues that might start an argument. Divorced parents don't have to be friends, but it's a great help to their children if they can cooperate on child-rearing issues.

- *Don't use your children as weapons.* Children suffer when they are forced to transmit angry messages or relay information, when they are asked to choose sides, or when family visits serve as a battleground. Parents who use their children this way are sacrificing the children's welfare for their own immediate satisfactions.
- *Change your children's lives as little as possible.* Any change is stressful—even a positive one—so the fewer adjustments children have to make, the more energy they have to cope with the major one. If you can avoid other major changes—like moving to a new neighborhood or taking a new, more demanding job—do so. If you have to make a big change, offer your children extra support and understanding.
- *Recognize the real conflict between your needs and your children's.* "This is a difficult issue to resolve," says Stephen L. Zaslow, M.D., a psychiatrist in private practice and director of the Long Island Institute of Psychoanalysis. "Right after a marriage breaks up, children need much more of the company of the parent they're living with. If that parent rushes into the dating scene, it can stir up anxieties about abandonment. But parents need time away from children's demands to pursue their own adult lives. This is a dilemma without an easy answer. All that parents can do is make a determined effort to meet everyone's needs."

Divorcing parents face a difficult situation. At a time when their children's needs are greatest, they are struggling to keep themselves together and have the least to give. Yet many parents find that summoning up extra strength to help their children helps strengthen them as well. Making the effort to see the positive aspect of the change, for parents and children alike, may be the most helpful approach to a family breakup.

STAYING ON FRIENDLY
TERMS AFTER DIVORCE

All the research on how children fare after divorce shows that children of every age do best—in personal adjustment, in school, in making friends, on virtually every psychological measure—when their parents cooperate and avoid open hostility. "Parents don't have to be good friends," says Judith S. Wallerstein, Ph.D., executive director of the Center for the Family in Transition in Corte Madera, California, who has followed sixty divorcing families over a ten- to fifteen-year period. "But they do have to be able to be civilized and to cooperate around the children. Continuing conflict is very frightening for children and creates havoc with their sense of security. Cooperation is doubly valuable: it provides a good environment for them, and it shows them good examples of rational people who act like adults."

Not surprisingly, divorced parents tend to be in closer touch with each other than divorced nonparents, and it's often the shared investment in their children's welfare that spurs them to put themselves out in ways that may inconvenience them but benefit the children (like spending holidays together and being generous with money and flexible on scheduling).

How, though, can ex-spouses, who often harbor deep grievances against each other, overcome their anger and hurt to let their positive feelings take over? As the rate of divorce climbed over the past two decades, social scientists have been looking carefully at postdivorce relationships and focusing attention on those formerly married people who don't throw out their friendship with their "His" and "Her" towels. These ex-spouses nurse each other in sickness and toast each other on special occasions. They ask each other's advice on issues ranging from major career decisions to problems with a current lover. They do favors for one another, are each other's most important support in times of crisis, and some still find sexual joy and release together.

Who are these people? They include people like Timothy Perper and Martha Cornog, whose wedding party four years ago included Tim's first wife Maria, as matron of honor, and Maria's boyfriend Bob, as best man. Both couples have dinner at each other's homes throughout the year and celebrate Christmas and other special occasions together.

Then there are Earl and Sue. For three years after they had split up, until Earl took a new job out of town and he and Sue formalized their divorce, they continued to do their banking through the same joint checking account they had opened early in their marriage, to submit a joint income tax return, and to split the tax payments on a piece of property they continued to own jointly.

And five years after Kathy and Ted's divorce, they call each other a couple of times a week and go out for dinner with each other every month or so to discuss their children, their jobs, and their new dating partners.

These people and others like them have a number of characteristics in common. They include the following:

- *Recognizing the other person's good qualities.* As Tim Perper told me, "Not being able to live with a person in marriage need not mean hatred and loathing afterwards. Maria and I had basic differences in our personalities and in our outlooks toward work and life, but we didn't forget that we liked each other."

  And Earl says of his former wife, "I still like her—I still *love* her—I just can't live with her. But I still want her in my life. We shared lots of experiences in fourteen years of marriage. She's part of my life, part of who I am, my best friend."

- *Recognizing that the qualities they* DON'T *like in each other are part of the other person's personality.* Kathy, a thirty-five-year-old secretary, told me, "The same traits that attracted me to Ted in the first place sowed the seeds of our divorce. I fell in love with his enthusiasm, his youthful rebelliousness, the courage that *I* didn't have to take risks and try new things. He showed me how to have fun, and in our ten years of marriage we never had a bad vacation. He was exciting to be with."

  But the kinds of risks that Ted took seemed increasingly irresponsible to Kathy. "Even after our two little girls were born, his first priority was having fun. Ted is a great

salesman—he can sell anything—but he was taking risks
at work that led him to change jobs six times in those ten
years, and he was buying all sorts of playthings that we
couldn't afford."

Since their divorce Kathy has been able to accept what
Ted can and can't do. For the past five years he has never
once sent the monthly child-support check without being
asked for it, but now that she isn't affected on a daily level,
his lack of responsibility doesn't bother her the way it used
to. "I know he's not acting this way just to make me miserable; this is who he is," she says now. "So I call him every
month to remind him, and he sends it out right away, and
when I see him I can enjoy his company and appreciate
what he can offer. He's more patient with the children
than I am, he takes them sailing and skiing—both of
which terrify me, and we have a lot of laughs together."

- *Trying not to hurt each other more than each has already been
  hurt.* "We didn't play dirty tricks on each other and we
  never called one another nasty names," said one ex-hus-
  band. And Alan Orenberg, a Middleton, Wisconsin, personnel recruiter, points to the "selective myopia" that
  helps him and his former wife stay friendly. "When you're
  married you learn how to fight, but after the divorce you
  learn how to avoid a fight. We're both on our best behavior when we talk now." He adds, "We still differ in the
  areas where we differed before, but we've both learned
  how to back off from our differences and to concentrate
  on what we like and respect about each other."
- *Understanding that simple unhappiness is enough of a reason to
  end a marriage.* Cynthia Laitman Orenberg, a medical
  writer in Madison, Wisconsin, who speaks to Alan almost
  every day about their children, about household problems, and just as one friend to another, says, "Marriage
  counseling helped me see that simple unhappiness was
  enough of a reason to end a marriage. It's easy to leave
  when you're married to a louse. But when your husband is
  a decent man and the two of you are just not right for each
  other, the temptation is always there to make him a terrible person, to find things to blame him for to justify what
  you're doing. This is something both Alan and I fought
  against."

- *Being fair, or even generous about money matters.* The ground is usually prepared for friendly divorces before any legal steps are taken, in the overall attitude adopted by both partners. The first major test is usually the division of property. Couples on good terms usually arrive at an amicable agreement, often going through their assets item by item, sometimes writing everything down as they go along, constantly trying to achieve fairness and take into account sentimental values as well as economic ones. These couples don't use money and property as weapons, don't focus on the good china as a symbol of bad feelings. They're not fighting over the spoils of battle—they're sharing the legacy of a happier past.

  "Of course, I would have loved her carved oak desk," one man told me. "We found it in a junk store, and I restored it so that it was now one of our most valuable pieces, but she loved it, too, and throughout our marriage it had been hers. So it would have been wrong for me to take it now." Sue and Earl urged each other to take more than either one wanted; Tim and Maria split a matched set of bowls so that each partner took one in a symbolic gesture of equality and division.

  Some feel that the relative meagerness of their material goods made cutting the marital pie easier; others believe that being on fairly equal financial footings helped; and still others credit each partner's lack of economic deprivation. The last explanation confirms the impression of Suzanne Jones, executive director of the Single Parent Resource Center in New York, who says, "It's very rare to find people in low economic brackets who have a friendly relationship. People who are struggling financially experience a lot of conflict around money, and the friendly divorce seems to be mostly a middle-class phenomenon."

- *Avoiding adversarial legal proceedings.* In the typical adversarial divorce, all good feelings between two people may dissolve as each person's attorney strives to fix blame so as to get the most for his or her client. Partners who want an amicable divorce do not hire lawyers with reputations as "hired guns" or "barracudas." Kathy, for example, was so upset at hearing her highly recommended lawyer talk about how he was going to "get" Ted that she walked out of his office and found someone else who agreed not to introduce rancor. Tim and Maria had one attorney represent them both. Earl rejected several lawyers who "all made heavy weather out of it and wanted to charge a lot of money," turned to the Yellow Pages and found an attorney who had both partners fill out and return the necessary papers; the lawyer sent them in, and in six weeks, for a fee of $75, the couple had their divorce. Others have turned to family mediation to work out a separation agreement, which each partner then checked out with their own attorneys. See the box "Family Mediation."

One of the first social scientists to explore the tie between divorced couples is Robert S. Weiss, Ph.D., now director of the Work and Family Research Unit of the University of Massachusetts in Boston, who writes, "Separation is an incident in the relationship of spouses, rather than an ending of that relationship."

"If you say all those years were rotten and evil and the person you were married to all those years is a terrible person, you have to lie to yourself and say that you were never happy—or you have to say that you were a fool," says Timothy Perper. "Either way you're doing damage to your feelings about yourself—and about this other person."

Professional therapists tend to agree. "Couples who can maintain friendly feelings are often freer to move on with their own lives. They find it easier to form new ties and to avoid living in the frustrations of the past," says Brooklyn family therapist Barbara Rothberg, Ph.D.

No one, of course, "falls out of love" easily. And no divorce comes about smoothly. Before any couple gives up their hopes and dreams for a shared life, there are invariably tears, angry words, hurt feelings, and a growing distance. There are places where each person rubs the other raw in an unceasing collision of differences. The very personality traits that may have been so appealing at first are now burdensome in the other's eyes: his stability becomes boring, her enthusiasm childish, his neatness compulsive, and her unconventionality eccentric. Then one day the gap between what each one wants in a mate and what the other person can give becomes too great.

FAMILY MEDIATION: WHAT IT CAN DO AND HOW TO FIND A MEDIATOR

Mediation is a cooperative problem-solving process in which a trained, objective person helps disagreeing individuals define and reach an agreement on the issues in dispute. This process is especially appropriate in situations in which the parties will have continuing relations, such as the workplace and the family. A family mediator can help a couple negotiate a separation agreement that will cover the division of assets and other financial arrangements; custody, visitation rights, and day-to-day care of children; and other issues that the two partners have trouble working out on their own. For mediation to work, spouses do not have to be on friendly terms, but they both do have to be willing to participate and cooperate.

Mediators are not necessarily attorneys or human relations professionals and do not make decisions, impose settlements, or give legal advice or psychological counseling. Agreements may be written up as informal working guidelines or filed with the court as legal contracts; in either case, they can be changed by mutual agreement. Depending on the complexity of the issues, mediation generally involves anywhere from one to ten hours of consultation. Fees are usually relatively modest and are often worked out on a sliding scale based on the family's income. The following organizations make referrals to mediators in various communities around the country:

- Academy of Family Mediators, P.O. Box 10501, Eugene, OR 97440 (503) 345–1205.
- Association of Family and Conciliation Courts, c/o Oregon Health Sciences University, Department of Psychiatry, Gaines Hall, Room 149, 3181 S.W. Sam Jackson Park Road, Portland, OR 97201 (503) 279–5651.
- American Arbitration Association, 140 West 51st Street, New York, NY 10020 (212) 484–4000.

And through the pain, one or both decide they don't want to live this way.

"In most divorces," says Ronnie Crane, a Long Island (New York) psychiatric social worker who has counseled hundreds of divorced men and women, "one person is the injured party. One wanted the divorce, and the other didn't. When this happens, the one who has been left is often consumed by a desire to get even to get over the misery of rejection and helplessness, and the one who left may feel so guilty that he or she justifies leaving the marriage by manufacturing anger toward the partner. Then the anger takes on a life of its own."

People end their marriages with enormous ambivalence," says Dr. Weiss. "The negative feelings are the ones fostered by the legal process, but the positive feelings are there, too, if only the couple can bring them to the surface." One way of doing this is, as Ronnie Crane counsels separating couples, "to search for your own generous and loving self, as well as the other person's." Divorced herself, she heeds her own counsel as she reminds her children—and herself—of her former husband's basic decency and personality strengths.

Those people who can find the right balance between moving on with their new lives and still holding onto the good parts of the old are usually blessed with self-confidence and a sense of comfort with who they are.

Not everyone, of course, is in such robust mental health. Further, the scars from some marriages are more inflamed than others, and some people have been so deeply hurt and disillusioned that they want to have as little as possible to do with those of whom they once expected so much.

But if you can keep your former spouse as a current friend, you can reap the benefits of having someone in your life who knows you very well, someone with whom you've shared experiences that no one else will ever understand in the same way, someone who will always be part of your children's lives and can share the challenges and the joys of parenthood, and, finally, someone who can offer continuity in your life.

HOW PARENTS ADJUST TO DIVORCE

Some years ago my friend Barbara's husband took a deep breath and told her that he was moving out of the house and out of their twenty-two-year marriage.

"At first I didn't think I could survive without Dan," Barbara told me. "And instead of feeling better over the next couple of years, I felt worse. I kept begging him to come back to me.

"When my friends told me I'd reach the point where I wouldn't even want him back, I'd shake my head in disbelief. But now I do feel that way." Barbara looked younger and happier than I had seen her look in years. I told her so.

"Finally," she said, smiling. "Finally, I feel like a whole person. I never want to live through anything like that again. At the same time, I have grown so much, I feel so free and so optimistic that I can't say I'm sorry I am where I am."

Barbara is not the only divorced person whose spirits have sunk lower and lower before they began to rise. This is a very common pattern, not only for divorced women, but for their husbands and children as well. There are, in fact, many predictable patterns to divorce (and its aftermath), as a major in-depth study shows. The study, conducted by E. Mavis Hetherington, Ph.D., a psychology professor at the University of Virginia, examined how people cope with difficult transitions. Dr. Hetherington and her colleagues spent thousands of hours on detailed interviews with ninety-six families. Forty-eight of the families were in the throes of a divorce, and forty-eight were intact (the intact families served as a comparison group). The researchers met with the families at regular intervals: two months, one year, and two years after the legal divorce.

Two Months Later

The study's most illuminating finding was its discovery that there are certain relatively predictable patterns in the ways people adjust to divorce. In a nutshell, things get worse before they get better. Two months after the divorce, euphoria often reigns for the partner who initiated the divorce, especially if there is a "transition" person. (While a third person doesn't break up a happy marriage, his or her support can provide the strength to end an unhappy one.) Both partners are likely to be living chaotic home lives, however, at this time, characterized by an irregularity in mealtimes, trouble sleeping, and an almost complete absence of routine. This departure from an accustomed orderliness in day-to-day living is often felt more keenly by the man, partly because he is usually the one who leaves his home and children and because he is usually less accustomed to handling the practical details of shopping, cooking, and cleaning. In any case, he often feels rootless and homeless, at sea about who he is.

One Year Later

One year after the divorce is the worst time of all for both men and women. "I never thought I would mind so much not being somebody's wife," says Joan. "It might be easier if I had a decent social life. I feel as if I'm married to Captain Kangaroo—he's the only adult man I ever see."

At this stage, three out of four women and a majority of men feel their divorce was a mistake. They see less of their married friends, who seldom call them; they are turned off by the casual sex implicit in their dating life (if, in fact, they are dating at all); and they are frenetically searching in all directions to improve their lives—night classes, creative workshops, self-improvement courses. They both feel like failures as parents—the man because he sees less of his children and the woman because she is often having trouble handling them, especially when they are sons. The adults also have problems on the job because they are under so much emotional strain that they have trouble concentrating on their work.

Two Years Later

By two years after the legal divorce, however, things are looking up for both partners. By now the husband is likely to be in better shape than his ex-wife, especially if he has an intimate relationship with a woman. He is more likely than his former wife to have remarried.

Divorced women still have problems centering on money and their social lives, but life is still usually much better than it had been the previous year. They are likely to have made new women friends who are a source of support; they are enjoying a better relationship with their children; and the percentage of women who feel their divorce was a mistake has reversed itself, so that only one in four now feels that way.

Those people who decide that divorce is their only answer should be very aware that change, even desirable change, is always stressful. It is unrealistic to replace the old myth of falling in love, getting married, and living happily ever after with a new myth of falling out of love, getting divorced, and living happily ever after. Coping with a major change in life—the adult's shift to a single status and the child's adjustment to the seeming loss of a parent—is never easy or painless.

HOW PARENTS CAN HELP THEMSELVES

You can take a number of concrete steps to make it easier for you to cope. Based on a number of studies and my talks with both single working parents and human relations professionals, the following seem to be the most valuable.

Ask for Help from Other People

The pioneer spirit with which this country was founded has left many of us with the feeling that we should be independent, that we should be doing things on our own, that we shouldn't have to ask for help from anyone. And yet throughout history, part of humankind's predilection for living in groups has been based on the ability of family, friends, and neighbors to help each other. Reaching out for this kind of help is especially important at a time of family crisis, like divorce. The box "Practical Strategies That Help Single Parents Cope" lists a number of ways that other people can help.

In a study of successful single-parent families conducted by Family Service Association of the Mid-peninsula in Palo Alto, California, almost all the parents listed family and friends as major sources of moral support and practical help. Time and again in my own conversations with single parents, I heard a variation of the theme expressed by Jean, a Cleveland, Ohio, community organizer: "I don't know how I would have managed without my women friends. They have come through for me time and time again, as shoulders to cry on when I was

PRACTICAL STRATEGIES THAT HELP SINGLE PARENTS COPE

- Sharing a baby-sitting co-op with friends
- Making good use of car pools for children's activities
- Dividing housework among family members
- Using outside household help when possible
- Allowing children to assume responsibility for jobs previously considered "adult"
- Keeping the standard of living within what is reasonable for one's income
- Explaining one's activities to one's children
- Spending time with children individually
- Planning enjoyable activities for parent and child to do together
- Respecting the privacy of the children
- Organizing a skills-exchange group with friends
- Getting together regularly with other single parents
- Organizing communal celebrations at holidays with other single parents, both with and without children
- Enlisting friends and relatives to go with you when you deal with schools or other community institutions
- Pursuing special interests through organizations, school, or hobbies

feeling blue, as people I could talk to who understood what I was going through, and just as companions to have fun with." Or, by Tom, a Las Vegas croupier, "When my wife left me, I could never have managed with the kids and my job if my sister hadn't come through. She saved our lives."

Single parents who don't already have a network of friends and families to call on have been getting together to form their own networks, through the help of community-support groups that are springing up around the country. The most well-known is Parents Without Partners (PWP) (see appendix "Helpful Organizations").

As one newly single parent told writer (and working parent) Ellen Klavan, "I've never been much of a joiner, so I was a little reluctant about going to a Parents Without Partners meeting. But I found a group with a lot of people at my stage and a few who had gotten through the initial bad time. It was so uplifting for me to see these people who had gone on with their lives in a really positive way. And I made lots of good friends I continue to see outside the group."

Most good-sized communities have other support groups. In New York, for example, the Single Parent Resource Center (see appendix "Helpful Organizations") has been offering a variety of services to parents since 1975, including peer counseling, information on public services, and help in life planning. It holds regular meetings, outings, and parties; maintains a library with books and articles on single parenthood, child support, custody, and other related topics; and keeps a list of single-parent programs around the country and helps those who want to start new groups. "What these support groups are saying is, We can't wait for professionals to help us; in fact, we don't often need professionals," says Suzanne Jones, executive director of the center. "We can help each other."

Other single parents have joined extended "families" of unrelated people. Marion Knight, for example, was a widow living with her two daughters in Cincinnati, Ohio. They had no relatives nearby, and for a long time Marion was concerned that the only men her girls ever saw were those who came to take her out to dinner. That was before she learned of and joined an extended family of nineteen unrelated people.

"Now the girls have a chance to relate informally to men of different ages," Marion told me. "They even have an adoptive grandmother. And I have grown very close to several people whom I can share problems and confidences with."

Whether you operate within a group like this one, which was formally organized by a religious congregation, or just with your own family, friends, and neighbors, you can often accomplish more together than any one family can do on its own. Single parents report, for example, benefiting from swapping baby-sitting with other parents, car-pooling, and taking turns marketing, cooking, and doing laundry for another family at the same time they do their own. One woman set up a skills-exchange group, in which members pooled their talents for home repairs, checkbook balancing, birthday-party planning, and so forth. No single-parent family need remain an island unto itself.

Get Help from Community Agencies

Schools, day-care centers, churches, scout troops, and other community institutions often respond positively when single parents spell out their special needs. Here are some suggestions specifically oriented toward your child's school:

- Early in the term, call your child's teachers. Explain your situation as a working single parent and assure them of your interest in your child's progress. Alert the teacher to any special problems your child has (her difficulty in adjusting to your spouse's death or his embarrassment about your recent divorce). A caring teacher often becomes the central stable figure in the life of a child whose home life has changed radically.
- Tell the teacher the times of day when you can come in for conferences. Some teachers will come in at 7:30 AM or even come to your home in the evening if your work schedule makes it impossible for you to get away during usual school hours. If you can't work out a time when the two of you can meet in person, you may be able to accomplish almost as much in a scheduled telephone conference.
- If your school is still sending letters home to "Mr. and

Mrs. John Smith,'' tell the teacher, principal's office, and PTA of your child's parental status. If your ex-spouse is still involved in your child's care, ask the school to send copies of all letters home to the other parent as well as yourself. Studies have shown that the more involved non-custodial parents are in their children's lives, the better off the children are. So anything that encourages this involvement is to the good.

- If teachers or other school personnel are still using terms like "broken home" to describe single parent–family homes and are holding up the intact nuclear family as the only "normal" kind, some consciousness raising is in order. It is perfectly appropriate for you to phone and/or write to point out that such characterizations wound your child and yourself. (Robbie Kleiman, age five, asked his mother, "Is our home broken? It doesn't *look* broken!" Carol explained that some people use that expression but reassured him, "There are lots of homes like ours. And they're still homes." And then she shook with anger at people who would say such things to a little child.)

- If your school schedules such parent-designated events as "Father and Son" banquets or "Mother and Daughter" sports nights, urge them to change these events so that a parent of either sex can participate. Even though some of these events may have long histories, tradition is no excuse for discriminating against a child who does not have a parent of the "right" sex.

- Ask your school's principal, social worker, psychologist, or guidance counselor about any special programs for children of single parents. Many schools conduct discussion groups, show films, and provide books specially geared to the concerns of children and divorce, and a growing number have begun to incorporate death education into the curriculum. Sensitive treatment of these issues can help a child over the worst of the rough spots.

Many single parents have found that in dealing with schools and other institutions—especially when you are questioning or trying to change some long-entrenched practice—it helps to bring someone with you. One of the hardest things about being single is the feeling that you have to fight all your battles alone. This needn't be so. No matter how busy your friends and relatives are, you can almost always find someone to spare a couple of hours to go with you on an important personal errand such as, for example, meeting with the principal of your child's school. If no one from your own personal circle can do this, maybe you can reach out to a single parent–support network, like the ones described above. A companion on these visits not only gives you moral support but also carries more weight with the person you're meeting with.

If your spouse is dead—or, though alive, does not take an active role in your child's life—you may want to make a special effort to encourage your child to form a close, stable relationship with an adult of the absent parent's sex. If a relative, family friend, or neighbor has the personality and the interest to become an important person in your child's life, you're lucky. If not, you may be able to enlist a teacher, a scout leader, a member of the clergy, or an older teenager to fill this void in your youngster's life. Or you can turn to the Big Brothers or Big Sisters organizations (see appendix "Helpful Organizations"), which enlist adult volunteers to spend time on a regular basis with fatherless boys and motherless girls.

Take Care of Yourself

Between caring for your child and doing your job (which you need more than ever now, not only for the money but also for self-fulfillment and the company of other adults), it's hard to find the time you need to take care of yourself. You're likely to feel so harassed that you'd readily agree with the divorced mother who told Dr. Hetherington, "I feel as if I'm being bitten to death by ducks."

But you owe it to yourself and to your children to spend some time and energy on self-nurturance. One way you can take emotional care of yourself is to give yourself a talking-to on days when you feel low. While these days this sort of affirmation goes by the impressive name of "cognitive therapy," it is what our grandparents referred to as "pep talks." For some statements that work for other parents, see the box " 'Pep Talks' That Single Parents Give Themselves."

"PEP TALKS" THAT SINGLE PARENTS GIVE THEMSELVES*

- I accept present reality.
- I try to give myself space and time to do things that make me feel good.
- I live in the present and don't dwell on the past.
- I try to be realistic in my expectations, remembering that I am only one average human being.
- I thrive on knowing that I make it or fail on my own skill, luck, stubbornness, or whatever.
- I cannot be a father and a mother, too.
- Other people cope with this, and so can I.
- I tell the truth about my feelings and don't feel guilty about being resentful or angry.
- I look for success in what I attempt and build on it.
- I will not blame myself for being a single parent or use not having a husband/wife as an excuse or a blame.
- I have made a conscious decision to succeed. If it's going to work, I'm going to have to make it work!
- Not every problem that my children have is due to the presence of only one parent in the home.

*These are some of the mental strategies evolved by successful single parents to keep themselves functioning positively, as reported to researchers in a study undertaken by Family Service Association of the Mid-peninsula, Palo Alto, California.

You need to be good to yourself for everyone's sake. The parent who is totally engrossed in family and work, one responsibility pressing hard upon another, robs children of a parent who's fun to be with and who shows them that life itself can be fun. Just as your body needs rest so that you can keep going physically, your soul needs a holiday so that you can keep going emotionally.

A handful of divorced couples share the care of their children through joint custody, which can take a variety of forms. In its "pure" version, it involves each parent's having custody of the child for about half the time. A more common arrangement is one in which the custodial parent (usually the mother) cares for the child during the week and the noncustodial parent (usually the father) takes over on weekends.

As one mother told me, "I'm glad Amy has such a good relationship with her father. He gives her a lot that I can't give her—partly because of money, because he can afford to take her places that I can't. But also because he has more patience than I do. Al can sit down and play with Amy for three hours at a stretch, which I could never do. So the fact that he takes her every weekend is great for her. It's also great for me. The sense of freedom I get on my weekends off is really delicious—these are the only times, for example, when I feel at all comfortable having a man spend the night."

If your ex-spouse can't or won't take over like this, maybe you can set up regular monthly visits when your children stay for a couple of days with your parents or your sister or brother and their families. Or you could swap one weekend a month with friends. You'll find taking care of their children a breeze when you realize the upshot will be a free weekend for you.

You're also entitled to a night out during the week, as well, without feeling as if you're neglecting your children. They can get along without you in the care of a friend, a relative, or a baby-sitter, and you can use the time to stoke up your own internal fires—by going out to a singles' event, by taking in a movie with a friend, or by pursuing some interest you may have ignored for years because your ex-spouse wasn't interested in it, say, square dancing or tennis or amateur theater.

The better you feel about your life, the better you'll be able to function, both as a parent and as a worker.

14

THE HEALTHY FAMILY

Over the past couple of decades, the American family has whirled through a dizzying succession of changes. As the very existence of this book suggests, "family" no longer means breadwinning father, aproned mother, 2.3 children, and a dog. And as Chapter 13 underscored, one common variation these days is that of a single parent raising one or more children. A family, however, can also come in many other guises. It may involve unmarried people living together, homosexual parents raising children conceived through artificial insemination, and various combinations of remarried people, along with their children from previous marriages and a complex network of relatives. As Joan Lawrence Baer of Basking Ridge, New Jersey, wrote in a letter to *The New York Times*, "Here a family celebration doesn't count unless my second husband's second wife's brother is present. Moreover, my first husband's half-brother's second wife's second husband is also godfather to my youngest child!"

Despite these changes and despite the increased tendency of government and various community agencies to take over many traditional family tasks, even in today's modern, high-tech world, the family still does many things better than any other institution in society. And most of us still find our families the center of our lives.

At their best, families do two things well. "A healthy family preserves the sanity and encourages the growth of the parents and produces healthy, independent children," says Jerry M. Lewis, M.D., director of research at Timberlawn Psychiatric Research Foundation in Dallas, Texas.

How do families perform these two vital tasks? A growing number of social scientists have been looking closely at families who seem to be doing a good job and have identified some of the ways they operate.

WHAT DO HEALTHY FAMILIES DO?

The healthiest families are made up of individuals who feel free to be different from each other, to disagree about tastes and values, to live their own lives, and to retain a measure of privacy. Families that encourage individuality have members who develop strong, interesting, distinctive personalities. They know where their identity ends and that of other family members begins.

"You can't talk in absolutes, of course, when you're looking at a family's emotional health," says Bloomington, Indiana, psychologist Laurence Barnhill, Ph.D. "Instead, you have to look for a balance. Too much togetherness and members don't feel like individuals; too much individuality and people feel isolated or alienated."

Happy families are not all alike, but they do share some common perspectives on life. They are generally positive thinkers: optimistic about the way their lives will turn out, trusting that other people will treat them well, and ready to take the initiative to change their lives. They often find help in dealing with life either through strong religious beliefs or through a set of ethical principles. The members of strong families show their commitment to each other in many ways.

They Are Dependable

For one thing, they can depend on each other. While they are not boringly predictable, they have a pretty clear idea of what to expect of one another. Members don't feel constantly off balance, wondering about each other's reactions, as members of the Dennis family often do.

Kate Dennis, for example, feels unsure about the support she gets from her husband. "Ted heard me scolding Bill after he messed up our new sofa with his dirty baseball mitt, and Ted started yelling at me that I was trying to turn Billy into a sissy by discouraging him from playing baseball. I felt he was encouraging Billy to be inconsiderate, and he was humiliating me by talking to me like that in front of Billy."

They Respect Each Other

While parents in healthy families do not always agree about issues involving their children, they do respect each other's feelings and opinions and act accordingly. And the children soon learn that they cannot play off one parent against the other.

Furthermore, both parents and children become sensitive to the issues that bother one another. While—being human—they sometimes do things that irritate, they don't do such things deliberately out of a wish to annoy or to prove that doing their own thing shows how independent they are.

Family members don't feel as if they have to be on guard against insults, sarcasm, ridicule, or other kinds of attacks. This sense of mutual trust makes their time together enjoyable, and so they plan for and look forward to being in each other's company.

They Communicate

The members of healthy families are accessible to each other. They are in close touch and they know how to reach and reach *out* to one another. Furthermore, when they do speak, they express their feelings and exchange information in a way that leaves no doubt about their meanings. They communicate both positive and negative feelings directly, avoiding blame and insult, and are spontaneous, not stilted and formal. In this way, they get to know each other intimately and are in touch with one another's feelings.

Problems, of course, crop up in all families. The healthiest families tend to recognize a pattern early, before it becomes overwhelming, and to take prompt steps to solve it.

They Solve Problems Together

Family members do not waste time and energy blaming and reproaching each other. They recognize that all people make mistakes, and they concentrate on what to do *now*. Furthermore, the healthiest families rarely arrive at solutions dictated by one person but instead participate jointly, generally under the shared leadership of both parents. Family members recognize that few solutions are perfect and are good at negotiating and compromising to find a choice everyone can accept.

The Baylor family, for example, found itself wrangling about household chores. Since Nora had gone back to teaching, her husband Ted and their twelve-year-old twins had agreed to do their share of the housework. But Ted kept forgetting to vacuum, Jessica was leaving the kitchen without doing the dishes, and Jason was ignoring the bathroom he had promised to clean.

Finally, Nora asked for a family conference. After everyone had aired their feelings of being overburdened, Jessica came up with the idea of a lottery. Together, the family listed all the jobs that needed to be done, drew up lists of four relatively equal workload assignments, and put the lists into a pot, which everyone drew from. Every Friday there is a new drawing. The new system is not perfect, but it *is* working.

They Keep Generational Boundaries

In the healthy family, the members of each generation are allied more closely with each other than with the members of

KEEPING IN TOUCH

Set up a bulletin board in a prominent place and get the entire family in the habit of checking it as soon as they come home. This is where you can keep

- a calendar showing dentist appointments, school plays, other family doings.
- notes letting each other know where you are and when you'll be back.
- important telephone numbers.
- special requests ("Please take hamburgers out of freezer").
- jokes and cartoons.
- school papers.
- kindergarten artwork.
- running shopping list.

Set aside special times when you phone home during the day or when your children can call you.

Slip notes into pockets or lunch boxes just to say "Hello," "I love you," or "Congratulations" for some achievement.

another generation. The parents have become independent of their own parents, they respect their children as individuals but are not their "equals" either as buddies or as full partners in the management of the family, and neither parent is aligned with a child against the other spouse.

A number of studies have found the strength of the parents' marriage a major element in total family health. While this is certainly important, we need to remember that much of the research on successful families has dealt only with intact nuclear families.

Furthermore, even in such well-conducted research as the Timberlawn study directed by Dr. Lewis, which found the strength of the parents' marriage the most important of several factors contributing to family health, a group of families emerged (termed *adequate*) in which the adults are lonely and unhappy in the marriage, but the children look just as healthy as those in the strongest families.

They Have a Sense of Humor

Light touches often prevent angry confrontations. The Wenner family, for example, engages in a lot of gentle teasing. Fourteen-year-old Jon might say, "Uh-oh, I'm in for it—Mom, you're breathing fire again." Or his father will begin a comment by saying, "I know this old dinosaur has a hopelessly old-fashioned attitude, but . . . ." In this way the family members can open the way to resolving an issue with goodwill all around.

HOW FAMILIES HANDLE DISCIPLINE

What *is* discipline? If you're like most parents, you hear this word and you think about spanking or fining or what may be the most dreaded punishment of all—a dark-as-night TV screen. But the principal meaning of discipline is far more global, covering just about everything you do for and with and to your children.

Discipline is *not* about punishment. What *is* it about? We get our clues from the word itself, which stems from the Latin for *knowledge* or *instruction*. The first definition for *discipline* in *The American Heritage Dictionary of the English Language* is: "Training that is expected to produce a specified character or pattern or behavior, especially that which is expected to produce moral or mental improvement." Not until the *fifth* meaning is there even a mention of punishment.

You discipline your children by making them your disciples, by teaching them character, self-control, moral behavior—in short, by teaching them how to grow up. And this is *hard*. Every parent struggles with the constant decisions involved in bringing up human beings who think well of themselves, who fulfill their potential, and who become happy, productive people. And every parent does it differently.

Thinking of discipline as an educational process doesn't make parenting any easier. But this view *can* help you stay on the sunny side of the parenting street. If you can look at day-to-day family adventures through this more positive lens, you can stop seeing them as challenges to come up with the right punishment to fit the wrong crime. Instead, you can look at them as opportunities to think about the kind of character you want your children to develop and the ways you can help them in this lifelong quest.

We all mix this up differently, of course, depending on the unique blend of ingredients in the pantries of our lives—the way we were brought up ourselves, the random genes we were born with, the genes our children were born with—and where and how we live.

Happily, many different child-rearing approaches can be "right." My own personal parenting metaphor is my mother's famous pot roast. My husband and children love brisket of beef cooked the way she used to make it. But I can't serve it to other family members who are vegetarians. Furthermore, even at my own table, succulent slices of meat with mushroom gravy may stoke appetites perfectly on a chilly winter Monday, but on a steamy summer Sunday we all crave a crisp, cool salad instead. So, too, with parenting: No one will ever write a child-rearing cookbook with recipes that work for all children at all times. This means that parents need to know how to vary the disciplinary diet. And how to improvise—how to take a pinch of this and a drop of that to create delicious moments and memories.

By and large, however, just as all serious cooks lean toward favorite cuisines, most parents follow their own favorite patterns of child rearing. The following popular patterns can all be right for different people in different circumstances; each one has its benefits and its drawbacks.

What Kind of Parenting Philosophy Do You Have?

- *"There's Gotta Be a Rule."* You set up a sturdy structure that outlines acceptable and unacceptable behaviors and spells out the consequences. Your children know in advance what kinds of parent-imposed rewards and punishments will follow what kinds of behaviors. But part of what makes bringing up children perpetually interesting is that even the most imaginative parent couldn't possibly anticipate everything a child might think of doing. So there's no way to draw up a set of rules elastic enough to fit every situation. You also run the risk of being too rigid, which may make your child rebel.

- *"Don't Stop the World."* You allow the natural consequences of children's behavior to occur, those consequences imposed by the demanding world beyond the family—the forces of nature or of society. You don't rush after a ten-year-old to remind her to wear her winter coat, but let her feel cold for the day. Nor do you rush to school to beg the principal to lift a thirteen-year-old's suspension for cutting classes. In this way, children learn valuable lessons from the natural results of their actions. However, you can't always stand back and allow natural consequences to take over. Is there a responsible parent who would dream of allowing a toddler to experience the natural consequence of running into the street or letting a teenager experiment with heroin?

- *"Don't Just Do Something—Stand There."* Under this "less-is-more" philosophy, inaction is the best action. You don't make a major issue over something that doesn't warrant it; your children experience the natural consequences of their behavior; and you save your energy for another battle on another day. There are times, however, when a responsible adult has to take action in the interests of keeping a child safe or teaching an important principle.

- *"I'm the Grown-Up."* The lines are bold and clear between the parent's authority as an adult and the child's place in the family, making it plain that some decisions are not for children to make and that they will be protected from wrong ones. This helps give your children a sense of their correct place in the world and asks only what they can handle. Yes, ask your first grader to put away his toys, but don't ask him whether he wants to go to Sunday School;

yes, expect your high schooler to wash the dishes—but no, don't ask her to decide whether the family should move to a new house. But children may be deprived of learning from their own mistakes if they're not given enough chances to make their own decisions.

- *"Do What I Do—Not Just What I Say."* You live by the values you profess, giving your children a model of self-disciplined responsible behavior. Like motherhood and apple pie, the parental practice of parental preaching is hard to be against. But the hard truth is that even the best of us parents don't always live up to our own ideals. And even when we do, our kids don't always notice—or care. Parents who never hit other people, take things that don't belong to them, drink or take drugs sometimes find their children going astray in these ways as well as in all sorts of never-dreamed-of transgressions. So sometimes you need to reinforce your virtuous example with vigorous talk. In other words, instead of just doing the right thing yourself, you need to explain to your children why certain ways of behaving are right for them, too.

- *"I Understand."* While explaining why you disapprove of what a child has done or plans to do, you acknowledge that the child thought that what she was doing seemed right at the time. This positive attitude lets children have a good opinion of themselves and fosters their ability to hear what you are saying. Of course, you could choke on your words if you don't believe them yourself—if, for example, you're facing a bully who repeatedly beats up little kids or a teenager who's been spending his leisure time joyriding in stolen cars.

- *"Be Prepared."* Successful child rearing often hinges on preventing confrontations rather than mopping up the emotional messes they cause. You may help your children manage their lives by controlling the environment (like "baby-proofing" the home) or by preparing them for potentially difficult circumstances (like giving a child watching TV five-minutes' notice before she has to get up to get ready for school). The proverbial ounce of prevention does more to preserve good family feelings than tons of after-the-fact "cures." Here again, though, even the most inventive parents can't possibly anticipate every scenario in the unpredictable drama of everyday life.

These seven approaches show just a sampling of possible positive ways to run a disciplined home. Good parents, like good kids, come in all shapes and sizes and all personalities, with all viewpoints on life and love and child rearing. Some of us like life to be as predictable as possible; some look for surprises in every day; some are funnier than others, some more spiritual, some more directive, some more laid-back. Happily, research has shown that children can thrive on a wide range of child-rearing styles. You can be strict or relaxed, do a lot or a little.

What *is* important is that your children grow up with a joyful feeling about themselves. People who feel good wearing their personalities and characters are happy people. This applies to parents, too, and since happy parents tend to raise happy children, it's important to remember that you don't need to fit anyone else's notion of what makes a "perfect parent." On some days, it's hard to remember this, but if you have love for your children, a willingness to assume the responsibility of parenthood, an eagerness to learn about how best to meet their needs and the flexibility to use what you've learned in ways that are right for yourself and your family, you have what it takes to be a good parent, no matter what your style.

MAKING FAMILY LIFE BETTER

What can you do if your family isn't functioning as well as you would like? You can take the initiative in making things better. Marilyn Caplan, for example, a divorced mother of two, felt that her family was not spending enough time together having fun. So she and her children sat down and each made a list of their current activities. They all went over their lists critically and scratched off those activities that were unimportant and unrewarding. In this way, they made time for special activities they could enjoy doing together.

Other families have improved their functioning by doing communication exercises they have found in one of the many books out on interpersonal communication, by involving the whole family in deciding where to go on vacation, or by taking the pressure off a "different" child to be just like everyone else.

Sometimes, however, problems seem too overwhelming to solve without outside help. If your family is sad and depressed much of the time, for example, or if you are always angry at each other, you may be too locked into self-defeating patterns to change them on your own. If you feel that the issues in your family are too difficult to handle by yourselves, you may want to seek professional counseling.

Practitioners of family therapy focus on treating problems by considering the entire family as the patient, rather than just one person. By helping the individual members to understand the way the family works as a whole, counselors can often help them—sometimes in only three or four visits—to see what each one is doing to live out self-defeating myths and carry on other unhealthy patterns, and what they can do to change these patterns.

Whether you opt to solve your problems by yourselves or with professional help, the most important first step is an honest look at how your family is functioning. It can be just as dangerous to deny the signs of emotional trouble as it is to deny the symptoms of physical illness. As painful as it is to explore the sources of trouble in your family life, such probing can in the long run yield a rich reward by offering all members of your family the opportunity to flourish in an atmosphere of love and support.

The health of a family bears no relationship to the occupations of the parents, or to whether they are working outside the home or in it, but rather to their attitudes toward themselves, the other family members, and life in general. Working parents, like parents at home full-time, can and do enhance the physical, intellectual, and emotional growth of their children. They do so in many different ways, some of which are discussed on the following pages.

BUILDING A WELL-STRUCTURED HOME

Most children seem to do best in a home in which the underlying values that govern the family's behavior are clearly stated, relatively constant, and agreed on by both parents. The rules set up to maintain these values are enforced consistently and equally firmly by both parents. The parents make a point of rewarding children for good behavior and try not to reward them, even unconsciously, for misbehaving. Activities in the household follow a relatively constant routine.

A firm foundation is important for all children. Children are happier when they know where they stand. They want to know what to expect of the world and what the world expects of them. They want to know what the rules are and when they are breaking those rules. They want to know what consequences to expect when they meet standards and what to expect when they do not. They need parents who will make decisions for them until they are ready to decide for themselves. They need an orderly routine as well as times to be free.

Young children generally do better when they know what their goals and limits are than when they have too much power—as, for example, in setting their own bedtimes or deciding whether they'll do their homework. Children who are faced with too many choices feel insecure, and if their work is accepted no matter whether it is good or bad, they are cheated out of a sense of achievement. Children who are indulged too much have trouble coping with the demands of school and neighborhood. When there's a big discrepancy between home and the outside world, children sometimes become fearful and too dependent on their parents.

Setting up a structure doesn't mean rearing children in an authoritarian way, so they won't develop responsibility for their own actions. It means instead that parents recognize their obligation to help children form acceptable standards of behavior and also to help them develop controls for meeting those standards. To do this, parents have to set realistic and reasonable expectations for the children's behavior—and then work out techniques that will help the children meet these expectations.

Setting Reasonable Expectations

You need to gear your expectations for your children to their age, their physical and emotional maturity, and their temperaments. You need to see them as individuals—and you need to avoid looking at brothers or sisters as carbon copies of each other. While most kids today are more capable than they're generally given credit for and can do more than we generally expect them to, we have to remember that they are not adults. This is especially important in the single-parent household, where more is often demanded of children.

One widowed father told me, "When Janice died, Laurie was only fourteen years old, but she was so capable that she soon became the woman of the house. Laurie did the cooking, made up the marketing list for me, looked after her two little brothers, and acted more like a wife than a teenage daughter. She was a lifesaver for me, but we both paid for it afterward.

"The folly of my having let her assume so much responsibility showed up when I remarried a couple of years later. Laurie was not about to replaced, and she effectively sabotaged my marriage to a very nice woman who was just no match for a young tigress defending her territory. I was furious at Laurie at the time, but now I see the role I played in taking advantage of her capabilities and in usurping those two years of her girlhood. I also see now how I let her run my life and didn't do what I could have to save the marriage."

Establishing Priorities

With so little family time available to them, working parents have to work hard at deciding how best to use it. Because you can't be with your children as much as you would like to be, you have to figure out which times are the most fruitful for you and them. As one father said, "It soon became clear to me that play with my children should occur during 'prime time' for them—times when they weren't exhausted, hungry, or keyed up from a long day."

You have to set priorities in other areas, too. Because you don't have time to do everything, you have to decide which is more important—a spotless house or a spur-of-the-moment trip to the zoo; peaceful, elegant dinners or boisterous family meals; wining and dining an out-of-town client who suddenly calls to announce her presence in town or keeping your date to take your daughter to her first professional baseball game. You won't always be happy with your choices, and the choices won't always be predictable (family won't always come before work or play, for example). But the fact that you make these choices in a context of overall priorities will make the decisions a little clearer.

Setting Predictable Routines

Most children find it comforting to live according to some sort of schedule. It is easier for them when they know that there are certain times for waking up, going to school, playing outside, doing chores, doing homework, watching television, eating meals and snacks, and going to bed.

Schedules will be different on weekends, of course, from during the week; different in summer and winter; and different for a ten-year-old than for a four-year-old. And while they should generally be fairly consistent, they should also be flexible enough to allow for special occasions. When possible, however, it's better not to shift the children's schedules around capriciously to suit your convenience. If, for example, six-year-old Polly has finally accepted an 8 PM bedtime, you shouldn't keep her out later than this because *you* feel like going shopping one night or because you're having such a good time visiting friends that you hate to leave. You have to respect her schedule if you expect her to respect it.

MAKING THE MOST OF FAMILY TIME

Just as you want to make the best use possible of the time you spend at work, you want to use to the fullest those hours you have to spend with your family. Your goal within the family is not, of course, the efficiency and productivity that you aim for on the job. It is rather the production of quite different results—the warm feeling on the part of every family member of being loved and respected, the enhancement of everyone's personal growth, closeness among family members, and shared good times. Here are some of the ways working parents do this.

Creating Family Time

Yes, quality is better than quantity when it comes to the time you spend with your family. But there has to be enough quantity at the right times for the quality to shine through. How, then, to find the time? Family time is not born, it is made. It is made by working parents who look at their lives and who figure out ways in which they can carve out niches of time—with a spouse, a child, the whole family—-that will make real contributions to their lives. Some ideas that have worked for other families are listed in the box "Creating Family Time." Maybe some with work for you.

Once you have found those minutes, hours, and days to be with your children, you've made quantitative progress. Now how do you make as much of this time as possible "quality" time?

- *Be there now.* Really there. We've all had the experience of being in one place physically, while our minds are miles away. "Are you listening to me or are you just saying, 'Uh-huh'?" is a question I have heard too many times over the years from my children. Youngsters quickly become adept at knowing when you're really hearing what they have to say and when you're nodding at their words but are really puzzling over the mistakes in last night's order sheet. If you *are* deeply immersed in your own thoughts, it's best to tell Johnny, "I have something on my mind now, but give me twenty minutes, and then I'll be all yours." And then *be* all his. If you learn to focus your energies on a work problem when you're dealing with that, and on your son when you're talking to him, you'll become more effective in both areas of your life.

- *Be available to them, even when you're not directly involved in an activity.* It's important for a child to know that when you're home and not officially working, she can come to you with a quick question, comment, or request for help without feeling as if she's bothering you. Researchers in the Harvard University Preschool Project found that the most competent children came from homes in which parents served as "designers" and "consultants." While the mothers in this study (many of whom worked outside the home) spent less than 10 percent of their time interacting with their babies, they were pretty much "on call" to them. While going about their daily routines, they made themselves available for a few seconds or minutes when needed to answer a question, label some object, help a toddler climb the stairs, or share in an exciting discovery.

  Children in such homes learn how to get attention from an adult and thrive on knowing that they will get help when they need it.

- *Have real conversations with them.* Make just as much of an effort to converse with your children as you would with an attractive new person you meet at a party. Take the initiative of starting a conversation. Talk about subjects you know they're interested in. Tell them stories about their earlier years or about your own childhood. Ask them how they feel about various issues. Encourage them to air their feelings about the people in their lives. Ask them what they like about their lives, what they don't like, what they'd like to change. Ask them what they like about a particular TV show, book, movie, or teacher.

- *Be affectionate.* At the end of every day, you should be able to answer "yes" to the questions, "Have you hugged your child today?" and "Have you kissed your child today?"

  "Too many people in our society suffer from 'skin hunger,' a deep-seated longing to touch and be touched," says Dr. Sidney Simon, professor of humanistic education at the University of Massachusetts. "We all need this kind of communication, which says, without words, 'I am here, you are here, and we care.'"

It's never too early or too late to start building these bridges of closeness with our children. Parents who wait too long

CREATING FAMILY TIME

- Push dinner back an hour later and devote your first hour home to playing or talking with your children. Stave off hunger pangs with nutritious snacks (celery, carrot sticks, cheese, or mugs of soup) or through a late-afternoon sandwich.
- Move closer to your place of work. Instead of spending an hour or two on the highway or the railroad, you can be spending it on the road to family closeness.
- Reserve one weekend day for family activity—a visit to the zoo, a ride in the car, a visit to another family with children, a get-together with extended family, or whatever else you and your children enjoy doing together.
- Take a child out to lunch from time to time—once a week if you work close enough to your home for the two of you to meet (even if it means having a baby-sitter or friend bring your child to you), or as a special treat during school vacations.
- Play hooky with a child. Stay home from work and keep a child out of school to work on a special project, go shopping, sneak off to a matinee, or take in a ball game. While this isn't something you'd do often (maybe no more than once a year), the delicious wickedness of it all may help to cement a bond between you and make the day even more enjoyable. (As my mother used to say when one of my children missed school, "So she'll be a professor a day later.")
- Find out what's important to your children. Since you can't be with them on every occasion, ask them to tell you which events mean the most to them. Molly may not care whether or not you come to hear the fifth-grade choir sing, but may long to have you in the gym for her two-minute stint in a two-hour gymnastic meet.

often regret the time they allowed to go by. This shows up dramatically in an interesting current development, the more intense reaction of fathers than of mothers to the "empty nest." By and large, middle-aged women do *not* become depressed when their youngest child leaves the parental home. On the contrary, after having given so much of themselves for some twenty years or so, they often breathe a sigh of relief to get some time and space for themselves. Many men, however, react to their children's leaving the home with regrets that they had not spent more time with them when they were younger.

Perhaps this disparity between the sexes exists because these women, following traditional mores, invested more of themselves in their children for so many years, while these men were devoting themselves to their jobs. When the fathers looked up one day, wanting to be more closely involved with their children, they saw their offspring on their way out the door. Such findings seem to imply that if both parents take a continuing, deeply involved interest in their children from the time they are small, neither one should be dismayed when, in the normal cycle of life, the nest is emptied.

Mealtimes

At one time, eating was the most popular activity shared by families, but for many families this is no longer true. Reports *Advertising Age,* "In one generation, we have gone from a traditional food-producing society to a food-grazing society—one where we eat wherever we happen to be." Americans spend about one-third of our food dollars away from home. In the average family, all members eat dinner together at home only about three times a week, and they get together for only half of their weekend meals. Still, a 1988 *New York Times* survey found that about seven out of ten people polled had eaten the previous evening's dinner with at least one of the people they lived with.

What this means is that we can no longer take for granted a considerable chunk of family time that was once a given. But this doesn't mean that it's a lost cause, either. Those of us who want to spend more time with our families can revive the tradition of shared family meals—or find other activities to do together. Because working parents have little discretionary time to devote to other activities and because the whole family has to eat anyway, it seems to make more sense to work out schedules that allow for more opportunities to break bread together—instead of just being satisfied with the crumbs. Here are some ways other parents have found to do this:

- Wake everyone up half an hour earlier so you can all sit down to breakfast together. The food can be just as simple as when it's taken on the run, but being together for twenty minutes at the same table encourages family sharing and closeness.
- Make a big production of Saturday or Sunday breakfast or lunch as a time when the family can experiment with new food and can enjoy each other's company in a leisurely atmosphere.
- See that the youngest children have an afternoon snack and a nap so they can stay up for a later meal with the parents and any older siblings.
- Try to schedule everyone's outside activities to allow for at least two "reserved" family dinners during the week; don't make any other social plans for those nights.
- Encourage each of your children to invite a close friend to join your family for dinner from time to time.
- Turn off your telephone, take it off the hook, or let your answering machine take messages during dinner, so your family time together won't be interrupted.
- Establish a time frame for dinner—anywhere from thirty minutes to an hour—which remains sacred. No matter what homework, meetings, or other activities await, and no matter how unhungry anyone may be, make it plain that all family members are expected to remain at the table for the allotted time.
- Make your dinner-table conversations so interesting that your family will *want* to linger. Some ways to do this are to use values-clarification strategies. The following and additional ones are in the book *Helping Your Child Learn Right from Wrong,* by Dr. Sidney B. Simon and Sally Wendkos Olds (see appendix "Recommended Reading"):

The Whip: Everyone gives a quick answer to one question. Some sample questions: What did you say or do in the last twenty-four hours that you're proud of? What was the high point (or low point) of your day? What is one thing you've changed your mind about recently? If there were a fire and you could save only one possession, what would it be? Who is one person you think you can learn something from? When did you last laugh out loud? What is the best thing you ever did for anyone?

The Seesaw: Everyone answers a question posing two alternatives and explains his or her answer in a minute or so. Sample questions: Are you more like the city or the country? A rose or a daisy? The heart or the brain? A TV set or a radio? A steak or a hamburger? A bubbling brook or a placid lake? A dog or a cat?

The Importance of Family Rituals

As adults, some of our favorite memories of family life when we were children revolve around activities that occurred over and over again in a way we could depend on. Usually these activities were special in some way to our own families. From my earliest childhood, for example, I remember hearing the unique whistle my father made up—the "Wendkos-family whistle." Whenever I heard it, I knew I was hearing my father or my brothers (my mother never learned to whistle), and my husband and I have carried on the same whistle, so our family can always find each other in a crowd.

The Leaf family fostered another tradition. At first, it was Martin, the father, who traveled often in connection with his work as an attorney. Then Louise, the mother, began to travel in her work as a city planner. As the three children began to go to camp and then away to college, there were more and more times when the five family members were not together for long stretches at a time. So their dinner-table ritual took on even more significance. Whenever all five Leafs are around the dinner table after not having eaten together for several days, they do a "family circle." Everyone crosses arms and holds hands with the people to the left and right. One

FAMILY RITUALS

- *Birthdays:* The birthday child gets to choose the family menu for breakfast and dinner, is excused from all chores for that day, and gets to stay up an hour later at night.
- *Weekends:* Every Sunday morning the entire family goes out on a local sight-seeing jaunt, eats out in an inexpensive restaurant or takes a picnic, and then comes home for the little ones to nap while the parents read the Sunday paper.
- *Bedtime:* One parent bathes a child; the other parent reads to her; and all three join in singing a favorite nursery song before she goes to sleep.
- *Holidays:* Each family member makes one gift for every other family member. The presents can be as simple as a woven potholder, as elaborate as a knitted sweater, or as personal as a pasted-up photo album.
- *Vacation:* A read-aloud book always goes along with the camping gear. Every night a different family member reads, knowing that the reader will always be the last one awake in the tent as the others, cozy in their sleeping bags after a long day of hiking, drop off to sleep, one by one.
- *Holidays:* Thanksgiving, Christmas, Passover, and other major days through the years are celebrated with aunts, uncles, cousins, and grandparents. This large security net makes the children feel safe, knowing that there are other adults, aside from their parents, who know them and love them.
- *Work:* A chain-store manager who regularly had to go back to work after supper took the whole family along. The small children carried boxes of clothing up from the basement and learned how to fill in the stock, take inventory, and straighten merchandise. They also learned how to work together, which they still do—whether it's working on the house, the yard, or the car.

person makes a wish, then squeezes the hand of the person on the right; that person then makes a wish and squeezes; and so on. When the last person has wished, the squeeze goes back in the other direction.

And Douglas Schwarz, a computer programmer in Concord, New Hampshire, has written of the rituals that his family shared with my family for many precious years as he was growing up:

"Christmas was unquestionably the family's most important holiday—so important, in fact, that we continued to gather and celebrate it for years even after my brother and I had moved out, and my parents had separated. . . . A true Schwarz Christmas involved all manner of time-tested family rituals. Glass-wax stencils on the den windows. The reading of Dickens's Christmas Carol around the dining room table, for as many nights as it took to finish it. Making Christmas bread. Composing elaborate 'hints' to write on the gift tags of each and every present.

"The rites of Christmas Eve were perhaps the most complex and wonderful of all. We almost always had friends over to help trim the tree. [This is where the Olds family often came in.] . . . Around six o'clock we would take a break to go down to the community Christmas tree, which the fire department decorated every year. There we would meet with most of our neighbors . . . and there, would sing Christmas carols.

Rituals, which can be built around mealtimes, holidays, birthdays, seasons of the year, vacations, or special situations within a family, play a major role in family life. They encourage a feeling of closeness, they foster a sense that "our family is special," and they lend a note of security in everyone's knowing what to expect. Dr. Gordon Shipman, Professor Emeritus at the University of Wisconsin and author of *Handbook for Family Analysis*, has studied the importance of family rituals and has found that they are much more likely to flourish in families that foster the growth of their members than in those that stymie the development of individual potential.

One measure of a family's health is its willingness to work together toward common goals, a necessity in the families of working parents. In the next chapter, we'll talk about some ways to encourage an all-for-one, one-for-all attitude.

15

THE COOPERATIVE FAMILY

───

I know a very special family who, years ago, instituted a very special ritual. Whenever anyone in the Simon household broke or spilled something, someone else in the family would immediately—without being asked—come running to help clean it up. To me, this simple practice, requiring little more than a few minutes and the willingness to give of oneself to help another, has always symbolized what is possible in family cooperation.

Happily, the Simon family is not unique. Many families live by an attitude of common caring and sharing. I couldn't count the number of working parents who told me how much their families helped them. The museum director who said, "My husband has always been my staunchest supporter. We've shared the shopping, the schlepping, the salary, and the social advantages of my job." The hospital technician who told me, "My wife is such a positive person that she always seems to figure out a way to get around whatever our current crisis is." The single mother who said, "I could never have made it intact through this last year without the help of my children. They seemed to grow up almost overnight and have come through for me again and again."

Most families do pull together when they see the need. Still, the biggest untapped natural resource in America today—its population of able-bodied youngsters—is not being mined as well as it could be. The rise in recent years of single-parent families and of two-job marriages has made children valuable once more for what they can do, not just for what they are. Years ago, people deliberately had large families so they would have a covey of clever hands and strong backs to work on the farm, to produce household goods, and to care for them in their old age.

As our economy changed and as child-labor laws were enacted, children did less and less and got more and more. In recent years, couples have not asked, "How many children do we need to help us do our work?" but "How much work do we have to do to afford to have a child?"

Now the pendulum is swinging back somewhat in the other direction, but as with men assuming a larger share of household tasks, the pendulum swings slowly. A recent University of Alabama study looked at the amount of time children ages six to seventeen spend preparing food, washing dishes, shopping, cleaning the house, doing yardwork, and taking care of car and pets. The results: School-age children spend about an hour a day on these tasks, and teenagers put in an average of about one hour and seventeen minutes a day. Although boys and girls do about the same amount of work, girls do more housework, and boys do more outdoor jobs. The most surprising finding is that in the families that need help the most—those in which the mother works full-time—children do the same amount of work or *less* than do children whose mothers work part-time or are at home.

Susan B. Lovett, the home economist who conducted this study, concluded that this probably reflects the fact that full-time working mothers are not training their children to do these chores—as well as the fact that they're not home to see that the chores get done. It's an old story. To teach someone how to do a job and to get him to do it sometimes seems like more work than doing it yourself. But those parents who do make the effort to get their kids to do their share usually reap the benefits eventually. So do the children, as they learn how to perform the chores of everyday life and as they absorb the philosophy that being part of a household implies not only privileges but responsibilities.

It's often easier to begin to get children involved by starting in the kitchen. Children rate cooking as their favorite household job. It's creative; giving people food often feels like giving them love; and everyone loves to eat. Also, it's easy to see the importance of help in the kitchen; we can't overlook the need for meals as easily as we can look away from dust balls under the bed. Some suggestions are listed in the box "Encouraging Children to Enjoy Cooking."

While most other household activities strike children (and grownups, too) as more of a yawn and a bore, they still need to get done. Working parents and their children report that all the following chores—and others—are often done by children:

- making beds
- emptying wastebaskets
- washing and folding laundry
- setting and clearing the table
- washing and drying dishes
- cleaning their own bedrooms
- doing their fair share of household cleaning, including dusting, sweeping, vacuuming, washing windows, and all the rest
- doing the marketing and other errands (Children too young to drive often bike or walk to the store and either take a taxi home or have a parent pick up the groceries.)
- feeding, walking, grooming, and otherwise caring for pets
- cleaning up the kitchen
- taking care of younger brothers and sisters from time to time
- mowing the lawn
- washing the car
- ironing their own clothes
- polishing silver
- sweeping leaves
- sewing and repairing their own clothes

Some children, of course, do much more than others. And some do it more cheerfully than others. Both the quantity and

ENCOURAGING CHILDREN TO ENJOY COOKING

- Start children of both sexes off young by having them work along with you. Preschoolers can help to mix cake and cookie batter, beat eggs, dip French toast, cut out cookies, shape hamburger patties, and so forth.
- Plan a birthday party around cooking. Keep the guest list small enough to avoid chaos in your kitchen and get another adult to help you. Provide the utensils and makings for one or two decorated cakes (or cupcakes) and give each child a job to do. As party favors, give everybody an apron. While the cakes are baking, give the children lunch or supper, or let them play games, and then serve their own creation.
- Observe safety and sanitary precautions and set a good example. Everyone should wash hands before and after handling food. You should be on hand when children begin using the stove, other hot and sharp appliances, and sharp tools, until you feel confident that they can handle them safely.
- Tell them how to put out an oven fire, how to treat a burn, and when and how to call for help.
- Stick to short, simple recipes.
- Make cooking a shared activity at first. Besides being an enjoyable way to spend quality time together, your children will learn from seeing how you do things.
- Start with easy and well-liked dishes like scrambled eggs, hot dogs and baked beans, hamburgers, salad, baked apples, oatmeal, and vegetables.
- Demonstrate the basic cooking techniques (boiling, broiling, baking, and frying) on your stove, toaster oven, microwave, and other equipment.
- Give them their own cookbook. When you buy one written especially for children, be sure it doesn't rely too heavily on sweets and on convenience foods with a lot of additives—both common failings.

Some good recent books are listed in the appendix "Recommended Readings."
- Teach them how to read a recipe, emphasizing the importance of reading the recipe through and assembling all ingredients before beginning to cook.
- Teach them to plan well enough in advance so that they'll have enough time to cook the dish (no midnight suppers!), and they'll have all the ingredients on hand (no having to dash out to the store in the middle of mixing).
- Give them a kitchen tour to show them where they can find—and put away—utensils and staples.
- Keep directions and rules to a minimum, emphasizing safety and convenience rather than neatness.
- Teach them to clean up and put away as they go along, but don't be so fussy that you squelch their enthusiasm.
- Keep planning sessions short and casual.
- Show them how to count backward to make everything come out together, as in this example:
  For a dinner planned for 6:00 PM:
  Chicken: Takes one hour to cook; put it in oven at 5:00.
  Baked sweet potato: Takes forty-five minutes; put it in at 5:15.
  Broccoli: Takes five minutes; boil water at 5:50; add broccoli at 5:55.
  Salad: Takes ten minutes to make; cut up ingredients and put them in salad bowl or plastic bag earlier in afternoon and refrigerate.
- *Eat what they cook and show your enjoyment (even if you have to fake it sometimes). Praise them lavishly, to them directly and to others, in the children's hearing.*

the quality of children's work show a direct relationship to the expectations and training they receive from their parents. How, then, do the most successful parents bring about a cooperative attitude and an effective work-sharing regime within the family? What can you learn from them?

COMMUNICATE AN ATTITUDE
OF FAMILY GIVE-AND-TAKE

"I sometimes feel as if I have two fathers and no mother," my daughter, then about fourteen years old, once said to me. Why? Because a "real" mother would sew on her buttons, drive her wherever she wanted to go whenever she wanted to go there, have her favorite foods always in front of her, and so forth. Because of the traditional role women have played in most families in this society, it didn't occur to this capable and bright adolescent that some of these tasks could just as appropriately be performed by her father—or even by herself.

My daughter bought society's definition of the good mother, hook, line, and sinker—except that the real catch dangling on the end of the line was me. I had undoubtedly fed this fancy over the years, and I now had a major job ahead of me: to disabuse all those in my family of the notion that I was their personal servant. I think I finally got the message across (at least most of the time), but it has not been easy. I know from speaking to so many other working parents that this is a pervasive problem in the families of working parents. The worst part of it is the fact that the woman herself accepts this definition.

Despite the rise in women's outside employment, this attitudinal barrier still keeps many women in a state of overwork and overworry—except for the one who've gone to their families and announced the necessity for a new order in the home. Whether they do this with sweet reasonableness, with hard logic, or with an "I'm-mad-as-hell-and-I'm-not-going-to-take-it-anymore" explosion, they're doing what almost always *needs* to be done. Change—especially change in a point of view ingrained over centuries, communicated in books, on television, in the movies, and throughout society—does *not* come without deliberate effort.

Sometimes, not much effort is required. Social worker Nancy Greenblatt told me about the family meeting she had with her children when she was first thinking about going back to school to get her master's degree in social work.

"I told my kids—they were nine, eleven, and thirteen then—what I wanted to do and that it would make some changes in our lives. My middle one told me, 'Don't worry, Mom. You're a lot nicer to have around when you're involved in something, anyway.' 'Yeah, you don't get on our backs so much,' my oldest chimed in.

"So, with that attitude, they were ready to pitch in. They all became independent from an early age. They rode their bikes everywhere, partly because they knew they couldn't count on me to drive them around. And they were really a strong backup in the house."

The basic approach that many women have used to enlist the full participation of their husbands in the work of the household, as outlined in Chapter 12, has also been adopted by many parents enlisting the support of their children. The three basic ingredients—love, communication, and encouragement—are just as important in dealing with children.

Another vital ingredient in the lives of many cooperating families is the recognized importance of the children within the family, an importance shown by the treatment they receive as valued members of the home team. They are, in effect, fully functioning members of a family partnership.

The same attitude that sociologist Robert Weiss found to work so well in single-parent families also operates to the benefit of many families with two working parents. This involves doing away with a hierarchical structure and running the family more democratically.

The parents, of course, do not abdicate their responsibilities to care for their children, to bring to family life the benefits of their maturity and experience, and to make those major family decisions that require adult judgment. They do, however, undertake a different kind of parenting, in which the marital partnership expands to take in the children as junior partners.

If your children are expected to share more of the responsibilities of running your household, it is only fair for them to share more of the decision making. If you have the courage to say to them, "This is your house, too. What do you want to do about the way it is run?" be prepared for some ingenious suggestions that may get your home humming to a new tune.

You may find that what, when, and where you eat undergo radical change, that jobs start getting done a different way and on a different timetable, and that you'll be doing a number of things as you never did them before. (Remember the old axiom: Ask a lazy man how to make a job easier? The same might apply to asking a youngster.)

THE FAMILY COUNCIL

One way many family partnerships run their operations is through that favorite tool of business, the weekly staff meeting. In the home setting, it's usually called a "family council." These councils are wonderful forums for dealing with all kinds of family issues—from the fun decisions like planning a New Year's Eve party and deciding on the next vacation, to the hairier ones like Mary Ann's playing with—and breaking—Richard's toys, or the failure of all the kids to do the jobs they're supposed to be doing.

An ongoing forum like this is a good idea for any family. It's especially useful in a family with working parents because it builds into the family structure a time when everyone, from the littlest toddler to the parents, can air their grievances, express their desires, and take part in family decisions.

The family council offers an ideal opportunity to get across the message that everyone in a family is a fully functioning member of that family, available to share in the goodies the family enjoys, and available to do the work that makes those goodies possible. As Sea Cliff, New York, public relations consultant Lilli Scott told me, "It's important to get across the sense that everyone has to earn the right to his or her comforts and conveniences and that we're all in this together."

Through these powwows, families talk about who will be doing what; they brainstorm to come up with imaginative solutions for sharing the jobs that *nobody* wants, and they keep an ongoing dialogue going. Families are living, breathing, changing entities. Even if you've devised what seems like the perfect solution to your housekeeping problems in January,

HOLDING A FAMILY COUNCIL

- Everyone in the family, from the littlest toddler to a visiting grandparent, takes part.
- Pick a time that's good for everyone. Usually a weekend morning or afternoon works out best.
- Allow an hour, but be prepared to end in as little as fifteen minutes, especially at the beginning when the format is new.
- Pick a chairperson to run the meeting and a secretary to take notes on decisions and actions to be followed through on. If necessary, pick a treasurer to handle any money matters. These posts should rotate so that everyone in the family gets a turn at each.
- Set an agenda for each meeting. Every member can contribute items to the agenda, which can cover topics such as
  - reading of minutes from the last meeting
  - calendar for the coming week (family plans and individual comings and goings)
  - allocation of chores for the coming week
  - money matters (allowances, pay for special jobs, major purchases)
  - old business
  - new business
- Use the first meeting to plan a fun-time family activity, either an immediate one that will take place on the same day, or one for the following weekend or the next family vacation.
- Establish a few simple rules:
  - Everyone who wants to speak will get a chance.
  - No one interrupts.
  - No one "puts down" anyone else. Everyone's point of view is listened to politely.
  - Disagreement is okay, as long as it occurs in a framework of mutual respect.
- A good way to end the meeting is with a game and/or refreshments.

by February you may need to take another look at the whole picture. With regular meetings, you can build flexibility into family systems. You can shift assignments in accord with everyone's day-to-day life. A change in a month's worth of afternoon rehearsals for the class play, the start of the field hockey season, a rash of out-of-town trips by one or both parents, a bout of flu, or any other change in anyone's life can prompt another look at the overall plan. Also, meeting on a regular basis gives you a chance to rotate chores and to talk about better ways of doing things.

Forming a family council does not mean that the parents are bound by what the children want, any more than the chief executive of a corporation is bound by the wishes of one or more department heads. It does mean that all family members are given an opportunity to express what they want, to air grievances, and to hear and talk about important family news, such as an impending move to another city or another neighborhood.

Some council meetings will ring with jokes and giggles. Others are bound to erupt in explosions of tears and shouting. It all depends on the topics on the floor, the moods of the conferees, and the current family climate. It's important to remember that the sadness and the anger have to come out in some way, and that providing a safe setting for their expression can do a lot to create strong bonds among the members of your family.

Some suggestions for forming and holding family councils are given in the box "Holding a Family Council."

START EARLY

It's unrealistic to expect children who have been waited on all their lives to suddenly snap to attention during their teens and become both responsible and competent. As one mother of three teenagers told me, "They're good kids, and they have good intentions, but they're just not in the groove. They're used to me doing everything for all of us—as I did before I went to work a couple of years ago. So now, while they're good-natured about taking on new jobs, they're not in the habit of thinking ahead; they forget all the time, and they don't know how to do a lot of things I expect from them. The worst part is that I have nobody to blame but myself!''

Adolescents and younger schoolchildren can, of course, learn quickly to make up for lost time. But it's a lot easier on the whole family when children begin doing their share as soon as they can. And that can come very early. It did in our family.

When our three girls were preschoolers, they were helping out in many small but appreciated ways. Even though an adult still had to be very much on the scene as overseer, the children's help on many tasks did eliminate the need for one of us to do them. Even more important in the long run, at an early, impressionable age they developed the attitude that they were expected to be participating, working members of the family.

What did they do? Three-year-old Jenny, armed with a bottle of juice, a diaper to tuck under her baby sister's chin, and a pillow to rest Dorri's head on, was an eager little nurturer. Our biggest problem was getting her to stop, even after the baby had drained the bottle. As for spoon feeding, five-year-old Nancy soon became expert at getting applesauce into Dorri's mouth, and as Baby and Big Sister were enjoying each other, the resident adult was able to tend to some other task. In a home with three little children, there was *always* some other task to be done.

Bathing the baby also became a family affair. While we weren't crazy enough to let preschoolers actually handle a slippery infant in a tub of water, Jenny at three could—and did—empty and wipe out the tub, and Nancy at five would often dry and dress Dorri. (Putting towel, clothes, and baby all on the carpeted floor made this a safe operation.)

They folded laundry, starting at age three to handle washcloths and diapers and gradually working up to the difficult stuff like shirts and pajamas. At age three they learned their way around the kitchen, starting with jobs like scooping out frozen orange juice concentrate and mixing it with water and setting the table. And at about age five, they learned how to handle a small kitchen knife, not too sharp, so they could cut cucumbers, celery, fruits, and sandwiches. By the time all three girls went to nursery school, at age three or four, they were making their own beds (after a fashion) before they left in the morning.

If all of this sounds as if it took twice as long to get everything done, it did. But while the children were doing some of these tasks, the parent or baby-sitter with them was able to do something else. We learned to gauge ourselves differently, to allow extra time for everything, and to take the trouble to teach the children how to do the little jobs that they could do and enjoyed doing. Besides, working with them—like mixing a batch of cookies or going to the store together—was also fun. Both big and little people enjoy doing these things together. As another mother said to me, "I've never had the patience to sit down and play games with my children, but if I feel we're accomplishing something together I get a big kick out of their company."

By the time our children had realized that what they were doing was *work,* they had already absorbed the idea that they were expected to do it. This doesn't mean, of course, that as they grew older there were no battles royal about chores left undone or done poorly, but the foundation was there, even if it was sometimes buried under more pressing matters like gymnastics practice, homework, parties, and all the other activities in their lives.

GIVE CREDIT WHEN CREDIT IS DUE

Most of us are guilty of going through life taking the good things for granted and remarking only on the things that go wrong. But those parents who either intuitively or consciously pat their children on the back when they catch them being good have a powerful tool for motivating the children to keep doing more and more.

"My children *should* be working in the house," you may say. "Why should I make a big deal out of praising them for doing what they're supposed to do, anyway?" By asking this question, you're not taking into account the basic principles governing the way people learn.

Most children, for example, have been taught that they should try to find the owner of any valuable property they may find in the street. In fact, the laws of our land generally prohibit a person from keeping property that is not rightfully his. Yet when children do find large sums of money and turn it in to the police, a laudatory newspaper story usually appears, commending the children and reporting some financial reward for them from the owner of the recovered property. In recognition that it is often difficult to do the right thing, it is perfectly appropriate to reward children when they do "what they are supposed to do." Another example of this principle are the lowered insurance rates that some companies offer to drivers with no traffic violations. Motorists are not supposed to violate the vehicle code; those who do are punished; those who accumulate no violations are only "doing what they are supposed to do." Yet it is only fitting that these people who do make special efforts should reap some benefits for doing so, aside from staying out of trouble.

In some families, rewarding children for good behavior comes naturally to parents. These parents are generous with their praises, their affection, and their attention. Other parents are chary of showing too much approval of a child for fear of spoiling her. Yet the more approval parents show their children for desirable behavior, the more the children are likely to act in those very ways. So be generous with your praise for jobs well done, even if it's only a made bed or an unloaded dishwasher. (Obviously, the age and ability of the child are relevant here. To show delight over the fact that a six-year-old remembered to hang up his coat may be appropriate; to act the same way with a sixteen-year-old would be ridiculous, and would also be sure to infuriate the sixteen-year-old.)

One extremely important reward for all of us is our sense of the importance of what we're doing. If we feel that our efforts are not making much of a contribution to our own lives, to those of the people we care about, or to society at large, we tend to shrug, say "What's the use?" and give up whatever we've been doing.

Many children get the feeling that the jobs they do are "make-work," assigned to them so they'll learn the virtues of responsibility and toil. As such, they have no sense of the work's importance. If, on the other hand, they feel that they are making valuable and valued contributions toward a smoothly running home, they are likely to put more of themselves into scrubbing that pan or sweeping that floor. This conclusion arises from research conducted by the Children's Time Study undertaken by several professors at the School of Law of the University of California, Berkeley. The study found that taking care of younger siblings is the one chore that children are most conscientious in carrying out, presumably because as Elliott A. Medrich, director of the study, writes in the book, *The Serious Business of Growing Up: A Study of Children's Lives Outside of School,* "Its necessity and value is more clear-cut and difficult to deny than the merits of bed-making or room-cleaning."

So show your appreciation for the work your children do. Tell them what good work they're doing. Tell them how their cooperation makes life easier for you. Be specific in your commendations by saying something like: "I'm so proud to invite friends over after you've polished the furniture so well"; "It was great the way I was able to concentrate on my work today—I didn't have to be distracted by worrying about what to make for dinner because I knew you were taking care of it!"; "Now that you did such a good job raking those leaves I won't have to do it this weekend, and we can go to a ball game together."

Whatever you do, don't sabotage your plan and undermine their efforts by redoing what they do. If they see that no matter how hard they worked, you still go in and rearrange the dishes in the dishwasher or give the dog "one touch-up brushing" or rake the lawn again, "just for good measure," they'll feel that their work was wasted. So even if the job they did wasn't perfect, remember it's better to have it done imperfectly by someone else than to have it done perfectly by you. Run to the nearest mirror, look in it and tell yourself a couple of dozen times, "Not everything has to be done my way."

In fact, one good rule to follow is that the person who does a particular job does it according to her own standards. If someone else feels that it isn't being done well enough, some job-swapping may be in order. So you may end up with the person who most enjoys food doing the cooking most of the time and the one who is most interested in appearance doing most of the laundry.

Watch out, though, that people don't get stuck in particular jobs, especially along gender-stereotyped lines, which can happen all too easily. To keep this from happening, and to enable both sexes to become proficient at the jobs usually associated with one gender or the other, the jobs should continue to be rotated to some degree. Frequent rotation also keeps boredom at bay.

EXPECT THE POSSIBLE

If you expect five-year-old Billy to make his bed like a Marine, sheets stretched so tautly that you can bounce a coin off them, you are doomed to disappointment, and you and Billy will have some hard times together. You always have to take into account a child's age, his physical dexterity and strength, and her levels of patience and persistence.

You also need to take a child's personality into account. It won't do you any good at all to tell your hyperactive, impulsive nine-year-old, "I don't know why you have so much trouble washing the dishes. Your brother used to do it all the time when he was even younger than you—and he did a better job, too." (Not only will you continue to get a poor dish-washing job, you'll also be sowing seeds of hatred and antagonism that are likely to outlive you, extending well into your children's old age. If you want your children to be teammates instead of opponents, you need to steer clear of fraternal and sororal comparisons.)

As Lilli Scott told me, "Trying to divide everything evenly was a losing battle. Everyone wound up keeping score. I found it was better to impart a sense of cooperation between my children and to let them trade off chores the way they wanted to, even if I thought one of them was getting the short end of the stick. This way, the kids ended up striking their own balances without interference and without relying on me to make every decision."

TEACH THEM HOW

It's also not fair to expect a child to know how to do something without ever having learned how. We often assume that our children know how to perform certain tasks because they've seen us do them so many times. But think of your children as being like passengers in a car being driven by someone else. You may travel the same route a dozen times, but it's very likely that you won't learn the route until you have to drive it yourself. Unless you're responsible for reaching your destination, you're apt to put your attention on the changing colors of the foliage or the joggers in the road or the clothes in the shop windows instead of on landmarks and mileage and turns. It's the same with children. And spouses. Chances are that they won't acquire the skill to change a tire, make a casserole, or iron a shirt simply by casual observation and osmosis. They have to be taught:

- Break the job down into its component parts. (See the example in the box "Cleaning Up After Dinner.")
- Go through the job with them, step by step.
- First, show them how to do each part.
- Second, have them do the job with you.
- Third, have them do it by themselves, under your supervision.
- Then they're on their own.
- Praise them enthusiastically for the parts they're doing right.
- Correct them tactfully as you point out what needs to be done differently the next time around.
- Be patient if they're slow.
- Use all the willpower you have to keep from redoing the job yourself.
- Define your standards clearly. Show the child what you

want done and give measurable criteria for how you want it done, so he'll know when he's met them.

CLEANING UP AFTER DINNER: A STEP-BY-STEP BREAKDOWN

1. Clear dishes, silver, and glassware from the table.
2. Put away condiments such as salt, pepper, and sugar.
3. Shake out tablecloth and put it back on the table or into the laundry hamper. Or wipe off and replace, or put away, place mats. Wipe off table.
4. Put away all leftovers and other food in refrigerator, freezer, or cupboard.
5. Scrape and dispose of garbage from dishes.
6. Rinse dishes, silver, and glasses and put in dishwasher if you have one. If not, wash these items.
7. Wash any items that do not go in the dishwasher (such as wooden-handled knives, large pots, or fine crystal) and either dry them and put them away, or leave them in the dish drainer to air-dry.
8. Pour detergent and hot water into any particularly greasy pans and let them soak overnight.
9. Run the garbage disposal unit if you have one.
10. Wipe off all kitchen counters.
11. Wipe off stove, including any food or liquid that may have spilled under the burners.
12. Scrub the sink.
13. Hang the dishrag and dish towel in a spot where they'll dry overnight.
14. Sweep the floor and pick up crumbs and stuff with dustpan.
15. Empty the garbage pail and take the garbage out to the incinerator or garage.
16. Reline the garbage pail.
17. Turn out the kitchen light.
18. Smile—you're all finished.

WHAT'S THE PAYOFF?

To pay or not to pay? That is the question working parents often ponder when deciding the fine line between family cooperation and exploitation of child labor. Most of the parents I spoke to do not pay their children for run-of-the-mill family chores, but consider the performance of most household tasks a shared responsibility that is part of the price of belonging to a family. As Lilli Scott says, "It's important to get across to them the ideas that one has to earn the right to his comfort and conveniences and that we're all in this together."

Most child-development authorities agree with Lilli. In Grace W. Weinstein's comprehensive and sensible book, *Children and Money* (see appendix, "Recommended Reading"), this eminent financial adviser (and working mother) says, "Excessive expectation of material reward is fostered by paying a child for every contribution to the family welfare; the result may be a child who won't lift a finger without pay." And as psychologist Dr. Lee Salk says, "The parent who pays a child for taking out the garbage is creating a monster."

It's not unreasonable, though, to pay a child for doing an especially burdensome or messy job, or one not directly involved with the life of the family, or one that keeps her from earning money outside the family. Many families do pay youngsters for washing the car, serving and cleaning up at an adults-only party, or baby-sitting on a weekend evening when the youngster could have earned money sitting for another family.

By and large, the payoff for children who share the work of the household is the self-respect they feel as contributing members of the family. As Sue Goldstein, age sixteen, told me, "I feel way ahead of a lot of my friends whose mothers wait on them or who have housekeepers to clean up after them. I know how to do everything: I can cook; I can handle tools; I can do the laundry. I've even stayed alone with my younger sister for a day or two when my mother has had to go on a business trip, and neither of us felt at all nervous because we know just what to do. I'm really pulling my weight in this family and that's a good feeling."

Another form of payoff is a feeling of pride in what the family does together. Because the Kelly family, for example, has been having guests over every couple of weeks, there's been a bigger push from everyone to get the house cleaned up for the company. Everyone enjoys the visits with friends and everyone enjoys showing off a clean, neat apartment.

MAKE SURE THEY FOLLOW THROUGH

Once your family has developed a plan that allots chores to everyone in the family, taking into account their various levels of ability, keep up your expectations that everyone will follow through and do what he is supposed to do.

Don't bail them out.

Don't say, "It's easier for me to do it myself than to nag." It may be easier this time, but in the long run persistence in the beginning will pay off in the end.

How, then, can you make sure that everyone does what she is supposed to do? There's no perfect solution, of course, but different families have come up with different approaches, depending on individual personalities and life-styles.

Memory-Jogging

We all tend to forget the things we don't want to do. (In fact, we sometimes forget the things we think we most want to do.) So once you've worked out a plan for household management, follow up with a plan for follow-through. Most families write it down in one or more places. Some post everyone's weekly work schedules on the family bulletin board; some on a chart magnetized to the refrigerator door; some on a large calendar (with big spaces for writing every day).

Instead of—or better yet, in addition to—writing it down, some families talk about it. They include chore division as a regularly scheduled item on the agenda of their weekly family council. Some allow a couple of minutes every evening after dinner to run through a quick review of who's doing what the next day, including who's cooking dinner, who has to go to the dentist, who needs a ride to dancing school.

Nancy and Ken Meyer of Chappaqua, New York, write out every job separately on three-by-five-inch index cards, and everyone in the family, including nine-year-old Mark, has his or her own stack of cards, to run through every day. Mark has been on this system since he was five. (For step-by-step instructions for setting up a color-coded card system that differentiates daily, weekly, and occasional chores, see the book, *Sidetracked Home Executives: From Pigpen to Paradise,* by Pam Young and Peggy Jones (see appendix "Recommended Reading"). These two sisters, who bill themselves as "reformed slobs," have devised a new and practical approach to household—and life—management.)

When They Fall Down on the Job

Okay, the agreement has been made, the memories have been jogged, and the job still doesn't get done. Mary dashed out of the house every morning this week without making her bed; Billy left a jumble of blocks all over the living-room floor two days ago, and they're still there; Andrea never did do the laundry last week, and no one has any clean underwear. What do you do?

It all depends. It depends on whether the culprit usually performs the job conscientiously and forgot just this once—or whether the exception is the time he *does* the job rather than the times he doesn't do it. And, of course, it all depends on what the job itself is.

Dr. Wayne Dyer, author of *What Do You Really Want for Your Children?* and a number of other best-selling self-help books, once told me of Evelyn, who came to him complaining that her twelve-year-old son George repeatedly neglected his job of taking out the garbage. She had reminded, scolded, and screamed, but nothing carried over to the next time, and she was determined that George would carry out this one simple task. "You have to stop stating your case in words," Dr. Dyer told Evelyn. "Devise some kind of behavioral strategy for dealing with the problem."

Dr. Dyer and Evelyn finally came up with a plan. The next time George went off to school, leaving the garbage in the kitchen, Evelyn marched up to his room, covered his bed with sheets of newspaper and emptied the bag of garbage right on top of the papers. Yes, there was an uproar when George set foot in his bedroom and found out where that smell was coming from. But yes, he did get that garbage off the bed and outside where it should have gone early that morning. And yes, he did learn that his mother meant business, especially when she said, smiling sweetly, without a hint of anger in her voice, "That's where the garbage will go every time I find it here in the kitchen when it's supposed to have been taken out." It landed on George's bed only one more time. When I expressed some question about my own ability to follow through on a program like this, Wayne had a ready answer: "If you say, 'Oh, I could never do that,' what you're saying by your refusal to take constructive action is that you're willing to go on emptying the garbage and being upset about it."

Another friend, educator Dr. Sidney Simon, takes a different tack. As he writes in his book, *Caring, Feeling, Touching,* "I'd like to relate something that parents often bring up in the workshops I give around the country. It seems that one of the major domestic problems of this nation is getting kids to put dirty socks and underwear in the laundry hamper. Parents say that they shout, they punish, they cajole, but nothing seems to work. The dirty socks and underwear continue to turn up in hallways, behind beds, and on closet floors. I suggest that a lot of energy can be saved and much more positive attitudes produced if the parents simply put the dirty underwear in the hamper themselves, but establish a rule that each time they do it, they are entitled to a five-minute back rub from the child who has played litterbug. Instead of occasioning an exchange of shouts and recriminations, the littered laundry sets off an exchange of kindnesses. And giving a five-minute back rub will build more character than any number of pieces of underwear picked up and put in the hamper."

Another approach allows natural consequences to take over. Suppose you have agreed that everyone in your family will take turns cooking dinner on weeknights. You have also agreed that the person doing the marketing will buy all the food for all the meals if she gets the lists before the regular weekly trip. If not, each cook is responsible for shopping for his own ingredients, as well as preparing the meal.

You have three children. Two of them consistently follow through on their cooking obligations, and even though the food wouldn't always rate four gourmet stars, it *is* edible. The third child, though, invariably forgets. "Oh, is this *my* night?" she gasps, twenty minutes before dinner time.

You can wave her in the direction of the pantry, the refrigerator, or the freezer, so she could whip up a tuna-noodle casserole, a bowl of spaghetti with canned meat sauce and frozen vegetables, or an omelet and salad. Or everyone could fix his or her own dinner. Or you could say, "The rest of us are hungry—so we'll go out to eat. I'm sure you can find something for yourself." The irritation the rest of the family expresses or the feeling of abandonment if she is left home alone while you all go out to eat may be enough to motivate the forgetful one to remember for the next time.

When everyone in the family is responsible for doing his own laundry, the minute Marc runs out of underwear or socks, he'll realize that it's up to him to think ahead next time.

DESIGN A COOPERATIVE ENVIRONMENT

"I found that adapting my home to my family's habits instead of vice versa cut down a lot of conflicts," Lilli Scott told me. Does your home environment work with you or against you? In the end, you're the one who decides whether it will be your friend or your adversary.

A cooperative home makes life easier for the entire family. It is easy to keep clean and easy to keep neat. By paring maintenance to a minimum, it keeps family conflicts over chores at a minimum, too, and so it helps you all get along better with each other. It also gives you more time to follow your own interests and to have fun.

How can you make your home cooperate with you? As an overall guideline, you might get into the habit of asking yourself one question before you buy anything for your home:

"Will this cooperate with our family?" Plush white carpeting wouldn't, for example, whereas a blue–green tweed might. Intricately carved dining-room chairs whose seats are covered in pale yellow velvet won't, while simple lines and easy-to-wipe-off seat coverings would. Here are some suggestions that other working parents have developed:

- Go all-or-nothing with rugs. Either pick them all up so you can sweep your floors quickly, or carpet from wall to wall so you can run over them quickly with a vacuum cleaner. The hardest, most time-consuming arrangement requires having to clean both bare floors and rugs in the same room.
- Set up a separate family/TV-viewing area away from the main living area where the family can eat and make other messes that don't have to be cleaned up right away.
- Install hooks within easy reach of the children in the entryway so they can hang coats, jackets, sweaters, and hats; in the bathrooms, for towels, washcloths, and shower caps; in their bedrooms, for pajamas, robes, sweaters, and jeans; in the rooms where they play, for dress-up hats and clothes, play jewelry and paint smocks; in the kitchen, for cooking utensils; and in the garage or workshop for tools. If you use a pegboard, you may want to tape the hooks so the children won't pull them out all the time. If you outline the shapes of tools and kitchen utensils, they're more likely to wind up at the right spots.
- Use shelves instead of closed cabinets or drawers wherever possible, because both big and little people tend to set things down rather than put them away.
- To make it easier for children to put their things away, color code or label their shelves and dresser drawers. Use words if they can read and pictures if they can't. (Using both words and pictures together will help teach them to read.)
- Make it easier for your children to put away their toys by using shelves instead of a toy box (in a box, toys get jumbled and broken and are hard to find; besides, the lid is a safety hazard for small children) and by replacing the boxes the toys originally came in with larger containers that don't require precision packing—old coffee cans or plastic refrigerator containers, for example, for crayons;

a fishing tackle box for Lego blocks; stackable vegetable bins for toys with a thousand pieces; flat shirt or dress boxes for paper dolls and craft papers; laundry baskets for trucks and cars; a shoe bag for small dolls and stuffed animals.

- Decorate dark. Use dark, tweedy, or multicolor designs for upholstery and carpeting; these don't show the dirt as much as light, smooth finishes.
- Replace bedspreads with quilts that don't need tucking in or straightening. With matching pillowcases and sheets, they dress up the bedroom decor and simplify bed-making for even the youngest member of the family.
- Decide upon a place for everything and show the children where the place is. When something starts to get too crowded—a closet, a shelf, or a drawer—go through it ruthlessly. You *can* throw out those torn boots you were saving for emergencies, those puzzles with missing pieces that no one plays with anymore, the stretched-out tee shirts in the back of the drawer. (Items like these are always available for next-to-nothing at thrift shops just in case you suddenly find a need for a stretched-out tee shirt with a big chocolate stain right on the front.) One useful test is the "rule of one year": if it hasn't been worn, played with, or looked at for a year, it doesn't deserve to take up space in your home.

Of course, no matter how ingenious your solutions, how good your planning, or how cooperative your family, you will have to keep reevaluating the way things are going. There is bound to be some backsliding, some discontent, some feeling that some family members are doing more than their share and others are doing less.

As Elliott A. Medrich emphasizes, "There are really no ready-made, easy solutions to the perpetual struggle for family cooperation. Children are never going to do all their chores perfectly and consistently, or without growling from time to time—it would be against their nature. But mutual respect, a willingness to compromise, fuller communication (that includes letting the kids know the importance of their contributions), plus an occasional dollop of crafty thinking, can certainly ease the conflict."

16

TIMESAVING TIPS FOR WORKING PARENTS

The suggestions in this chapter come from the experiences of other working parents and from the advice of time management experts. You are probably already doing some of the things outlined, and you probably don't want to do some of the others. Not all of them, of course, will work out well for your own situation. But a number of them probably will. And even if these particular approaches are not for you, you'll find that as you read about different ways of doing things, you'll come up with your own innovative ways of saving time, energy, and sanity. Good luck!

TIME IS MONEY!*

These suggestions can be applied to your paid work as well as to your unpaid work of home management.

*Suggestions for saving time culled from the book of the same name, *Time Is Money! The Key to Managerial Success,* by Ross A. Webber (Free Press, 1980).

- Every evening, write down the six most important tasks for the next day in order of priority. Every morning, do them in the order listed.
- Make a list of ten things you want to do. Do the first two for sure and do the others when you can.
- Take five sheets of paper. List:
  1. the activities of your job
  2. these activities arranged by importance
  3. the same activities arranged by urgency
  4. the same activities arranged by how easily they can be delegated
  5. the people you need to see to do these activities
     This lets you see which activities are urgent and important and should be done at once, which you can farm out, and where to start to do them.
- Keep a log for two weeks, writing down everything you do as you do it. Look back to see what's necessary and what isn't, what you yourself have to do, and what you can delegate.
- Set deadlines for tasks, in minutes, hours, or days.
- Reward your progress by giving yourself a treat (a lunch out, an hour's pleasure reading, a favorite TV show).
- Involve your family in your work by talking to them about it, thus narrowing the gap between work life and family life.
- Allow time for the unexpected. Says Dr. Ross A. Webber, a professor of management at the University of Pennsylvania, "To imply that time is wasted just because it is used in an unplanned way is a distortion of values, a misguided overconcern for time."
- Try Alan Lakein's "life-control" plan. Every year on your birthday list goals for your lifetime, for the next five years, and for the next six months; take the three most important from each and then the three most important from the nine remaining. Allot specific blocks of time for activities that will help you reach those goals. Do one activity every day.
- Master time anxiety by taking off your wrist watch on weekends.

FINDING TIME WHEN THERE ISN'T ANY

- Put a price on your time. Figure out what it's worth and which laborsaving devices and services are worth the cost in dollars for the savings in hours.
- Think about the kinds of services you can pay someone else to do. Some common examples are laundry, cooking (buying cooked foods from a local store, caterer, or the freezer department), house repairs, clothing alteration, yard work, and housecleaning. You might also be able to hire a teenage or adult neighbor, or one of your own children, to do various errands: wait in line at the motor vehicle bureau, sit in your home to wait for a delivery or repairman, or do your marketing.
- Open charge accounts with stores that deliver groceries, drug items, dry cleaning, laundry, liquor, and whatever else you can buy this way.
- When you delegate chores, give up the responsibility for remembering to see that it gets done, along with giving up the need to do the actual chore.
- Consolidate your trips. Plan your errands so that you do several in the same neighborhood. Make appointments for your children and yourself to see the dentist on the same day. While you're waiting, you can do some of the portable tasks suggested in the next section. You can also use the time for social catching up with your children.
- Learn how to work with small blocks of time so that you can complete small tasks or make inroads in large ones. If you don't have time to clean out an entire file drawer, do half, leave a marker where you stopped, and do the rest another time.
- Learn how to do two things at once. Some of the things you can do while talking on the phone or watching TV: water plants, polish nails or shoes, fold laundry, sew on buttons, mend, knit, balance your checkbook, go over bank statements, open the mail, do exercises, cook, and wash dishes.
- Wake up an hour earlier than the rest of the family. In that

quiet time you may be able to accomplish far more than you could later in the day when you have to cope with distractions.

• Invest time in teaching everyone in your family how to run all the appliances (stove, dishwasher, clothes washer, and dryer) and how to prepare basic meals.

• Teach your caregiver to drive.

• Kick the habit of reading the daily newspapers from front to back. Learn how to skim to get the important news and the latest developments in your own field. Catch up by listening to an all-news radio station while you exercise, dress, or drive.

WAYS NOT TO WASTE WAITING TIME

(In the dentist's waiting room, the haircutting shop, your car, or anywhere else you have to sit for a while)

• Catch up on business or personal reading. Always carry your own reading matter so you won't have to read three-year-old *National Geographics.*

• Write a letter. Always keep a few sheets of stationery, some envelopes, and some stamps with you.

• Plan your schedule for the next day, week, or month.

• Take a cat-nap. Ten or fifteen minutes of sleep can often keep you going for hours.

• Clean out your handbag or briefcase.

• If you're in the car, clean out the glove compartment, clean all the inside windows and the rearview mirror, and get rid of debris on floor and seats (remember to keep window-cleaning spray and paper towels in the trunk).

• Use what writer Phyllis LeFarge calls "third time." "First time" is time spent working; "second time" is time spent taking care of home and family; and "third time" is the time you have to let your mind meander about your life, your feelings, and your idle thoughts.

TAKING THE WRINKLES OUT
OF DOING THE LAUNDRY

- Send out shirts, tablecloths, and clothes with stubborn stains and spots instead of struggling with them yourself.
- Have each family member do her own laundry; if anyone falls down on the job, he will be the one who runs out of clean clothes.
- Pay a child to do the laundry for the entire family.
- Never iron. If anything really needs to be pressed, throw that item out or give it away.
- Hang up blouses, shirts, dresses, and slacks immediately after removing them from the dryer to let the wrinkles hang out.
- If clothes come wrinkled from staying in the dryer too long, rerun the dryer for five or ten minutes (a waste of electrical energy, but a savings in human energy).
- Assign your children to fold laundry while they're watching TV.
- If one person does everyone's laundry, each individual's clothes should be put in a separate pile so everyone can pick up her pile and put away her own clothes.
- Have every family member keep a laundry hamper or bag in his bedroom. Each person's laundry can be washed separately (in cold water, so the colors won't run) and then stay together. No sorting will be necessary this way.
- Use the washing machine as a hamper for white clothes, the bathroom hamper for colored clothes. You can then run the washer when it's full, without having to sort by color.
- Don't run the washing machine or the dryer (or the dishwasher, for that matter) when no one is home. If the machine leaks or short-circuits, you could have big troubles. Do run them while you're doing something else nearby.
- When you change your bed linens, strip the bed in the morning, launder the sheets and cases, and put the same ones back on the bed later on. This eliminates the need to fold and put them away. All you need is one extra set of sheets and cases for each bed for emergencies.

- Do the same thing with your towels and washcloths: Wash and dry them and hang them right back on the same hooks. No folding, no putting away.
- Buy different-patterned sheets for each size bed for instant recognition.
- Color code underwear and socks as much as possible, giving each family member a distinctive color or pattern, again for instant recognition. If all your children insist on wearing white socks, have them sew different color threads in the toes or dab them with a permanent marker to identify them.
- Label the shelves in your linen closet (e.g., *flat single sheets, fitted single, pillowcases, flat doubles, fitted doubles, washcloths, guest towels, bath towels, etc.*). Whoever puts the linens away will know the right spot for everything.
- Don't use separate face towels and hand towels for family. Let everyone use their bath towels for everything.
- Make a rule that what goes in the wash inside out (like socks, underwear, and tee shirts) comes out inside out. Everyone straightens out her own clothes.
- If you have clothes that have to be washed by hand (you shouldn't have, if you shop carefully, but we all make mistakes), put some suds in the bathroom or kitchen sink and let your preschooler swish them about. Your child will enjoy the water play, and your blouse, shirt, or underwear will come clean painlessly.
- Or take your hand laundry into the tub or shower with you. A quick couple of squeezes or rubs with a mild bar soap and both you and your clothes will emerge clean.

MAKING MARKETING MORE MANAGEABLE

- Make a master list of the foods you usually buy and make a stack of photocopies. Group items by category and, if you use the same market all the time, by location in the store. Leave space for write-ins. Include brand names, sizes, and quantities if other people besides yourself do the shopping. Post a photocopy on the family bulletin board or on the front of the refrigerator, with a pencil hanging nearby, to check items you need to buy.

- Always keep an extra container of staples or of items that can live for a long time in the freezer or the refrigerator, so you'll be unlikely to run out. Whoever opens the spare container checks it off on the shopping list.
- Make up a week's menus ahead of time. Figure out what foods you'll need for the entire week and shop only once. Have the bagger separate the perishables and put away immediately anything that goes in freezer or refrigerator.
- Hang a pad and pencil in the bathroom to keep a running list of bathroom supplies you need to replace.
- Don't go to the store for one item, if at all possible. Learn how to substitute for the items you most often run out of. The world won't come to an end if a favorite food isn't available every single day.
- When loading your cart, keep similar items together, (like frozen foods, refrigerated items, produce, etc.). It will be easier to unload and bag, by category, and to put away at home.
- Use the baby seat in the cart for perishables if you don't have a baby in it.
- If you do have a small child with you, buy him a healthful snack to keep him occupied. Cheese, raisins, and animal crackers are favorites.
- When unloading, place all items price-side-up or code-side up to speed the cashier's job.
- If you need special clearance for cashing a check, get it before you get in line so you won't have to wait (and won't keep other busy working parents behind you in line waiting).
- Pick a line where a bagger is helping the cashier; it will move more quickly. Pick a cashier you know; a new one will be slower.
- Help the clerk bag the groceries. You'll get out faster, and you can pack your items according to the way you'll put them away (all frozen foods together, produce, refrigerated items, etc.).

- A long line with a lot of small orders usually moves more quickly than a shorter line with bigger orders.
- Put the heavier items (cans, bottles, cleaning supplies) on the counter first, so they can go in the bottoms of the bags.
- Give the cashier your coupons before she begins ringing up your order.
- If you can find a supermarket that accepts phoned-in orders, gets your order ready for pick-up, or delivers it to you, the extra service may well be worth a nominal extra charge.
- When putting foods away, put the newest items in the back so you'll always use the oldest ones first.
- Freeze meats in amounts you'll need for one meal. Divide ground beef into individual patties, wrap separately in waxed paper, and put several patties in a plastic bag and freeze. When it comes time to cook them, you can take out the exact amount you need. The hamburgers will thaw more quickly, and you won't have any waste.
- When you hard-boil eggs, mark the date on them in pencil. You'll be able to tell them apart from raw eggs and you'll be able to use the oldest ones first.
- Label the shelves where you store your canned goods, so whoever puts them away will know where to put canned soups, fruits, vegetables, tomato sauces, and so forth.
- Label all your frozen foods.
- Use plastic wrap instead of aluminum foil to cover foods so you'll have fewer "mystery" packages in your refrigerator.
- Steer clear of so-called convenience foods, which are expensive, loaded with additives, and often no easier to use than the real thing.
- Market during your lunch hour, in the evening with your spouse, or whenever you have an hour between other activities and you find yourself near a market. The least crowded times are Monday (don't go till after 11:00 AM to be sure shelves are restocked after the weekend) through Wednesday during the day; most evenings; and Sunday. The worst days are Friday and Saturday.
- Buy nonperishables (like paper goods, canned goods, bottled goods, and cleaning supplies) in large amounts if you

have the storage space. Buying by the case will save you time, and it may save you money if your grocer will give you a discount, as some do.

- Call ahead if you want special cuts of meat. Or, go to the butcher as soon as you enter the store, and then do the rest of your shopping while he's cutting and wrapping your order. This way you won't have to wait.
- Choose items with clearly marked prices so the cashier won't have to stop to ask someone else about the prices.
- Market for staples every other week. On the alternate week, just pick up perishables like produce, dairy products, meats, and bread.
- If a hired person or your children are doing the marketing, teach them how to choose produce; to avoid soft or icy frozen foods; to avoid rusty, swollen, and banged-up cans; to count their change; to be sure everything they put on the counter gets into the bag they carry out of the store; and to check the expiration dates on the package.
- Also tell them what to do if the market doesn't have the exact size or brand you've specified or usually use.

HOT TIPS FOR MEALTIMES

- Divide cooking equally among all members of the family, so each bears responsibility for planning, marketing for, cooking, serving, and cleaning up after meals.
- Institute a "cook's day off" once a week. Have everyone in the family prepare his or her own meals, whenever they feel like eating. As long as you have on hand such staples as canned soups, tuna fish, eggs, and cheese, putting a meal together can be easy and fast. No one has to think about feeding the family, and everyone can enjoy the freedom to eat according to his or her own schedule.
- Instead of a heavy, fattening, time-consuming Sunday or holiday meal, consider a do-it-yourself salad and/or sandwich bar, followed by the fixings for making your own sundaes. No one will have to spend hours in either prep-

aration or cleaning up, and you'll still enjoy the family togetherness.

- Use a crock pot or put up meals in the morning before you go to work. Or a microwave oven for fast cooking at mealtimes.
- "Eat out" at home once a week. Serve prepared food—pizza, fried chicken, hamburgers, or special dishes from the delicatessen—on paper plates. It's more expensive than cooking yourself, but cheaper, easier, and less time consuming than taking several children out to a restaurant. You can make it a healthier meal by providing your own salad, vegetables, and a fruit dessert.
- Switch your family to eating the day's big meal at lunchtime. If you're all eating lunch out anyway, you can eat a more substantial meal at midday and be satisfied with a light supper in the evening. This policy of eating "like a king at breakfast, like a prince at lunch, and like a pauper at supper" is easier on the cook and healthier for everyone.
- When you're cooking a main dish that freezes well, cook enough for two or three meals and freeze the extra for work-free dinners another time.
- As long as your diet is balanced overall, every single meal doesn't have to be balanced. Take advantage of seasonal treats by, for example, making an entire meal out of farm-fresh buttered corn-on-the-cob one evening or of fresh asparagus another. From the health standpoint, animal protein is overrated, anyway. Your family's protein needs can be met with legumes and cheeses and with small amounts of meat, fish, and poultry. For good suggestions on putting together an easy and nutritious eating plan, see the excellent book written by one working mother, *Jane Brody's Nutrition Book* (Bantam, 1982).
- Plan a cold-main-dish meal once a week. Eat leftover poultry or meat, accompanied, if you wish, with hot vegetables and rolls. In winter, you can add hot soup.
- Keep chopped onion and green pepper in your freezer, so you can easily add them in cooking. You can either buy them already chopped and bagged from your grocer's freezer, or you can mince a quantity yourself and freeze it.

- Save time and vitamins by not peeling potatoes (unless they have green skin or eyes), tomatoes, eggplant, zucchini, and carrots. A fast scrubbing will get rid of the dirt and make any of these vegetables ready for cooking and eating.
- Hire your children to cook and bake for you. If they're like most youngsters, they're likely to consider cooking fun, to have more time than you do and to enjoy the idea of earning a little pocket money. Even young children can make delicious cookies, brownies, and other goodies.
- Do your messiest kitchen work, such as husking corn, grating cabbage, or peeling potatoes—if you insist—over sheets of newspaper, outdoors when the weather permits. When you're finished, you can dump the whole mess, papers and all, right into the garbage can.
- Freeze small amounts of leftovers in an easy-to-use form. If you have just a little bit of everything, put it in a TV tray, and you'll have an individual meal for a time when someone's eating home alone. Or if you have just a slice or two of meat, make and freeze half a sandwich. Come some lunchtime, two or three half-sandwiches of different varieties can constitute an interesting lunch-box surprise.
- Use natural convenience foods rather than the prepared kinds. One survey found that working women serve fewer convenience foods than their at-home counterparts, partly because portion sizes are often inconvenient, prepared foods are 15 percent to 100 percent more expensive than similar dinners made at home, and often they don't save that much time. This shows sensible thinking, especially since there are such naturally convenient foods—foods that take a minimum of time to prepare—as vegetables, salads, hamburgers, hot dogs, pasta, cheese, eggs, liver, steak, and lamb chops. All of these are fast and easy to cook and good to eat. For the food value you get, a sirloin steak can be a better dollars-and-cents value than a packaged macaroni-and-cheese dinner.
- Finally, *never* NEVER prepare an elaborate meal—even for company—unless you enjoy doing it so much that it constitutes an enjoyable leisure-time hobby. You don't have to prove anything to anybody. You don't have to be

supercook as well as superworker. Between your grocer's freezer and nearby specialty stores, you can purchase complete meals that are as good as—or better than— those you could make yourself. Depending on your time schedule, it may well be worth spending the extra money to buy it. Often, the difference is not as great as you might think.

TEN TRICKS FOR GETTING THE FAMILY UP AND OUT IN THE MORNING

1. Give each child his or her own alarm clock. Set them for the little ones and show the older ones how to do it themselves. If you can swing the expense, give them clock radios so they can wake up to music or a favorite personality.
2. About ten minutes after the alarms should have gone off, play loud music that everyone likes. Rock, folk, Sesame Street, and John Philip Sousa marches are all good choices.
3. Wake up half an hour earlier yourself. You won't miss the extra sleep; your mornings will be less hectic, and everyone will be in a better mood.
4. Stagger wake-up times if there's only one bathroom.
5. Do whatever you can the night before, like preparing lunches, setting the breakfast table, choosing everyone's clothes, measuring out the coffee, and taking baths and showers.
6. Prepare a quick-and-easy breakfast.
7. Stack books and other items to take to school and work at a "launching pad," a special place near the door where you all leave the house. Set aside a special corner for each family member and get everyone in the habit of checking his spot before leaving the house. Leave reminder notes here, too. Do as much as you can the night before.
8. Simplify the children's clothing (see list following).

9. Keep all the daily suplies—toothbrush and toothpaste, soap, washcloth, and towel; mirror, comb, and brush— at a level low enough for the children to reach easily.
10. Make a list for each child of the things he has to do every morning, photocopy the lists so there's a fresh one every day, have the children check off their lists every day, award gold stars each day they do everything, and give small rewards for ten gold stars. The list might include: make bed, brush teeth, pack lunch, take homework, feed cat, etc.

HOW TO SIMPLIFY CHILDREN'S CLOTHING AND MAKE IT EASIER FOR THEM TO DRESS

- Buy them clothes that fasten in front.
- Check for fasteners they can manage themselves. Zippers are easier than buttons, for example.
- Never buy anything that needs ironing. Beware of labels that say, "light touch-up recommended."
- If shoelace-tying is a problem, substitute narrow elastic for laces. Or buy shoes that close with Velcro.
- Sew buttons on with elastic thread. It stretches and makes buttons go through buttonholes more easily.
- Attach metal rings to boot zippers to make them easier to pull.
- Clip mittens to coat sleeves (clips designed just for this are sold in dime stores), or pin or sew them to a sturdy string that you run through both sleeves of a coat or jacket.

TAKING CARE OF YOURSELF

- Find a haircutter who can get you out within an hour so you can get your hair cut during your lunch hour. Or look for one that stays open evenings, or one where you can take your child along on a Saturday.

- Keep your hair dryer on a hook in the bathroom or in a special case instead of putting it away each time.
- Get your hair cut in a way that's easy to take care of. Very short or very long hair is usually easier than an in-between length.
- Treat yourself to one professional makeup session. Then learn how to put on your daily makeup in five minutes or less.
- Take a bath or shower with your little one. It's a relaxing social time, an extra chance to be together, and an enjoyable way to accomplish part of your daily routine. (While some psychiatrists discourage parental nudity in front of children, others say that if you feel comfortable and unembarrassed, your children are not likely to suffer any ill effects.)
- Keep small containers of cosmetics in your purse or briefcase so you can apply quick touch-ups when needed. If you've rushed out of the house, you may be able to apply cosmetics on the commuter train (I see people doing it all the time on the Long Island Rail Road) or when your carpool is stuck in traffic.

BUYING YOUR CLOTHES

- Open a charge account with every store you shop at. This will help you to shop easily by mail or phone. Have packages delivered to a neighbor, a friend, or your place of business if no one is at your home during the day.
- Shop from newspaper ads and catalogs to save a trip to the store.
- In your personal telephone book, devote one page to the stores where you shop by phone. Write in the special shop-by-phone number for each one, the general store number (for times when you have special questions), and your charge-account number. When you call, you'll have all the

information handy. If one store doesn't have what you want, you can go right down the list.

- Shop for yourself when you take your children to buy their clothes. It may require only a quick detour into another department, and it will give you an interested stake in the shopping expedition and your children the fun of rendering their opinions. (Although you may get tired of hearing such opinions as: "Yuch! Does that make you look fat!" or "Don't you think that outfit is too *young* for you?")
- To get quick, personalized service, get to know a salesperson in a favorite store. Then, when you need to make a major purchase like a suit or coat, you can call first and find out whether there's a good supply in stock. Before you get there, the salesperson can pull out the things that might interest you, and you can try them on right away.
- At the beginning of each season, check the fashion magazines and newspaper ads and decide what you need to fill out your wardrobe. Then take one or two days for blitz shopping to get everything.
- Shop for clothes when you're out of town on business trips and have an odd hour or two between appointments.
- Many better department stores have personal shoppers. If you call them first and make an appointment to meet them, they'll do a lot of the work of gathering separates and accessories from different departments, to await your arrival in the store.
- Make a note of sizes and brand names of standard items like socks, underwear, pajamas, bras, and stockings so you can order them by phone.
- When you find a special style of shirt, sweater, blouse, jeans, slacks, or skirt that fits you particularly well, buy two or three at a time, in different colors and fabrics.

ORGANIZING YOUR PERSONAL TELEPHONE NUMBERS FOR GREATER EFFICIENCY

1. Use a small loose-leaf directory (available at stationery stores and dime stores).

2. Write all numbers in pencil (so you can easily correct for changed addresses, phone numbers, and names that go from single to married or vice versa).

3. Line up some entries by category, rather than alphabetically, such as doctors, department stores (write your charge-account number under each), baby-sitters, household workers (plumber, electrician, etc.), and other categories you call often (tennis or bridge players, grocery stores, movie theaters, restaurants, etc.). Arranging numbers this way helps you locate someone quickly when you can't remember the last name right away. It also lets you go right down the list of department stores when you shop by phone.

4. On the first or last page, write down information you need to refer to from time to time, such as Social Security numbers for everyone in the family and checking account numbers.

5. Of course, if you have a personal computer, you can keep all this information there.

CATCHING UP WITH CORRESPONDENCE

• Keep the names and addresses of the friends and family you correspond with or send Christmas cards to on three-by-five-inch index cards or in your personal computer. This works out much better than an address book for changing names and addresses and telephone numbers; for recording the births and names of children; and for writing down dates of birthdays and anniversaries.

• When you have an extra fifteen minutes in a shopping area, buy a quantity of greeting cards—birthday, anniversary, get-well, and general friendship. When you want to send one, you won't have to rush out to buy the kind you need.

• Or don't send cards. Drop a quick note or postcard or make a fast telephone call instead. These more personal gestures will probably be appreciated even more. (They'll cost a lot less, too.)

- In the front of your card box, keep a card for each month. Record all the birthdays and other dates you want to remember for, as an example, January. At the beginning of the month address the appropriate cards. At the end of the month move January's card to the back of the pile and start on February.
- Drop a quick postcard from time to time just to let friends know you're thinking of them. Chances are they don't have any more time to read long letters than you have to write them, so they're likely to appreciate a couple of lines and the thought.
- Evaluate your Christmas-card list. Are you still interested in all the people who are on it? If they live within fifty miles, do you make any effort to see them during the year? If not, do you still feel you have a relationship worth preserving through the annual card? If the only communication you receive from someone is a once-a-year card with their names printed on it, with no personal note, is this a real connection? You may feel your time is better spent cultivating and nurturing fewer deep friendships rather than keeping up many superficial acquaintances.
- Pay a child to address and stamp your Christmas envelopes. While you're sitting down together with her, you can be writing personal notes to slip inside the envelopes.
- Get labels printed up with your name and address. You can get 1000 for $1.49,* and they come in handy as return-address stickers on letters and Christmas cards, on mail-order forms, to identify your books and other belongings, and whenever you need to send out a self-addressed envelope.
- Another good use for these labels is in sending mail to someone you write to often (such as a child at college, your parents in another city, or your closest long-distance friend). Instead of writing the same address over and over, you can order a quantity of labels printed up with someone else's name and address. (I just threw out the rest of the supply left from one daughter's college years. That dollar forty-nine was one of the best investments I ever made!)

*From Walter Drake & Sons, Inc.; 94 Drake Building; Colorado Springs, CO 80940.

17

MAKING LIFE BETTER FOR ALL WORKING PARENTS—INCLUDING YOU

In 1988 pediatricians T. Berry Brazelton, Penelope Leach, and Benjamin Spock all spoke at the Boston Parents' Paper Family Forum at Harvard University. As Nicola Knipe reported in the *Boston Parents' Paper,* they came together "to plant the seeds of political activism in parents who were at their wits' end to find enough time even to shop for groceries. Instead of offering some magic formula to 'have it all' and be happy, they turned the tables and said there *is* no answer—no secret, no formula—unless parents make one themselves. Unless parents organize, and get their voices heard, and make their needs known, nothing will change. Only we, the parents, can do it."

Because the working parent's scarcest commodity is time and because dreams about what could be often have to give way to dealing with what is, most of the focus in this book is on

377

what you can do that directly affects your everyday life. Still, you *are* part of a growing force in this country. You're important as a worker, as a voter, as a consumer, as a citizen. And you can take actions that can give you more of the societal supports that you should have. You have every right to make demands on the government supported by your taxes, the employer supported by your labor, and the community organizations supported by your charitable contributions.

These and other forces in society can and should be doing much more than they are now. The following pages suggest some of the courses that you might pursue to make life better for you, for other working parents, and eventually for your children, who will probably be working parents, too. Besides these specific suggestions, you may want to contact and join some of the organizations listed in the appendix, "Helpful Organizations," many of which are advocacy groups for parents and children. For information on what they offer and the ways you can benefit from, or work to advance, their services, write directly to the agencies that seem most pertinent to your own situation.

Meanwhile, you can take steps like the following.

MAKING CHANGES AT WORK

What You Can Do

- *Do a great job.* The more valuable you are as an employee, the more likely your employer is to listen to—and act on—what you have to say. This is true not only in terms of making individual exceptions to company policy but also in terms of changing company policy.
- *Join with fellow workers.* If you're a member of a union, mobilize support there. If not, talk to other workers who have similar concerns and set up a committee.
- *Gather information.* Find out how many working parents are in your organization, how many two-paycheck work-

ers, how many single parents. Then find out from other workers what benefits they would like and what other similar companies are doing.

- *Go to your company's human resources department.* With a couple of your committee members, meet with a company representative in personnel. This is the department that would be aware of lateness and absence caused by child-care problems, of requests for maternity and paternity leaves, and of time lost because of excessive afternoon telephone contact between workers and their school-age children.
- *Ask for what your group wants.* Some companies follow some of the following policies. All of them are valid to request.

What You Might Ask For

- Equal opportunity for both sexes in employment, payment, promotion, and family-related policies.
- Paid maternity and paternity leaves, so that one or both parents can be home for a baby's first few months.
- The acceptance of part-time employment as a professional, permanent option, prorating health and other benefits to equal those offered full-time employees.
- Flexible scheduling that would allow employees to work during a core period—say, from 10 AM to 3 PM—and to schedule the rest of their time around their personal needs.
- Flexibility around lunch hours, so that workers can work through lunch one day and take two hours on another.
- Enough notice about overtime requests so that workers can make suitable child-care arrangements.
- Paid leave for family emergencies, recognizing that a child's illness is as valid a reason for absence from work as a parent's illness.
- Provision for letting employees do some work at home.
- Sponsorship of lunchtime seminars on career–family issues.
- Support for child care. Between 1978 and 1986, employer-supported child care programs went from 100 to more

than 3000 around the country, according to a survey by the Conference Board in New York City. Such support can take one of the following forms:

- Set up an on-site day-care center if there are enough parents who want the service, if they live near enough to work that they do not have to take small children on crowded public transportation during rush-hour traffic, and if the employer understands this effort as a contribution to the community rather than a way to boost company profits. (Chances are that the center would not make money, even if it did reduce employee turnover and absenteeism, because good day care is expensive. However, more and more employers have established such centers in efforts to attract more women workers and to help both male and female employees with their child-care problems.)
- As part of a "cafeteria benefits plan," subsidize child care by offering the option of child-care vouchers or tax exclusions so parent employees can purchase the kind of care they want.
- Support child-care services in the community by contributing funds and/or services to a local clearinghouse or information and referral agency. If none exists, help start one.
- Designate one or more employees as child-care coordinators, who can help other parents with their questions and problems, including how to get the child-care tax deduction or a child-care subsidy.
- Reimburse parents for child care when workers have to travel or work at other than their usual schedules.

MAKING CHANGES IN YOUR NEIGHBORHOOD

What You Can Do

- *Go to established agencies and institutions.* Some that offer services to the families of working parents are schools, churches and temples, day-care centers, United Way or Community Fund, senior citizens groups, Girl and Boy Scouts, and League of Women Voters.

- *Go first to those to which you belong.*
- *Enlist one or two other working parents to go with you.*
- *Make your requests for services like the following.*

What You Might Ask For

- A child-care clearinghouse (information and referral agency) that would provide lists of centers, nursery schools, family day-care providers, and baby-sitters.
- Free or low-cost workshops, seminars and courses for parents, baby-sitters, care-giving relatives, day-care and nursery-school workers, and family day-care providers.
- A resource center where family day-care providers can rent or borrow toys, equipment, child-care literature, and other materials.
- A center for children with minor illnesses.
- A center for disabled or chronically ill children.
- An infant-care center.
- A pick-up service to provide transportation for children who have to be picked up from school or preschool to go to a center or baby-sitter.
- After-school centers where children can play and do homework.
- Emergency in-home care by a trained worker who can care for sick or injured children, parents, and caregivers.
- A "block parent" program, designating at least one adult on every block to be available on call for emergency assistance around the clock at times of family crisis.
- Services for single parents, including discussion groups, social and educational programs, and help in obtaining public and private services.

MAKING CHANGES IN YOUR TOWN OR STATE

What You Can Do

- Press all candidates for election for their stands on issues that affect families of working parents. Tell them what you want. Vote for the ones who take the best stands.
- Contact your elected representatives on the city council or state assembly and press them to do what you want. Legislators do pay attention to what their constituents ask. They take their mail and phone calls seriously. You don't have to write a lengthy letter with overpowering arguments. Even a postcard stating your position on a particular issue or bill counts. So instead of putting off writing until you can compose a persuasive letter, just jot a few lines on a card, letter, or telegram and get it out.
- Follow the news about proposed bills and services and express your opinion forcefully.

What You Might Ask For

- Better public transportation so children can be more independent and so families can take advantage of more opportunities and services.
- Evening and/or weekend hours for government offices so that parents will not have to take time off from work to apply for child-care subsidies, get food stamps, go to family court, and take care of other important business.
- A comprehensive plan of community-based child care, which would offer a variety of services keyed to the needs of people in your area.
- Use of public school buildings and faculty in preschool, after-school, and summer programs and availability of full-day preschool and kindergarten sessions.
- Elimination of the "catch-22" situation that traps many parents. A mother goes to work because her family needs

her income, but as soon as she does well enough to get a raise, she has to take her child out of a government-sponsored child-care center—even if she can now pay the full cost of the child's care. Children should not have to leave familiar centers or day-care homes when their parents' incomes exceed eligibility requirements. Parents should be allowed to increase their share of the cost for the child's care.

- Registration of day-care providers instead of licensing. Licensing frightens many caregivers: They are worried about losing their privacy and losing income. As a result, they have no contact at all with the government resources that could help them give better care. Under voluntary registration, caregivers list their names with a state or local agency, agree to meet health and safety standards, and inform parents of those requirements. The agency distributes its list of caregivers but warns parents that they have to see that the homes meet state standards.

- Better working conditions and pay for caregivers, to attract and keep well-qualified workers. The state should increase child-care subsidies so that day-care workers can receive salaries and fringe benefits that are equivalent to those in local public schools.

- The inclusion of childcare in any welfare reform initiative, so that mothers receiving aid can go to school, get job training, and go to work.

MAKING CHANGES ON THE NATIONAL LEVEL

What You Can Do

- As with action on local and state levels, pressing all candidates for election for their stands on issues that affect the families of working parents can show them the impact that working parents can have on their ability to be elected.

Tell them what you want. Vote for the ones who take the |best stands.

- Contact your U.S. senators and members of the House of Representatives. National legislators, too, pay attention to their mail and phone calls. Again, you don't have to write a long letter but can make your position clear with a few lines on a card, letter, or telegram.
- Follow the news about proposed bills and services and express your opinion forcefully.
- Work for the election of more women to public office. Since Norway elected a woman as prime minister, child-care subsidies and paid parental leave both increased.
- Dramatize issues in innovative ways. In Iceland women workers called a boycott; even its woman prime minister did not show up for work, and the work world came to a virtual standstill.

What You Might Ask For

- A minimum-income level for every family with young children, as every other major industrialized nation in the world has. Parents should have the option to stay at home to care for young children. If our society acknowledged that taking care of children—even one's own children—is valuable work, parents could choose freely whether to do this or work outside at some other job.
- A central federal agency in charge of child care. This would plan and coordinate all funding, research, information, and action involving child care. At present this work is divided among various government departments, and one often doesn't know what another is doing. A central agency would train state and local officials, develop minimum standards for child care, support research, coordinate day-care planning, serve as an information clearinghouse, and educate parents and caregivers.
- A major financial investment in child care, safe from the ups and downs of politics.
- Larger tax deductions and/or tax credits for child care, which should revert to covering children up to age fifteen. Tax refunds to families at low-income levels.

- Tax deductions for household-cleaning help for working parents.
- Tax incentives for employers to support child care.
- Direct child-care subsidies to parents on a sliding-scale basis.
- Job-protected parental leave upon the birth or adoption of a child.
- Change labor, immigration, and social policies to make it easier for working parents to find caregivers.
- Less red tape in applying for child-care subsidies.
- Become a model employer by setting up model day-care facilities for the children of federal employees, with good working conditions and adequate pay scales for caregivers.

Some of the provisions described in this chapter are already available to some parents. Employers, community groups, and government agencies have begun to respond to your requests and needs. As more of you join together and mobilize your combined strength, you will bring about more changes in society. Society needs you; it needs your work in the labor force, and it needs your children. You are the face of America today, and your country must pay as much attention to nurturing you as you devote to fostering the healthy development of your children.

APPENDIX

—

—

RECOMMENDED READING

Books For Parents

Becoming Parents: Preparing for the Emotional Changes of First-Time Parenthood, by Sandra Sohn Jaffe and Jack Viertel (Atheneum, 1980). A powerful and perceptive detailing of the experiences and emotions of six real couples during their first babies' first year.

The Boys and Girls Book About Divorce, by Richard Gardner, M.D. (Bantam, 1977). A sensitive guide written by a child psychiatrist, who speaks directly to the children of divorced parents, presenting in clear, straightforward terms many of the issues that trouble children, such as anger, blame, fear, and divided loyalties.

Children and Money: A Parents' Guide, by Grace W. Weinstein (New American Library, 1987). A commonsense discussion of both practical and psychological implications of lessons in money matters from tots to teens, including allowances, payment for chores, first jobs, banking and credit. This updated edition of an award-winning book includes new information on single-parent families and step-families.

The Complete Book of Breastfeeding, by Marvin S. Eiger, M.D., and Sally Wendkos Olds (Workman, Bantam, 1987). A comprehensive, easy-to-read guide for new parents that offers suggestions for the working nursing mother and for the father who wants to be closely involved in family life.

Cradles of Eminence, by Victor and Mildred Goertzel (Little, Brown, 1978). An absorbing study of the childhoods of some 400 prominent persons that seeks to relate early life factors to eventual success in life—and finds a high proportion of single-parent childhoods among successful people. It brings together biography, autobiography, and professional literature about gifted children and adults.

Day Care for Sick Children (Day Care and Child Development Council of Tompkins County, Inc., 306 N. Aurora St., Ithaca, NY 14850, 1976). A twenty-four-page booklet with information for your caregiver on childhood illness, when to call the doctor, and activity ideas for sick children.

Family Politics, by Letty Cottin Pogrebin (McGraw-Hill, 1983). A lively profamily book by a feminist who compares traditional and contemporary families, identifies the strengths and weaknesses of various kinds of families, and urges changes in light of the needs and interests of parents and children today.

401 Ways to Get Your Kids to Work at Home, by Bonnie Runyan McCullough and Susan Walker Monson (St. Martin's Press, 1981). Creative strategies on getting your children to do their share of the housework. (Example: Guessing game. Tell your child to put away ten items in a room, then you have to guess what has been put away.)

Going It Alone: The Family Life and Social Situation of the Single Parent, by Robert S. Weiss (Basic Books, 1981). In this book, a sociologist who has done extensive research on single-parent families offers sensitive insights into the way things are and suggestions for making them better. His discussion of the various kinds of overload that single parents have to deal with is especially good.

Helping Your Child Learn Right from Wrong, by Dr. Sidney B. Simon and Sally Wendkos Olds (McGraw-Hill, 1977). The subtitle, "A Family Guide to Establishing Values That Children Can Live with Now and as Adults," summarizes the theme of this book, and the more than eighty gamelike exercises it describes help to make talking about values an absorbing, fun-filled family activity.

How to Make Love to the Same Person for the Rest of Your Life (and Still Love It!), by Dagmar O'Connor (Doubleday, 1985; Bantam, 1986). This lively little book by a Masters-and-Johnson-trained sex therapist suggests ways that couples can get around problems like being "too busy for sex" and feeling more like Mommy and Daddy than lovers.

How to Start and Run a Successful Home Typing Business: A Complete Step-by-Step Business Plan, by Peggy Glenn (Aames-Allen Publishing Co., P.O. Box 453, Huntington Beach, CA 92648, 1983). An exhaustive and practical look at what it takes to set up and run this kind of enterprise.

Know Your Child, by Stella Chess, M.D., and Alexander Thomas, M.D. (Basic Books, 1987). This book by an eminent husband-and-wife (and working parent) team is a sometimes scholarly, often reassuring book that evaluates the major research in child development over the past thirty years. The authors emphasize the importance of the child's own personality in shaping his or her own life and show how parents can avoid problems by matching their own expectations and attitudes to their children's temperament. There's a particularly thoughtful chapter on working mothers and their children.

Live-In Child Care: The Complete Guide, by Barbara Binswanger and Betsy Ryan (Dolphin: Doubleday, 1986). A guide full of suggestions for evaluating the kind of live-in caregiver you want—and then for finding, interviewing, and hiring someone—and making the arrangement work.

The Parents Book About Divorce, by Richard Gardner, M.D. (Bantam, 1979). A practical volume by a child psychiatrist, who covers such issues as telling children about a divorce, dealing with their problems both before and after the separation, and handling the quandaries of the adults themselves, including problems revolving around money, dating, remarriage, and relationships with other people.

Raising a Hyperactive Child, by Mark A. Stewart, M.D., and Sally Wendkos Olds (Harper & Row, 1973). The long section in this book called "How to Help Your Child at Home" offers many suggestions for establishing a healthy climate in the home, for raising children's self-esteem, for setting up reasonable rules, and for encouraging children to form good habits. Parents can use the reward system it describes to motivate their children to take better care of themselves and to pitch in with household chores.

Remaking Motherhood: How Working Mothers Are Shaping Our Children's Future, by Anita Shreve (Viking, 1987). A research-based book by an award-winning journalist that delves into the risks and rewards of "a new kind of mothering" and finds that children of working mothers, in general, are not "deprived" but enriched. The book covers the working mother as a new role model; the effects of mothers' employment on daughters and sons, including stresses and strains; the new working father; and the single working mother.

School's Out—Now What? Creative Choices for Your Child, by Joan M. Bergstrom, Ed.D. (Ten Speed Press, 1984). A practical guide for parents to help children ages six through twelve use their time out of school creatively and in ways that will advance their development. While some of the activities demand parental time and effort, special attention is given to the situations of working parents and self-care children. The book is full of good ideas, checklists, and anecdotes. It also has a superb bibliography for both parents and children.

Sharing the Kitchen: A Cookbook for Single Parents and Children, by Sharon Cadwallader (McGraw-Hill 1979). Written with the special needs of the working parent who has little time but great interest in providing good, nutritious meals for the family. Recipes are fast and easy, with most able to be prepared by parent or child alone, or working together.

Sidetracked Home Executives: From Pigpen to Paradise, by Pam Young and Peggy Jones (Warner, 1981). Two sisters tell how they reformed their sloppy ways to run enviably well-organized homes and families. Reading about their former selves has to make you feel superior—because *nobody* could be as chaotic as they once were! Their system, built on three-by-five-inch cards, is the basis of workshops around the country.

The Socially Competent Child: A Parents' Guide to Social Development—From Infancy to Early Adolescence, by Anita Gurian and Ruth Formanek (Houghton Mifflin, 1983). Two psychologists draw on the latest research to provide practical suggestions for helping children to make friends with children their own age and to get along with adults. Many quotations and anecdotes about children make this lively reading.

The Stressproof Child: A Loving Parent's Guide, by Antoinette Saunders and Bonnie Remsberg (Holt, Rinehart & Winston, 1984). A practical guide for parents to help children deal with stress. It provides suggestions for helping children develop self-esteem, as well as guidelines on recognizing signs of stress in children and techniques for dealing with it.

The Two-Paycheck Marriage, by Caroline Bird (Rawson, Wade, 1982). A fascinating in-depth report on "the most important revolution of our times: the march of wives into the workplace." This extensively researched book shows how the two-earner family pattern is changing our society and is both reassuring and supportive of those who are part of this revolution.

The Very Best Child Care and How to Find It: A Parent's Guide for Locating Quality Care for Your Infant or Toddler, by Danalee Buhler (Prima Publishing, 1989). A comprehensive look at various kinds of child care, with especially interesting discussions of care for infants, health and safety, child abuse, and children with special needs. Contains excellent resource lists, including the name and address of every state agency concerned with licensed child care.

What Color Is Your Parachute?, by Richard N. Bolles (Ten Speed Press, 1989). Far and away, the best book on life–work planning to be found, this manual humorously and effectively helps you to zero in on the kind of job/career you want and offers a goldmine of tips for achieving it.

Women and Home-Based Work: The Unspoken Contract, by
Kathleen Christensen (Henry Holt, 1988). A look at how it
really is for women working at home today. Based on a national survey of 14,000 women working at home and in-
depth interviews with 100 of them, the book tells the story of
a range of workers, describing both the joys and the problems, and in its summary chapter offering practical suggestions for making this kind of work work out.

Working Parent Food Book, by Adeline Garner Shell and
Kay Reynolds (Sovereign, 1979). A cookbook with recipes
for one-pot dinners, cook-ahead main dishes, and "throw-
together" meals, as well as a lot of good tips for saving time
in food preparation.

Books For Kids

***Alone After School: A Self-Care Guide for Latchkey Chil-
dren and Their Parents,*** by Helen L. Swan and Victoria
Houston (Prentice-Hall, 1985). A balanced and comprehensive manual with a workbook approach and separate sections
for parents, schoolchildren, and young teens. It raises questions to help parents decide whether eight- to fifteen-year-
olds are ready to stay alone and to help the children learn
how to deal with various situations that can arise. It's full of
checklists, quizzes, and charts.

Alpha-Bakery, by Gold Medal Flour (General Mills, 1987,
$1 from P.O. Box 5401, Dept. 849, Minneapolis, MN
55460). Sensible and good baking book, best for eighth
graders and older.

Dinner's Ready Mom, by Helen Gustafson (1986; $8.95
from Celestial Arts, P.O. Box 7327, Berkeley, CA 94707).
Good for older teenagers, especially good at showing how to
time cooking so everything comes out at the same time.

***In Charge: A Complete Handbook for Kids with Working
Parents,*** by Kathy S. Kyte (Knopf, 1983). This helpful, easy-
to-read little book can help schoolchildren, young teens, or
baby-sitters get organized, cope with crises (both minor and

major), cook, and take care of their clothes. It emphasizes the normality of the self-care situation and offers guidelines for using family conferences to set rules, chores, and procedures.

Kids Can Cook, by Dorothy R. Bates (1987; $9.95 from the Book Publishing Co., P.O. Box 99, Summertown, TN 38483). Good recipes, with the easiest ones marked. Good for eighth graders and older.

Kids Cooking, by Vicki Lansky (Scholastic, Inc., 1987). Clear step-by-step instructions make this good for fourth graders and older.

The Little Gourmet Cookbook for Children (1986; $10.45 from Auxiliary of Children's Hospital of Philadelphia, 1 Children's Center, 34th St. and Civic Center Blvd., Philadelphia, PA 19104). Good recipes, most useful for twelve-year-olds and up.

My First Baking Book, by Rena Coyle (Workman, 1988). A book that fourth graders can use on their own. Good step-by-step drawings.

My First Cookbook, by Rena Coyle (Workman, 1985). Good ingredients and good recipes, but best used with an adult's help.

Once Upon a Recipe, by Karen Greene (New Hope Press, 1987). Simple and nutritious recipes, with tie-ins with children's literature, for sixth graders and older.

HELPFUL ORGANIZATIONS

American Council of Nanny Schools
Delta College
University Center, MI 48710
(517) 686–9417
This coalition of nanny schools (twenty-four at this writing) will send you a list of the schools, indicating which ones have placement services. The council accredits schools, holds conferences, issues a newsletter to give continuing education,

and is currently developing a national competency test for nannies. Its newsletter provides a variety of child-care tips, and at $5 a year is worth subscribing to for your nanny, as well as yourself.

Association of Part-Time Professionals
Flow General Building
7655 Old Springhouse Road
McLean, VA 22102
(703) 734–7975
A national professional association that works with employers, workers, and community groups to promote part-time professional positions. National members receive a newsletter and discounts on various publications (dues $20); Washington-area members receive a local newsletter, access to a job-referral service, and the opportunity to attend the group's workshops (dues $35).

Big Brothers/Big Sisters of America
230 North 13th Street
Philadelphia, PA 19107
(215) 567–2748
Some 465 Big Brothers/Big Sisters agencies across the country match up, in one-to-one friendships, adult volunteers and school-aged children who need stability and companionship. Most of the children live with a single parent. The organization provides a professional backup for the volunteers, who can turn to them for advice and help. Local programs can be located through telephone directories, social service agencies, or this national office.

Child Care Action Campaign
99 Hudson Street—Suite 1233
New York, NY 10013
(212) 334–9595
This national coalition of leaders from various institutions and organizations serves as an advocacy group to set in place a national system of child care using both public and private resources. It offers information on many aspects of child care through individual information sheets, a bimonthly

newsletter, and audio training tapes for family day care providers. Annual membership fee is $20. For a list of individual information sheets on such topics as using the child-care tax credit; care for sick children, infants and toddlers, and schoolchildren; and sexual abuse in child care, send a self-addressed stamped envelope (SASE). Nonmembers send another SASE for up to three information sheets; members can get all thirty-seven.

Children's Defense Fund
122 C Street, N.W.
Washington, DC 20001
(202) 628–8787
This advocacy group aims to make the world a better place for children through education, lobbying, and organizing. It publishes a monthly newsletter, an annual in-depth analysis of the nation's investment in children, and a series of special reports. Among its major concerns are child care, prenatal care, and the prevention of adolescent pregnancy. Its list of publications is available on request.

Coalition of Labor Union Women
15 Union Square
New York, NY 10003
(212) 242–0700
This organization of trade unionists promotes the rights of working women and is very active in pressing for family legislation. Its book, *Bargaining for Child Care: A Union Parent's Guide* (1989, $5), presents both actual and model contract language for use in collective bargaining. It can provide general assistance, including referring union members to key contacts within their own unions.

Girl Scouts of the United States of America
830 Third Avenue
New York, NY 10022
(212) 940–7500
In recognition of the many school-age children who are home alone after school, Girl Scout councils have instituted the program, "Safe and Sound at Home Alone," for both

scouts and nonscouts, girls and boys. The program involves a series of activities that can be used in troop meetings, after-school programs, evening programs for families, in-school programs, on cable TV, or by children at home, either alone or with a friend or sibling. The program materials, along with consultation with a Girl Scout representative, are available for a nominal feel.

National Association of Child Care Resource and Referral Agencies (NACCRRA)
2116 Campus Drive S.E.
Rochester, MN 55904
(507) 287–2020
This professional organization of resource and referral agencies provides services to its member agencies and acts as a clearinghouse for information about child-care services around the country. It maintains a referral service for parents, along with procedures for handling complaints.

National Association for Family Day Care (NAFDC)
815 Fifteenth St., N.W.—Suite 928
Washington, DC 20005
(202) 347–3356
This organization accredits family day-care providers, based on an in-depth evaluation by a team of a parent, a provider, and a representative from NAFDC. It also publishes a newsletter, holds national and local conferences, lobbies on children's issues, and issues national directories of family day-care agencies, associations, and support groups. Membership for parents and providers is $12.

National Association for the Education of Young Children (NAEYC)
1834 Connecticut Avenue, N.W.
Washington, DC 20009
(202) 232–8777 or (800) 424–2460
This professional association in the field of early childhood programs accredits child-care centers and preschools around the country, holds both regional and national meetings, and distributes publications for both professionals and parents (listed in its resources catalog).

National Black Child Development Institute
1463 Rhode Island Avenue, N.W.
Washington, DC 20005
(202) 387–1281
This national nonprofit organization focuses on child care, health, education, and child welfare. It holds conferences, conducts tutorial programs, and helps homeless children find adoptive families. Members ($20 for individuals) receive the quarterly publication *The Black Child Advocate*, updates on laws and public policy, and discounts on other publications (like "Teens, Television and Telephones" and "Giving Your Child a Good Start in School").

National Foundation for Consumer Credit
8701 Georgia Avenue, #507
Silver Spring, MD 20910
(301) 589–5600
This organization maintains a library on consumer credit and distributes educational materials. It can also put you in touch with local agencies that help with credit-related problems.

Parents Without Partners
8807 Colesville Road
Silver Spring, MD 20910
(301) 588–9354
This international, nonprofit membership organization is concerned with the welfare and interests of single parents and their children. It issues a number of publications, including the monthly magazine *The Single Parent*, offers scholarships for high school students, and provides such other benefits as insurance and an auto club. PWP's 800 local chapters in North America and Europe are the heart of the program, helping single parents and their children with educational meetings for both adults and children and recreational activities for the whole family.

School Age Child Care Project (SACC)
Center for Research on Women
Wellesley College
Wellesley, MA 02181
(617) 431–1453, ext. 2546
SACC offers consultation, both on the phone and on-site, to parents and community organizations that want to offer after-school care and help to children. It also trains policy-makers and child-care personnel, holds workplace seminars for parents, and publishes books and a newsletter. A packet that includes a bibliography and resource lists, plus relevant articles and a sample SACC newsletter is $5, including post-age and handling.

Single Parent Resource Center
1165 Broadway
New York, NY 10001
(212) 213–0047
This nonprofit organization mainly serves the tristate area of New York, New Jersey, and Connecticut, offering peer counseling, information on public services, and help in life planning. It helps in the start-up of single-parent groups and programs, gives seminars for corporations and businesses for single-parent employees, issues publications and serves as a clearinghouse of information.

Woman's Workshop
P.O. Box 843
Coronado, CA 92118
(619) 437–1350
This national quarterly newsletter ($16 for one year; sample issue, $5) is an idea exchange for at-home mothers who want to work part-time or from home now or plan for future work through education or volunteering. It features profiles of women who have pursued outside interests and who offer advice to others who want to follow in their footsteps. Upon receipt of a self-addressed stamped envelope, it will send a brochure with a list of pertinent books.

INDEX

OTHER SUCCESSFUL-PARENTING BOOKS FROM PRIMA

The Very Best Child Care and How to Find It
by Danalee Buhler

This is the first book to focus on child care for infants and toddlers (from birth to three years old). Danalee is herself a mother and a child care professional. Included are such topics as:

- The different types of child care: advantages and disadvantages
- Basic health and safety issues—including checklists
- Dealing with the child care disease cycle
- Nannies and other caregivers
- Infant programs
- Toddler programs
- How to spot child abuse
- Child care options for physically and emotionally handicapped children
- Much, much more .... U.S. $8.95

Raising Self-Reliant Children in a Self-Indulgent World
by H. Stephen Glenn and Jane Nelsen, Ed.D.

Authors Stephen Glenn and Jane Nelsen are real people with real answers. Each is a parent with many children. They *know* that parenting in today's affluent society isn't easy. As renowned educators whose seminars are attended by over 250,000 people annually, they offer a fresh approach to raising children.

In this book you'll learn why so many children today feel irrelevant and alienated. Why, when you give them everything you never had, they appear ungrateful. But most of all, you will learn how to involve your children in activities and discussions that will help them feel capable and worthwhile .... U.S. $9.95

PLEASE TURN PAGE FOR ORDERING INFORMATION

FILL IN AND MAIL...TODAY

PRIMA PUBLISHING & COMMUNICATIONS
P.O. Box 1260 WP
Rocklin, CA 95677

USE YOUR VISA/MC AND ORDER BY PHONE
(916) 624-5718
Mon.–Fri. 9–4 PST (12–7 EST)

Dear People at Prima,

I'd like to order copies of the following titles:

_____ copies of **The Working Parents' Survival Guide**
at $10.95 each for a total of . . . . ._____

_____ copies of **Raising Self-Reliant Children**
at $9.95 each for a total of . . . . ._____

_____ copies of **The Very Best Child Care**
at $8.95 each for a total of . . . . ._____

Subtotal	_____
Postage & Handling	**$2.50**
Sales Tax	_____
TOTAL (U.S. funds only)	_____

☐ Check enclosed for $ _____, payable to Prima Publishing
   Charge my ☐ MasterCard ☐ VISA

Account No. _____ Exp. Date _____

Signature _____

Your Name _____

Address _____

City/State/Zip _____

Daytime Telephone _____

GUARANTEE
YOU MUST BE SATISFIED!
You get a 30-day, 100% money-back guarantee on all books.

Thank you for your order.